Cardinal Beran Library
St. Mary's Seminary
9845 Memorial Drive
Houston, Texas 77024

SAINT MARY'S SEMINARY LIBRARY
9745 Memorial Drive
Houston 24, Texas

KARL MARX
DICTIONARY

KARL MARX DICTIONARY

Edited by

Morris Stockhammer

PHILOSOPHICAL LIBRARY

New York

Copyright, 1965
by Philosophical Library, Inc.
15 East 40th Street, New York, N. Y.

All rights reserved

Library of Congress Catalog Card Number 65-10660

PRINTED IN THE UNITED STATES OF AMERICA

To Mona and Elliott

Foreword

Karl Marx was born in Trier, Germany, in 1818 and died in London in 1883. During his later years he became an important social philosopher and a radical political leader, and is renowned today as the father of modern communism.
The son of a jurist, Marx had originally intended to follow his father's profession, but his study of law was terminated by a growing interest in philosophy. He finally decided to devote all his time to philosophy and took a Ph. D. degree in 1842. Shortly thereafter he became editor of a radical newspaper. This paper was suppressed by the German government, and in 1843 Marx left Germany to settle in Paris. It was here that he encountered Friedrich Engels, who was to be his life-long friend and patron. Having become a confirmed socialist, Marx published, in 1848 and with the aid of Engels, the famous *Communist Manifesto*, in which he set forth the basic tenets of his radical philosophy. Returning to Germany in 1848 in order to participate in revolutionary movements there, he met with official disapproval and was forced to flee the country after two years. He found exile in London in 1850 and remained in the British capital for the rest of his life, existing most of the time in dire circumstances and supporting himself with odd journalistic assignments as well as with the occasional financial contributions of Engels. In 1867 he published the first volume of his monumental work *DAS KAPITAL*, which was eventually to change the shape of the world.
DAS KAPITAL, subsequently published in three volumes, has exerted an enormous influence on the modern world. Marx combined a powerful and profound mind with a capacity for inexhaustible research and study. He made himself thoroughly familiar with all traditional and contemporary economic philosophies, and used this knowledge as a frame of reference for his study of the British economic system. As a result of his disenchantment with the conditions that existed in his time in England,

he repudiated all existing socialistic theories as either utopian or unsocialistic and developed a dynamic theory of social change which became the basis of *scientific socialism* and *dialectical materialism.* It is from these that most forms of socialism and communism are derived today.

Objective critics have tended to consider Marx as one of the greatest of economic theorists, one whose views cannot be lightly discounted, but whose system, like all systems, is seriously hampered by its rigidly doctrinaire nature.

M. S.

LIST OF ABBREVIATIONS

A.	Address at two sittings of the International Working Men's Association
C.	*Capital* (1, 2, 3, 4)
C. C.	*Contribution to the Critique of Hegel's Philosophy of Right*
C. M.	*Communist Manifesto*
C. W.	*Civil War in France*
D. E.	*Differences between the Philosophy of Democritus and the Philosophy of Epicurus*
D. T.	Articles in the N. Y. *Daily Tribune*
E. B.	*The Eighteenth Brumaire of Louis Bonaparte*
G. I.	*German Ideology*
G. P.	*Critique of the Gotha Programme*
H. F.	*Holy Family*
H. P.	*Demonstration in Hyde Park*
I. Q.	*The Indian Question*
J. Q.	*Papers on the "Jewish Question"*
L. A.	Leading Article of No. 179 of *Koelnische Zeitung*
M.	Manuscripts of 1844
P. E.	*A Contribution to the Critique of Political Economy*
P. P.	*Poverty of Philosophy*
T. F.	*Theses on Feuerbach*

All references are made to Karl Marx's Works "Gesamtausgabe" and to their translations by Moore and Aveling.

A

ABOLITION OF PROPERTY
The abolition of existing (private) property relations is not at all a distinctive feature of communism. . . . The distinguishing feature of communism is the abolition of bourgeois (private) property.—C. M.

ABSOLUTE KNOWLEDGE
Mind, this thinking returning home to its own point of origin—the thinking which, as the anthropological, phenomenological, psychological, ethical, artistic and religious mind is not valid for itself, until ultimately it finds itself, and relates itself to itself, as absolute knowledge in the hence absolute, i.e., abstract mind, and so receives its conscious embodiment in a mode of being corresponding to it.—M.

ABSOLUTE SURPLUS-VALUE
The surplus-value produced by prolongation of the working day, I call absolute surplus-value.—C. 1.

ABSORPTION OF LABOR
The means of production are at once changed into means of absorption of the labor of others. It is now no longer the laborer that employs the means of production, but the means of production that employ the laborer. Instead of being consumed by him as material elements of his productive activity, they consume him as the ferment necessary to their own life-process, and the life-process of capital consists only in its movement as value constantly expanding, constantly multiplying itself.—C. 1.

ABSTRACT THINKER
The abstract thinker learns in his intuition of nature that the entities which he thought to create from nothing, from pure abstraction, are nothing else but abstractions from characteristics of nature.—M.

The transition from logic to natural philosophy is difficult to effect for the abstract thinker.—M.

ABSTRACTION
Don't think, don't ask me, for as soon as you think and ask, your abstraction from the existence of nature and man has no meaning. Or are you such an egoist that you postulate everything as nothing, and yet want yourself to be?—M.

ACCELERATION
Political economy occasionally identifies the *acceleration of accumulation* due to increased productiveness of labor with its acceleration due to increased exploitation of the laborer.—C. 1.

ACCIDENTS
The very fact that the number of accidents, though still very high, has decreased markedly since the inspection system was established, and this in spite of the limited powers and insufficient numbers of the inspectors, demonstrates the natural tendency of capitalist exploitation. These human sacrifices are mostly due to the inordinate avarice of the mine owners. Very often they had only one shaft sunk, so that apart from the lack of effective ventilation there was no escape were this shaft to become obstructed.—C. 3.

ACCUMULATION
The accumulation and concentration of instruments of production and of work people preceded the development of the division of labor inside the factory.—P. P.

The accumulation of wealth at one pole is at the same time accumulation of toil, slavery, ignorance, mental degradation at the opposite pole.—C. 1.

ACCUMULATION OF CAPITAL
Employing surplus-value as capital, reconverting it into capital, is called accumulation of capital.—C. 1.

The first condition of accumulation of capital is that the capitalist must have contrived to sell his commodities, and to reconvert into capital the greater part of the money so received.—C. 1.

Accumulation, where private property prevails, is the concentration of capital in the hands of a few; it is in general an inevitable consequence if capitals are left to follow their natural course, and it is precisely through competition that the way is cleared for this natural destination of capital.—M.

The accumulation of large capitals is generally accompanied by a corresponding simplification of fixed capital relative to the smaller capitalists.—M.

Accumulation is in general an inevitable consequence if capitals are left to follow their natural course.—M.

While the capitalist of the classical type brands individual consumption as a sin against his function, and as "abstinence" from accumulating, the modernized capitalist is capable of looking upon accumulation as "abstinence" from pleasure.—C. 1.

The accumulation of large capitals proceeds much more rapidly than that of smaller capital, quite irrespective of competition.—M.

Accumulation of capital is increase of the proletariat.—C. 1.

ACQUISITION
Those of the members of bourgeois society who work acquire nothing, and those who acquire anything do not work.—C. M.

ADDITIONAL LABOR
The laborer adds fresh value to the subject of his labor by expending upon it a given amount of additional labor, no matter what the specific character and utility of that labor may be.—C. 1.

ADDRESS TO THE LEAGUE
It was the address to the League which we have written together—actually nothing but a plan of war against democracy.—Ltr. to Engels.

ADULTERATION
The capitalist's fanatical insistence on economy comes to the surface also conversely in the adulteration of the elements of production, which is one of the principal means of lowering the relation of the value of the constant capital to the variable capital, and thus of raising the rate of profit.—C. 3.

AGE
Differences of age and sex have no longer any distinctive social validity for the working class. All are instruments of labor, more or less expensive to use, according to their age and sex.—C. M.

AGRARIAN EQUIPMENT
The equipment of the bigger landowner does not increase in proportion to the size of his estate.—M.

AGRICULTURAL PRICE
So long as necessity compels the purchase of all the agricultural products put upon the market, the market price is determined by the highest cost of production.—P. P.

AGRICULTURAL REVOLUTION
In the sphere of agriculture, modern industry has a more revolutionary effect than elsewhere, for this reason, that it annihilates the peasant, that bulwark of the old society, and replaces him by the wage laborer. Thus the desire for social changes, and the class antagonism are brought to the same level in the country as in the towns.—C. 1.

AGRICULTURE
The earth itself is an instrument of labor, but when used as such in agriculture implies a whole series of other instruments and a comparatively high development of labor.—C. 1.

The big proprietors who with the comfortable incomes have mostly given themselves over to extravagance are, for the most part, not competent to conduct large-scale *agriculture*.—M.

AGRICULTURE, CAPITALISTIC

All progress in capitalistic agriculture is a progress in the art, not only of robbing the laborer, but of robbing the soil; all progress in increasing the fertility of the soil for a given time is a progress toward ruining the lasting sources of that fertility. The more a country starts its development on the foundation of modern industry, like the United States, for example, the more rapid is this process of destruction.—C.1.

AGRICULTURE, INDUSTRIAL

The power of industry over its opposite is at once revealed in the emergence of agriculture as a real industry, most of the work having previously been left to the soil and to the slave of the soil, through whom the land cultivated itself. With the transformation of the slave into a free worker—i.e., into a hireling—the landlord himself is transformed into a captain of industry, into a capitalist.—M.

If the use of machinery in agriculture is for the most part free from the injurious physical effect it has on the factory operative, its action in superseding the laborers is more intense, and finds less resistance.—C. 1.

AGRICULTURE, RATIONAL

The moral of history, also to be deduced from other observations concerning agriculture, is that the capitalist system works against a rational agriculture, or that a rational agriculture is incompatible with the capitalist system (although the latter promotes technical improvements in agriculture), and needs either the hand of the small farmer living by his own labor or the control of associated producers.—C. 3.

AGRICULTURE, SCIENTIFIC

The irrational, old-fashioned methods of agriculture are replaced by scientific ones. Capitalist production completely tears asunder the old bond of union which held together agriculture and manufacture in their infancy.—C. 1.

ALIENATION OF LABOR

The worker puts his life into the object; but now his life no longer belongs to him but to the object. Hence, the greater his activity, the greater is the worker's lack of objects. Whatever the product of his labor is, he is not. Therefore the greater this product, the less is he himself.—M.

The more the worker spends himself, the more powerful the alien objective world becomes which he creates over against himself, the poorer he himself—his inner world—becomes, the less belongs to him as his own.—M.

What constitutes the *alienation of labor?* The fact that labor is external to the worker, i.e., it does not belong to his essential being; that in his work, therefore, he does not affirm himself but denies himself, does not feel content but unhappy, does not develop freely his physical and mental energy but mortifies his body and ruins his mind. The worker therefore only feels himself outside his work, and in his work feels outside himself. He is at home when he is not working, and when he is working he is not at home. His labor is therefore not voluntary, but coerced; it is forced labor. It is therefore not the satisfaction of a need; it is merely a means to satisfy needs external to it. Its alien character emerges clearly in the fact that as soon as no physical or other compulsion exists, labor is shunned like the plague. External labor, labor in which man alienates himself, is a labor of self-sacrifice, of mortification.—M.

The external character of labor for the worker appears in the fact that it is not his own, but someone else's, that it does not belong to him, that in it he belongs, not to himself, but to another.—M.

The object which labor produces—labor's product—confronts it as something alien, as a power independent of the producer. The product of labor is labor which has been congealed in an object, which has become material: it is the objectification of labor. Labor's realization is its objectification. In the conditions dealt with by political economy this realization of labor appears as loss of reality for the workers; objectification as loss of the object and object-bondage; appropriation as estrangement, as alienation.—M.

If the product of labor is alienation, production itself must be active alienation. In the estrangement of the object of labor is merely summarized the estrangement, the alienation, in the activity of labor itself.—M.

The alienation of the worker in his product means not only that his labor becomes an object, an eternal existence, but that exists outside him, independently, as something alien to him, and that it becomes a power on its own confronting him; it means that the life which he has conferred on the object confronts him as something hostile and alien.—M.

ALONENESS
As soon as I am not alone, I am another—another reality.—M.

AMERICA
One of the most indispensable conditions for the formation of the manufacturing industry was the accumulation of capital facilitated by the discovery of America and the introduction of its precious metals.—P. P.

ANIMAL PRODUCTION
Admittedly animals also produce. They build themselves nests, dwellings, like the bees, beavers, ants, etc. But an animal only produces what it immediately needs for itself or its young. It produces one-sidedly, whilst man produces universally. It produces only under the dominion of immediate physical need, whilst man produces even when he is free from physical need and only truly produces in freedom therefrom.—M.

ANIMAL WORSHIP
Does not animal worship debase man below the animal, does it not make the animal man's god?—L. A.

ANONYMOUS
The pamphlet must first be published anonymously, so that the public believes that its author is a great general. In the second printing, you mention yourself in a six-line preface. This then will be a triumph for our party.—Ltr. to Engels.

ANTAGONISM, SOCIOLOGICAL
The bourgeois relations of production are the last antagonistic form of the social process of production—antagonistic not in the sense of individual antagonism, but of one arising from the social conditions of life of the individuals; at the same time the productive forces developing in the womb of bourgeois society create the material conditions for the solution of that antagonism.—P. E.

ANTAGONISM OF INTERESTS
We find that the hostile antagonism of interests is recognized as the basis of social organization.—M.

ANTIQUATED
The antiquated tries to maintain and re-establish itself within the new order.—Ltr. to Bolte.

ANTIQUITY
In antiquity, material productive labor bore the stigma of slavery and was regarded merely as a pedestal for the idle citizen.—C.4.

ANTI-SEMITISM
What is stated as theory in Jewish religion, namely, contempt for theory, art, history and man as an end in himself, is an actual and conscious point of view, held to be virtuous by the man of money. Even the relations between the sexes, between man and woman, become an object of commerce. The law of the Jew, lacking all solid foundation, is only a religious caricature of morality and of law in general, but it provides the formal rites in which the world of property clothes its transactions.—J. Q.

APHORISTIC STYLE
The wealth and diversity of the subjects to be treated could have been compressed into *one* work only in a purely aphoristic style; whilst an aphoristic presentation of this kind, for its part, would have given the impression of arbitrary systematizing.—M.

APOSTASY
Every philosophy of the past without exception was accused by the theologians of apostasy.—L. A.

APPRECIATION AND DEPRECIATION
Appreciation and depreciation are self-explanatory. All they mean is that a given capital increases or decreases in value as a result of certain general economic conditions, for we are not discussing the particular fate of an individual capital. All they mean, therefore, is that the value of a capital invested in production rises or falls, irrespective of its self-expansion by virtue of the surplus-labor employed by it.—C. 3.

APPROPRIATION
Communism deprives no man of the power to appropriate the products of society: all that it does is to deprive him of the power to subjugate the labor of others by means of such appropriation.—C. M.

ARISTOCRACY
In order to arouse sympathy, the aristocracy were obliged to lose sight, apparently, of their own interests, and to formulate their indictment against the bourgeoisie in the interest of the exploited working class alone. Thus the aristocracy took their revenge by singing lampoons on their new master, and whispering in his ears sinister prophecies of coming catastrophe.—C. M.

ARMY
The ancients first completely developed salaries in the army.—Ltr. to Engels.

ART
If you want to enjoy art, you must be an artistically cultivated person.—M.

Capitalist production is hostile to certain branches of spiritual production, for example, art and poetry. If this is left out of account, it opens the way to the illusion of the French in the eighteenth century which has been so beautifully satirized by Lessing. Because we are further ahead than the ancients in mechanics, etc., why shouldn't we be able to make an epic too? And the *Henriade* in place of the *Iliad*!—C. 4.

ASIATIC AGRICULTURE
In Asiatic empires we are quite accustomed to see agriculture deteriorating under one government and reviving again under some other government. There the harvests correspond to good or bad governments, as they change in Europe with good or bad seasons.—D. T.

The artificial fertilization of the Asiatic soil, dependent on a central government, and immediately decaying with the neglect of irragation and drainage, explains the otherwise strange fact that we now find whole territories barren and desert that were once brilliantly cultivated, as Palmyra, Petra, the ruins in Yemen, and large provinces of Egypt, Persia, and Hindustan; it also explains how a single war of devastation has been able to depopulate a country for centuries, and to strip it of all its civilization.—D. T.

ASIATIC ECONOMICS
An economical function developed upon all Asiatic governments: the function of providing public works.—D. T.

ASIATIC GOVERNMENT
There have been in Asia, generally, from immemorial times, but three departments of government: that of finance, or the plunder of the interior; that of war, or the plunder of the exterior; and, finally, the department of public works.—D. T.

ASIATIC SOCIAL REVOLUTION
England, it is true, in causing a social revolution in Hindustan, was actuated only by the vilest interests, and was stupid in her manner of enforcing them. But that is not the question. The question is, can mankind fulfill its destiny without a fundamental revolution in the social state of Asia? If not, whatever may have been the crimes of England she was the unconscious tool of history in bringing about that revolution.—D. T.

ASSOCIATION, AGRARIAN
Association, applied to land, shares the economic advantage of large-scale landed property, and first brings to realization the original tendency inherent in land division, namely, equality.—M.

ASSOCIATION, CLASSLESS
In place of the old bourgeois society, with its classes and class antagonisms, we shall have a (classless) association, in which the free development of each is the condition for the free development of all.—C. M.

ASSOCIATION, WORKERS'
The revolutionary combination of laborers is due to association. —C. M.

ATHEISM
Atheism is a negation of God, and postulates the existence of man through this negation.—M.

Atheism and communism are no flight, no abstraction; they are not a losing of the objective world begotten by man—of man's essential powers given over to the realm of objectivity; they are not a returning in poverty to unnatural, primitive simplicity. On the contrary, they are but the first real coming-to-be, the realization become real for man, of man's essence, of the essence of man as something real.—M.

AUTHORITY
All combined labor on a large scale requires, more or less, a directing authority, in order to secure the harmonious working of the individual activities, and to perform the general functions that have their origin in the action of the combined organism, as distinguished from the action of its separate organs.—C. 1.

AUTOMATON
To work at a machine, the workman should be taught from childhood, in order that he may learn to adapt his own movements to the uniform and unceasing motion of an automaton.—C. 1.

AUXILIARY MATERIAL
The use of flour in the cotton industry may serve as an illustration of the importance of a price reduction for an article which is not strictly a raw material but an auxiliary and at the same time one of the principal elements of nourishment.—C. 3.

AVARICE
The only wheels which political economy sets in motion are avarice and the war amongst the avaricious—competition.—M.

At the historical dawn of capitalist production—and every capitalist upstart has personally to go through this historical state—avarice, and the desire to get rich, are the ruling passions.—C. 1.

AVERAGE
The intelligible and the necessary wants to be recognized only as a blindly working *average.*—Ltr. to Kugelmann.

AVERAGE PROFIT
Experience shows that if a branch of industry, such as, say, the cotton industry, yields unusually high profits at one period, it makes very little profit, or even suffers losses, at another, so that in a certain cycle of years the average profit is much the same as in other branches. And capital soon learns to take this experience into account.—C. 3.

Average profit is the basic conception, the conception that capitals of equal magnitude must share *pro rata* to their magnitude in the total surplus-value squeezed out of the laborers by the total social capital; or that every individual capital should be regarded merely as a part of the total social capital, and every capitalist actually as a shareholder in the total social enterprise, each sharing in the total profit *pro rata* to the magnitude of his share of capital.—C. 3.

The average profit coincides with the average surplus-value produced for each 100 of capital. In the case of the average profit the value of the advanced capital becomes an additional element determining the rate of profit.—C. 3.

B

BACHELOR
He is an old bachelor through and through, anxiously concerned about his conservation and preservation.—Ltr. to Engels.

BACON
The real founder of English materialism and all modern experimental science was Bacon. For him natural science was true science and physics based on perception was the most excellent part of natural science.—H. F.

In Bacon, its first creator, materialism contained latent and still in a naive way the germs of all-around development. Matter smiled at man with poetical, sensuous brightness. The aphoristic doctrine itself, on the other hand, was full of the inconsistencies of theology.—H. F.

BAIT
Every product is a bait with which to seduce away the other's very being, his money; every real and possible need is a weakness which will lead the fly to the gluepot.—M.

BAKUNIN
On the whole Bakunin is one of the few fellows whom after sixteen years I find to have developed, not backwards, but further.—Ltr. to Engels.

Theory is for Bakunin only a secondary affair, merely a means to a self-asserting end. The less he is a scientist, the more he is an intriguer.—Ltr. to Bolte.

BALANCE OF TRADE

It is possible that the export trade to India and the import trade from India may approximately balance each other, although the volume of the import trade is determined and stimulated by the export trade. The balance of trade between England and India may seem equilibrated or may disclose slight oscillations in either direction.—C. 2.

BALANCE OF WAGES

The prices of labor are much more constant than the prices of provisions, often they stand in inverse proportion. In a dear year wages fall on account of the fall in demand, but rise on account of the rise in the prices of provisions—and thus balance. In any case, a number of workers are left without bread. In cheap years wages rise on account of the rise in demand, but fall on account of the fall in the prices of provisions—and thus balance.—M.

BANK OF ENGLAND

The Bank of England, being a public institution under government protection and enjoying corresponding privileges, cannot exploit its power as ruthlessly as does private business.—C. 3.

The power of the Bank of England is revealed by its regulation of the market rate of interest. In times of normal activity, it may happen that the Bank cannot prevent a moderate drain of gold from its bullion reserve by raising the discount rate because the demand for means of payment is satisfied by private banks, stock banks and bill-brokers, who have gained considerably in capital power during the last thirty years. In such case, the Bank of England must have recourse to other means.—C. 3.

If the export of precious metal (gold) assumes a larger scope and lasts for a longer period, then the English bank reserve is affected, and the English money-market, particularly the Bank of England, must take protective measures. These consist mainly in raising the interest rate. When the drain on gold is considerable, the money-market as a rule becomes tight, that is, the demand for loan capital in the form of money significantly exceeds the supply and the higher interest rate follows quite naturally from this; the discount rate fixed by the Bank of England corresponds to the situation and asserts itself on the market.—C. 3.

BANKER
In society, a general or a *banker* plays a great part, but mere man, on the other hand, a very shabby part.—C. 1.

BANKING SYSTEM
By means of the banking system the distribution of capital as a special business, a social function, is taken out of the hands of the private capitalists and usurers. But at the same time, banking and credit thus become the most potent means of driving capitalist production beyond its own limits, and one of the most effective vehicles of crisis and swindle.—C. 3.

The banking system, so far as its formal organization and centralization is concerned, is the most artificial and most developed product turned out by the capitalist mode of production. —C. 3.

BANKS, BRITISH
Banks create credit and capital by (1) issuing their own notes, (2) writing out drafts on London running up to 21 days, but paid in cash to them immediately on issue and (3) paying out discounted bills of exchange, which are endowed with credit primarily and essentially by endorsement through the bank—at least as far as concerns the local district.—C. 3.

BARTER
The direct barter of products attains the elementary form of the relative expression of value in one respect, but not in another.— C. 1.

In the direct barter of products, each commodity is directly a means of exchange to its owner, and to all other persons an equivalent, but that only insofar as it has use-value for them. At this stage, therefore, the articles exchanged do not acquire a value-form independent of their own use-value, or of the individual needs of the exchangers.—C. 1.

BAYLE, PIERRE
Pierre Bayle did not only prepare the reception of materialism and the philosophy of common sense in France by shattering metaphysics with his skepticism. He heralded atheistic society,

which was soon to come to existence, by proving that a society consisting only of atheists is possible, that an atheist can be a respectable man and that it is not by atheism but by superstition and idolatry that man debases himself.—H. F.

BEAUTY
Man also forms things in accordance with the laws of beauty—M.

BEGGARY
A section of the working class falls into the ranks of beggary just as necessarily as a section of the middle capitalists falls into the working class.—M.

BEING
The less you are, the more you have; the less you express your own life, the greater is your alienated life—the greater is the store of your estranged being.—M.

A being which does not have its nature outside itself is not a natural being, and plays no part in the system of nature. A being which has no object outside itself is not an objective being. A being which is not itself an object for some third being has no being for its object; i. e., it is not objectively related. Its being is not objective.—M.

An unobjective being is a nullity—an un-being. Suppose a being which is neither an object itself, nor has an object. Such a being, in the first place, would be the unique being: there would exist no being outside it—it would exist solitary and alone. For as soon as there are objects outside me, as soon as I am not alone, I am another—another reality than the object outside me. For this third object I am thus another reality than it; that is, I am its object. Thus, to suppose a being which is not the object of another being is to presuppose that no objective being exists.—M.

BELLUM OMNIUM
In the animal kingdom, the bellum omnium contra omnes more or less preserves the conditions of existence of every species.—C. 1.

BEQUEST
A very happy event—yesterday we were informed of the death of the 90-year-old uncle of my wife. My mother-in-law thus saves 200 Thalers, and my wife will get approximately £100 or even more, if the old dog did not bequeath to his housekeeper that portion of the money, which is not a *fidei commis*.—Ltr. to Engels.

BIG CAPITALIST
If the big capitalist wants to squeeze out the smaller capitalist, he has all the advantages over him which the capitalist has as a capitalist over the worker. The larger size of his capital compensates him for the smaller profits, and he can ever bear temporary losses until the smaller capitalist is ruined and he finds himself freed from this competition. In this way, he accumulates the small capitalist's profits.—M.

The big capitalist introduces for himself some kind of organization of the instruments of labor.—M.

The big capitalist always buys cheaper than the small one, because he buys bigger quantities. He can therefore well afford to sell cheaper.—M.

BISMARCK
I had written about ten days ago telling Schweitzer that he must make a front against Bismarck, that even the appearance of a flirtation with Bismarck on the part of the workers' party must be dropped. He has thanked me by "all ready" philandering with Pissmarck more than ever.—Ltr. to Engels.

BONDAGE, ECONOMICAL
In reality, the laborer belongs to capital before he has sold himself to capital. His economical bondage is both brought about and concealed by the periodic sale of himself, by his change of masters, and by the oscillations in the market price of labor-power.—C. 1.

BOOKKEEPING
Apart from the actual buying and selling, labor-time is expended in bookkeeping, which besides absorbs materialized labor such as pens, ink, paper, desks, office paraphernalia.—C. 2.

Bookkeeping includes the determination of prices, or the calculation of the prices of commodities.—C. 2.

Bookkeeping, as the control and ideal synthesis of the process of production, becomes the more necessary the more the process assumes a social scale and loses its purely individual character. It is therefore more necessary in capitalist production than in the scattered production of handicraft and peasant economy, more necessary in collective (communist) production than in capitalist production.—C. 2.

BOREDOM
The mystical feeling which drives the philosopher forward from abstract thinking to intuiting is boredom—the longing for a content.—M.

BOURGEOIS ACCOMPLISHMENT
The bourgeoisie has been the first to show what man's activity can bring about. It has accomplished *wonders* far surpassing Egyptian pyramids, Roman aqueducts, and Gothic cathedrals; it has conducted expeditions that put in the shade all former Exoduses of nations and crusades.—C. M.

BOURGEOIS ARGUMENTS
"Undoubtedly," it will be said, "religious, moral, philosophical and juridical ideas have been modified in the course of historical development. But religion, morality, philosophy, political science, and law constantly survived this change. There are, besides,

eternal truths, such as Freedom, Justice, etc., that are common to all states of society. But communism abolishes eternal truths, it abolishes all religion, all morality, instead of constituting them on a new basis; it therefore acts in contradiction to all past historical experience."—C. M.

BOURGEOIS CHEAPNESS
The cheap prices of its commodities are the heavy artillery with which it batters down all Chinese walls, with which it forces the barbarians' intensely obstinate hatred of foreigners to capitulate.—C. M.

BOURGEOIS CONVERSION
The bourgeoisie has stripped of its halo every occupation hitherto honored and looked up to with reverent awe. It has con-

verted the physician, the lawyer, the priest, the poet, the man of science, into its paid wage-laborers.—C. M.

BOURGEOIS DUPLICITY
The relations of productions in which the bourgeoisie exists have not a single, a simple character, but a double character, a character of duplicity; in the same relations in which wealth is produced, poverty is produced also; in the same relations in which there is a development of productive forces, there is a productive force of repression; these relations produce bourgeois wealth, that is to say the wealth of the bourgeois class, only in continually annihilating the wealth of integral members of that class and in producing an ever-growing proletariat.—P. P.

BOURGEOIS INSTITUTIONS
State, church, etc., are only justified insofar as they are committees to superintend or administer the common interests of the productive bourgeoisie; and their costs—since by their nature these costs belong to the overhead costs of production—must be reduced to the unavoidable minimum.—C. 4.

BOURGEOIS INTERNATIONALISM
Just as the bourgeoisie has made the country dependent on the towns, so it has made barbarian and semi-barbarian countries dependent on the civilized ones, nations of peasants on nations of bourgeois, the East on the West.—C. M.

BOURGEOIS MISCONCEPTION
Selfish misconception induces you to transform into eternal laws of nature and of reason the social forms springing from your present mode of production and form of property.—C. M.

BOURGEOIS SELF-CONTRADICTION
Modern bourgeois society is like the sorcerer, who is no longer able to control the power of the nether world whom he has called up by his spells. For many a decade past the history of industry and commerce is but the history of the revolt of modern productive forces against modern conditions of production, against the (private) property relations.—C. M.

BOURGEOIS SELF-DESTRUCTION
The weapons with which the bourgeoisie felled feudalism to the ground are now turned against the bourgeoisie itself.—C. M.

BOURGEOIS SOCIETY
The conditions of bourgeois society are too narrow to comprise the wealth created by them. And how does the bourgeoisie get over these crises? On the one hand by enforced destruction of a a mass of productive forces; on the other, by the conquest of new markets, and by the more thorough exploitation of the old ones. —C.M. *See* Bourgeois self-contradiction.

BOURGEOIS THINKING
Your very ideas are but the outgrowth of the conditions of your bourgeois production and bourgeois property.—C. M.

BOURGEOISIE
By bourgeoisie is meant the class of modern capitalists, owner of the means of social production and employers of wage-labor.— C. M.

What the *bourgeoisie* produces, above all, are its own gravediggers. Its fall and the victory of the proletariat are equally inevitable.—C. M.

All the English bourgeoisie may be forced to do will neither emancipate nor materially mend the social conditions of the mass of the Indian people, depending not only on the development of the productive powers, but on their appropriation by the people. But what they will not fail to do is to lay down the material premises for both. Has the bourgeoisie ever done more? Has it ever effected a progress without dragging individuals and peoples through blood and dirt, through misery and degradation?—D. T.

BOURGEOISIE, MODERN
In proportion as industry, commerce, navigation, railways extended, in the same proportion the bourgeoisie developed, increased its capital, and pushed into the background every class handed down from the Middle Ages. The modern bourgeoisie is itself the product of a long course of development, of a series of revolutions in the modes of production and of exchange. —C. M.

The modern bourgeoisie is the necessary offspring of the feudal form of society.—C. M.

The modern bourgeois society that has sprouted from the ruins of feudal society has not done away with class antagonisms. It has but established new classes, new conditions of oppression, new forms of struggle in place of the old ones.—C. M.

The bourgeoisie compels all nations, on pain of extinction, to adopt the bourgeois mode of production; it compels them to introduce what it calls civilization into their midst, i.e., to become bourgeois themselves. In a word, it creates a world after its own image.—C. M.

BOURGEOISIE, ORIGIN OF
From the burgesses of the Middle Ages the first elements of the bourgeoisie were developed.—C. M.

BOURGEOISIE, REVOLUTIONARY
The bourgeoisie, historically, has played a most revolutionary part. The bourgeoisie, wherever it has got the upper hand, has put an end to all feudal, patriarchic, idyllic relations. It has pitilessly torn asunder the motley feudal ties that bound man to his "natural superiors," and has left remaining no other nexus between man and man than naked self-interest, than callous "cash payment." It has drowned the most heavenly ecstasies of religious fervor, of chivalrous enthusiasm, of philistine sentimentalism, in the icy water of egotistical calculation.—C. M.

BOYCOTT
If you break through the webs of routine thought, you are always sure to be "boycotted" in the first instance; it is the only arm of defense which in their first perplexity the *routiniers* know how to wield. I have been "boycotted" in Germany for many years.—Ltr. to Danielson.

BRAVERY
He who can buy bravery is brave, though a coward.—M.

BRITISH COLONIALISM
The profound hypocrisy and inherent barbarism of bourgeois civilization lies unveiled before our eyes, turning from its home,

where it assumes respectable forms, to the colonies, where it goes naked. They are the defenders of property, but did any revolutionary party ever originate agrarian revolutions like those in Bengal, in Madras, and in Bombay? Did they not, in India, to borrow an expression of that great robber, Lord Clive himself, resort to atrocious extortion, when simple corruption could not keep pace with their rapacity? While they combated the French Revolution under the pretext of defending "our holy religion," did they not forbid, at the same time, Christianity to be propagated in India, and did they not, in order to make money out of the pilgrims streaming to the temples of Orissa and Bengal, take up the trade in the murder and prostitution perpetrated in the temple of Juggernaut? These are the men of "Property, Order, Family, and Religion."—D. T.

It was the British intruder who broke up the Indian hand-loom and then destroyed the spinning-wheel. England began with driving the Indian cottons from the European market; it then introduced twist into Hindustan and in the end inundated the very mother country of cotton with cottons. But at the same time the population of Dacca decreased from 150,000 inhabitants to 20,-000. This decline of Indian towns celebrated for their fabrics was by no means the worst consequence. British steam and science uprooted, over the whole surface of Hindustan, the union between agriculture and manufacturing industry.—D. T.

The antagonism of the various races, tribes, creeds and sovereignties continued to be the vital principle of British supremacy.—D. T.

BRITISH EAST INDIA COMPANY
The true commencement of the East India Company cannot be dated from a more remote epoch than the year 1702, when the different societies, claiming the monopoly of the East India trade, united together into one single company. Till then the very existence of the original East India Company was repeatedly endangered, once suspended for years under the protectorate of Cromwell, and once threatened with utter dissolution by parliamentary interference under the reign of William III. It was under the ascendancy of that Dutch Prince, when the Bank of England sprang into life, when the protective system was

firmly established in England, and when the balance of power in Europe was definitively settled, that the existence of an East India Company was recognized by Parliament.—D. T.

The East India Company commenced by attempting merely to establish factories for their agents, and places of deposit for their goods. In order to protect them they erected several forts.—D. T.

European despotism was planted upon Asiatic despotism, by the *British East India Company,* forming a more monstrous combination than any of the divine monsters startling us in the Temple of Salsette.—D. T.

BRITISH IMPERIALISM
The Roman *divide et impera* was the great rule by which Great Britain, for about one hundred and fifty years, contrived to retain the tenure of her Indian Empire. The antagonism of the various races, tribes, castes, creeds and sovereignties continued to be the vital principle of British supremacy.—D. T.

BUILDING BUSINESS
In the London building business, which is carried on mainly on credit, the building contractor receives advances in accordance with the stage of construction reached. None of these stages is a house, but only a really existing constituent part of an inchoate future house; hence, in spite of its reality, it is but an ideal fraction of the entire house, but real enough to serve as security for an additional advance.—C. 1.

BULLION
The only difference between coin and bullion is one of shape, and gold can at any time pass from one form to the other.—C. 1.

BUREAUCRACY
A race brought up in *bureaucracy* has to take a lesson in "self-help."—Ltr. to Engels.

BUYING AND SELLING
This talk about free selling and buying, and all the other "brave words" of our bourgeoisie about freedom in general, have no

meaning when opposed to communistic abolition of buying and selling.—C. M.

BYZANTINE STATE
The Byzantine state was the properly religious state, for there dogmas were matters of state, but the Byzantine state was the worst of all states.—L. A.

C

CAPITAL
Capital is not a personal, it is a social power.—C. M.

Capital is stored-up labor.—M.

The essential condition for the existence, and for the sway, of the bourgeois class is the formation and augmentation of capital. —C. M.

Capital is the governing power over labor and its products. The capitalist possesses the power, not on account of his personal or human qualities, but inasmuch as he is an owner of capital. His power is the purchasing power of his capital, which nothing can withstand.—M.

People who do not own capital, tackle it quite differently than the owner, who anxiously weighs the limitations of his private capital in so far as he handles it himself.—C. 3.

As a matter of history, capital, as opposed to landed property, invariably takes the form at first of money; it appears as moneyed wealth, as the capital of the merchant and of the usurer. But we have no need to refer to the origin of capital in order to discover that the first form of appearance of capital is money. —C. 1.

CAPITAL, SIZE OF
The larger size of his capital compensates the biggest capitalist for the smaller profits.—M.

CAPITAL, SOCIAL CHARACTER OF
Capital announces from its first appearance a new epoch in the process of social production.—C. 1.

To be a capitalist is to have not only a purely personal, but a social status in production. Capital is a collective product, and only by the united action of many members, nay, in the last resort, only by the united action of all members of society, can it be set in motion.—C. M.

The social character of capital is first promoted and wholly realized through the full development of the credit and banking system.—C. 3.

By means of the banking system the distribution of capital as a special business, a social function, is taken out of the hands of the private capitalists.—C. 3.

CAPITAL AND PRODUCTION
With the accumulation of capital, the specifically capitalistic mode of production develops, and with the capitalistic mode of production the accumulation of capital.—C. 1.

On the one hand it is the tendency of capital to reduce to a dwindling minimum the labor-time necessary for the production of commodities, and therefore also the number of the productive population in relation to the amount of the product. On the other hand, however, the capitalist mode of production has the opposite tendency to accumulate, to transform profit into capital, to appropriate the greatest possible quantity of the labor of others. It strives to reduce the norm of necessary labor, but to employ the greatest possible quantity of productive labor at a given norm.—C. 4.

We have seen not only how capital produces, but how it itself is produced, and how, as an essentially altered relation, it emerges from the process of production and how it is developed

in it. On the one hand capital transforms the mode of production; on the other hand this changed form of the mode of production and a particular stage in the development of the material forces of production are the basis and precondition, the premise, for its own formation.—C. 4.

We have seen that it is a law of capitalist production that its development is attended by a relative decrease of variable in relation to constant capital, and consequently to the total capital set in motion.—C. 3.

CAPITALISM
If large capital is opposed by small capitals, it crushes them completely.—M.

CAPITALIST
The capitalist himself only holds power as the personification of capital.—C. 4. *See* Italian Bookkeeping.

Except as personified capital, the capitalist has no historical value. . . . And so far only is the necessity for his own transitory existence implied in the transitory necessity for the capitalist mode of production.—C. 1.

CAPITALIST ACCUMULATION
So far as accumulation of capital takes place, the capitalist must have succeeded in selling his commodities, and in reconverting the sale-money into capital.—C. 1.

CAPITALIST ACCUMULATION, LAW OF
The greater the industrial reserve army in proportion to the active labor army, the greater is the mass of a consolidated surplus population, whose misery is in inverse ratio to its torment of labor. The more extensive, finally, the lazarus-layers of the working class, and the industrial reserve army, the greater is official pauperism. This is the absolute general law of capitalist accumulation.—C. 1.

CAPITALIST AIM
The capitalist's aim is to produce not only a use-value, but a commodity also; not only use-value, but value; not only value, but at the same time surplus-value.—C. 1.

CAPITALIST CONFLICT
The means—unconditional development of the productive forces of society—comes continually into conflict with the limited purpose, the self-expansion, of the existing capital. The capitalist

mode of production is, for this reason, a historical means of developing the material forces of production and creating an appropriate world-market, and is, at the same time, a continual conflict between this its historical task and its own correspondin the spider-web of usury.—C. 3.

CAPITALIST EXPLOITATION
In a social order dominated by capitalist production even the non-capitalist producer is gripped by capitalist conceptions. Balzac, who is generally remarkable for his profound grasp of reality, aptly describes in his last novel, *Les Paysans*, how a petty peasant performs many small tasks gratuitously for his usurer, whose goodwill he is eager to retain, and how he fancies that he does not give the latter something for nothing because his own labor does not cost him any cash outlay. As for the usurer, he thus fells two dogs with one stone. He saves the cash outlay for wages and enmeshes the peasant, who is gradually ruined by depriving his own field of labor, deeper and deeper in the spider-web of usury.—C. 3.

CAPITALIST GOALS
Our capitalist has two objects in view: in the first place, he wants to produce a use-value that has a value in exchange, that is to say, an article destined to be sold, a commodity; and secondly, he desires to produce a commodity whose value shall be greater than the sum of the values of the commodities used in its production, that is, of the means of production and the labor power, that he purchased with his good money in the open market.—C. 1.

As in religion man is governed by the products of his own brain, so in *capitalist production*, he is governed by the products of his own hand.—C. 1.

CAPITALIST PRODUCTION
Capitalist production only then really begins . . . when each individual capitalist employs simultaneously a comparatively large number of laborers; when consequently the labor-process is carried on on an extensive scale and yields, relatively, large quantities of products. A greater number of laborers working

together, at the same time, in one place (or, if you will, in the same field of labor), in order to produce the same sort of commodity under the mastership of one capitalist, constitutes, both historically and logically, the starting point of capitalist production.—C. 1.

Fanatically bent on making value expand itself, the capitalist ruthlessly forces the human race to produce for production's sake; he does force the development of the productive powers in society.—C. 1.

Wherever it takes root capitalist production destroys all forms of commodity production which are based either on the self-employment of the producers, or merely on the sale of the excess product as commodities. Capitalist production first makes the production of commodities general and then, by degrees, transforms all commodity production into capitalist commodity production.—C. 2.

The real barrier of *capitalist production* is capital itself. It is that capital and its self-expansion appear as the starting and the closing point, the motive and the purpose of production; that production is only production for capital and not vice versa, the means of production are not mere means for a constant expansion of the living process of the society of producers. The limits within which the preservation and self-expansion of the value of capital resting on the expropriation and pauperization of the great mass of producers can alone move—these limits come continually into conflict with the methods of production employed by capital for its own purposes, which drive toward unlimited extension of production, toward production as an end in itself, toward unconditional development of the social productivity of labor.—C. 3.

CAPITALIST PRODUCTION, LAWS OF
In theory it is assumed that the laws of capitalist production operate in their pure form. In reality there exists only approximation; but this approximation is the greater, the more developed the capitalist mode of production and the less it is adulterated and amalgamated with survivals of former economic conditions.—C. 3.

CAPITALIZATION
The formation of a fictitious capital is called capitalization. Every periodic income is capitalized by calculating it on the basis of the average rate of interest, as an income which would be realized by a capital loaned at this rate of interest.—C. 3.

CASTE
The division of labor has made castes. But castes are the inconveniences of the division of labor; then it is the division of labor which has engendered inconveniences. *Quod erat demonstrandum.*—P. P.

CAVE
Man is regressing to the cave dwelling, etc.—but he is regressing to it in an estranged, malignant form. The savage in his cave—a natural element which freely offers itself for his use and protection—feels himself no more a stranger, or rather feels himself to be just as much at home as a fish in water. But the *cellar dwelling* of the poor man is a hostile dwelling.—M.

CELLAR DWELLING
The worker's crude need is a far greater source of gain than the refined need of the rich. The cellar dwellings in London bring more to those who let them than do the palaces; that is to say, with reference to the landlord they constitute greater wealth, and thus (to speak the language of political economy) greater social wealth.—M.

CENSORSHIP
What do we need censorship for, when the philosophical press discredits itself in the public eye?—L. A.

CENTRAL BANK
The central bank is the pivot of the credit system.—C. 3.

CENTRALIZATION
Competition and credit are the two most powerful levers of centralization.—C. 1.

CENTRALIZATION, POLITICAL
The bourgeoisie has agglomerated population, centralized means of production, and has concentrated property in a few hands. The necessary consequence of this was political centralization.

Independent, or but loosely connected, provinces, with separate interests, laws, governments and systems of taxation, became lumped together in one nation, with one government, one code of laws, one national class-interest, one frontier and one customs tariff.—C. M.

CENTRALIZATION OF CAPITAL
One capitalist always kills many.—C. 1.

The centralization of capital is essential to the existence of capital as an independent power. The destructive influence of that centralization upon the markets of the world does but reveal, in the most gigantic dimensions, the inherent organic laws of political economy now at work in every civilized town.—D. T.

Centralization supplements the work of accumulation, by enabling the industrial capitalists to expand the scale of their operations. The economic result remains the same, whether centralization is accomplished by the violent means of annexation, by which some capitals become such overwhelming centers of gravitation for others as to break their individual cohesion and attracting the scattered fragments, or whether the amalgamation of a number of capitals, which already exist or are in process of formation, proceeds by the smoother road of forming stock companies.—C. 1.

CENTRALIZATION PROPER
Capital grows in one place to a huge mass in a single hand, because it has in another place been lost by many. This is centralization proper, as distinct from accumulation and concentration.—C. 1.

CHANGE
The philosophers have only interpreted the world, in various ways; the point, however, is to change it.—T. F.

CHARGES, IDEOLOGICAL
The charges against communism made from a religious, a philosophical, and, generally, from an ideological standpoint, are not deserving of serious examination.—C. M.

CHARM OF WORK
Owing to the extensive use of machinery and the division of labor, the work of the proletarians has lost all individual character, and, consequently, all charm for the workman. He becomes an appendage of the machine, and it is only the most simple, most monotonous, and the most easily acquired knack that is required of him.—C. M.

CHEAP BUYING
The big capitalist always buys cheaper than the small one, because he buys bigger quantities.—M.

CHEMICAL INDUSTRY
Every advance in chemistry not only multiplies the number of useful materials and the useful applications of those already known, thus extending with the growth of capital its sphere of investment. It teaches at the same time how to throw the excrements of the processes of production and consumption back again into the circle of the process of reproduction, and thus, without any previous outlay of capital, creates new matter for capital.—C. 1.

CHILD LABOR
In the automatic factories, as in all the great workshops, where machinery enters as a factor, or where only the modern divisions of labor are carried out, large numbers of boys are employed up to the age of maturity. When this term is once reached, only a very small number continue to find employment in the same branches of industry, whilst the majority are regularly discharged.—C. 1.

CHILDREN, EXPLOITATION OF
Do you charge us with wanting to stop the exploitation of children by their parents? To this crime we plead guilty.—C. M.

By the action of modern industry, the proletarian children are transformed into simple articles of commerce and instruments of labor.—C. M.

CHINESE WAR
All we want is to study the first Chinese war, an event, so to say, of yesterday. The English soldiery then committed abomi-

nations for the mere fun of it; their passions being neither sanctified by religious fanaticism nor exacerbated by hatred against an overbearing and conquering race, nor provoked by the stern resistance of a heroic enemy. The violations of women, the spittings of children, the roastings of whole villages, were then mere wanton sports, not recorded by mandarins, but by British officers themselves.—D. T.

CHRISTIAN SOCIALISM
Nothing is easier than to give Christian asceticism a socialist tinge. Has not Christianity declaimed against private property, against marriage, against the state? Has it not preached in the place of these, charity and poverty, celibacy, and mortification of the flesh? Christian socialism is but the holy water with which the priest consecrates the heart-burnings of the aristocrat.—C. M.

CHRISTIANITY
Was it not Christianity before anything else that separated church and state?—L. A.

When the ancient world was in its last throes, the ancient religions were overcome by Christianity.—C. M.

CIRCULATION, VELOCITY OF
The velocity of circulation of the money-capital advanced by the merchant depends (1) on the speed with which the process of production is renewed and the different processes of production are linked together; and (2) on the velocity of consumption.—C. 3.

CIRCULATION OF BLOOD
One of the savants of Paul de Kock may tell me that the circulation of my blood is a condition for my enrichment.—C. 4.

CIRCULATION OF CAPITAL
Time of circulation and time of production mutually exclude each other. During its time of circulation capital does not perform the functions of productive capital and therefore produces neither commodities nor surplus-value.—C. 2.

CIRCULATION OF COMMODITIES
The *circulation of commodities* is the starting point of capital.—C. 1.

Circulation, or the exchange of commodities, begets no value.—C. 1.

The circulation of commodities differs from the direct exchange of products (barter), not only in form, but in substance. . . . The process of circulation does not, like direct barter of products, become extinguished upon the use values changing places and hands.—C. 1.

CIRCULATION OF MONEY
Money, as the medium of circulation, keeps continually within the sphere of circulation, and moves about in it.—C. 1.

The money does not vanish on dropping out of the circuit of the metamorphosis of a given commodity, It is constantly being precipitated into new places in the arena of circulation vacated by other commodities.—C. 1.

CIRCUMSTANCES
The materialist doctrine forgets that it is men that change circumstances.—T. F.

Circumstances make man just as much as man makes circumstances.—G. I.

CIVIL RIGHTS
Human rights fall under the category of political freedom, of civil rights, which by no means presupposes the abolition of religion.—J. Q.

CIVIL SOCIETY
According to Hegel the civil society is a "spiritual animal kingdom," as according to Darwin the spiritual animal kingdom represents a civil society.—Ltr. to Engels.

The anatomy of civil society is to be sought in political economy.—P. E.

Society, as it appears to the political economist, is civil society, in which every individual is a totality of needs and only exists for the other person, as the other exists for him, insofar as each becomes a means for the other. The political economist reduces everything to man, i.e., to the individual whom he strips of all determinateness so as to class him as capitalist or worker.—M.

CIVILIZATION
The bourgeoisie, by the rapid improvement of all instruments of production, by the immensely facilitated means of communication, draws all, even the most barbarian, nations into civilization.—C. M.

Just as the savage must wrestle with nature to satisfy his wants, to maintain and reproduce life, so must civilized man, and he must do so in all social formations and under all possible modes of production.—C. 3.

CLASS DUALISM
Our epoch, the epoch of the bourgeoisie, possesses this distinctive feature; it has simplified the class antagonisms. Society as a whole is more and more splitting up into two great hostile camps, into two great classes directly facing each other: Bourgeoisie and Proletariat.—C. M.

The final consequence is . . . the abolishment of the distinction between capitalist and landowner, so that there remain altogether only two classes—the working class and the class of the capitalists.—M.

CLASS RENEGADE
Just as, at an earlier period, a section of the nobility went over to the bourgeoisie, so now a portion of the bourgeoisie goes over to the proletariat, and in particular, a portion of the bourgeoisie goes over to the proletariat, and in particular, a portion of the bourgeois ideologists, who have raised themselves to the level of comprehending theoretically the historical movements as a whole.—C. M.

CLASS STATE
The state is only justified insofar as it is a committee to superintend or administer the common interests of the bourgeoisie.—M.

CLASS STRUGGLE
Every class struggle is a political struggle.—C. M.

If the conditions, under which the *class struggle* rages, were always propitious, world history would be easily achieved. Indeed, it would be very mystical if "accidents" were not involved.—Ltr. to Kugelmann.

Here and there the contest (between proletariat and bourgeoisie) breaks out into riots.—C. M.

The history of all past society has consisted in the development of class antagonism, antagonism that assumed different forms at different epochs. But whatever form they may have taken, one fact is common to all past ages, viz., the exploitation of one part of society by another.—C. M.

The history of all hitherto existing society is the history of class struggles. Freeman and slave, patrician and plebeian, lord and serf, guild-master and journeyman, in a word, oppressor and oppressed, stood in constant opposition to one another, carried on an uninterrupted, now hidden, now open fight, a fight that each time ended, either in a revolutionary reconstitution of society at large, or in the common ruin of the contending classes.—C. M.

The proletariat goes through various stages of development. With its birth begins its struggle with the bourgeoisie. At first the contest is carried on by individual laborers, then by the working people of a factory, then by the operatives of one trade, in one locality, against the individual bourgeois who directly exploits them.—C. M.

The development of class antagonism keeps even pace with the development of industry.—C. M.

CLASS UNIFICATION
A section of large landowners become simultaneously industrialists.—M.

CLASS WAR
In depicting the most general phases of the development of the proletariat, we traced the more or less veiled civil war, ranging within existing society, up to the point where that war breaks out into open revolution, and where the violent overthrow of the bourgeoisie lays the foundation for the sway of the proletariat.—C. M.

CLASSES
The existence of classes is connected with particular, historic phases in the development of production.—Ltr. to Weydmeyer.

The first question to be answered is this: What constitutes a class—and the reply to this follows naturally from the reply to another question, namely: What makes wage-laborers, capitalists and landlords constitute the three great social classes? At first glance—the identity of revenues and sources of revenue. There are three great social groups whose members, the individuals forming them, live on wages, profit and ground-rent respectively, on the realization of their labor-power, their capital, and their landed property. However, from this standpoint, physicians and officials, e.g., would also constitute two classes, for they belong to two distinct social groups, the members of each of these groups receiving their revenue from one and the same source.—C. 3.

CLASSICAL ECONOMY
Accumulation for accumulation's sake, production for production's sake: by this formula classical economy expressed the historical mission of the bourgeoisie.—C. 1.

CLASSLESS SOCIETY
In a future society, the antagonisms of classes will have ceased, there will no longer be classes.—P. P.

If the proletariat during its contest with the bourgeoisie is compelled, by the force of circumstances, to organize itself as a class, if, by means of revolution, it makes itself a ruling class, and, as such, sweeps away by force the old conditions of production, then it will, along with these conditions, have swept away the conditions for the existence of class antagonism, and of classes generally, and will thereby have abolished its own supremacy as a class.—C. M.

CLIMATE
The more unfavorable the climate, the more congested is the working period in agriculture, and hence the shorter is the time in which capital and labor are expended. Take Russia for instance. In some of the northern districts of that country field labor is possible only from 130 to 150 days throughout the year, and it may be imagined what a loss Russia would sustain if 50 out of the 65 millions of her European population remained without work during the six or eight months of the winter, when agricultural labor is at a standstill.—C. 2.

CLOCK
The clock is the first automatic machine applied to practical purposes.—Ltr. to Engels.

CLOTHING
Wherever the want of clothing forced them to it, the human race made clothes for thousands of years, without a single man becoming a tailor. But coats and linen, like every other element of material wealth that is the spontaneous produce of nature, must invariably owe their existence to a special productive activity, exercised with a definite aim, an activity that appropriates particular nature-given materials to particular human wants.—C. 1.

Whether the coat be worn by the tailor or by his customer, in either case it operates as a use-value.—C. 1.

COAL
When a coal mine supplies coal to an ironworks and gets from the latter iron which enters into the operations of the coal mine as means of production, the coal is in this way exchanged for capital to the amount of its own value, is exchanged as capital for coal.—C.4.

COIN
That money takes the shape of coin springs from its function as the circulation medium.—C. 1.

COINING
Coining, like the establishment of a standard of prices, is the business of the state.—C. 1.

COLONIALISM
The discovery of America, the rounding of the Cape, opened up fresh ground for the rising bourgeoisie. The East Indian and Chinese markets, the colonization of America, trade with the colonies, the increase in the means of exchange and in commodities, generally, gave to commerce, to navigation, to industry, an impulse never before known, and thereby, to the revolutionary element in the tottering feudal society, a rapid development.—C. M.

COMBINATION, SOCIOLOGICAL
Combination among the capitalists is customary and effective; workers' combination is prohibited and painful in its consequences for them. Besides, the landowner and the capitalist can augment their revenues with the fruits of industry; the worker has neither ground-rent nor interest on capital to supplement his industrial income. Hence the intensity of the competition among the workers. Thus only for the workers is the separation of capital, landed property and labor an inevitable, essential and detrimental separation. Capital and landed property need not remain fixed in this abstraction, as must the labor of the workers.—M.

COMMERCE
The commerce of the world almost entirely turns upon wants arising not from individual consumption but from production. —P. P.

Commerce increased the misery of the masses in those countries whose principal export was raw produce.—Ltr. to Danielson.

COMMODITIES, KNOWLEDGE OF
The use-values of commodities furnish the material for a special study, that of the commercial knowledge of commodities.—C. 1.

COMMODITY
A commodity appears, at first sight, a very trivial thing, and easily understood. Its analysis shows that it is, in reality, a very queer thing, abounding in metaphysical subtleties and theological niceties.—C. 1.

A commodity is, in the first place, an object outside us, a thing that by its properties satisfies human wants of some sort or another. The nature of such wants, whether, for instance, they spring from the stomach or from fancy, makes no difference. Neither are we here concerned to know how the object satisfies these wants, either directly as means of subsistence or indirectly as means of production.—C. 1.

Commodities have only one common property left, that of being products of labor.—C. 1.

A thing can be useful, and the product of human labor, without being a commodity. Whoever directly satisfies his wants with the produce of his own labor, creates, indeed, use-values, but not commodities. In order to produce the latter, he must not only produce use-values, but use-values for others, social use-values.—C. 1.

COMMODITY, PRODUCTION OF
The division of labor is a necessary condition for the production of commodities, but it does not follow conversely that the production of commodities is a necessary condition for the division of labor.—C. 1.

COMMODITY, THE WORKER AS
The worker becomes all the poorer the more wealth he produces, the more his production increases in power and range. The worker becomes an ever cheaper commodity the more commodities he creates. With the increasing value of the world of things proceeds in direct proportion the devaluation of the world of men. Labor produces not only commodities: it produces itself and the worker as a commodity—and does so in the proportion in which it produces commodities generally.—M.

COMMODITY, VALUE OF
The value of a commodity represents human labor in the abstract, the expenditure of human labor in general.—C. 1.

The value of each commodity is determined by the quantity of labor expended on and materialized in it, by the working-time necessary, under given social conditions, for its production.—C. 1.

Commodities, in which equal quantities of labor are embodied, or which can be produced in the same time, have the same value. The value of one commodity is to the value of any other, as the labor-time necessary for the production of the one is to that necessary for the production of the other.—C. 1.

COMMODITY MAN
Production does not simply produce man as a commodity, the commodity man, man in the role of a commodity; it produces him in keeping with this role as a spiritually and physically dehumanized being.—M.

COMMON INTEREST
The common interest is appreciated by each only so long as he gains more by it than without it. And unity of action ceases the moment one or the other side becomes the weaker, when each tries to extricate himself on his own as advantageously as he possibly can. Again, if one produces more cheaply and can sell more goods, thus possessing himself of a greater place in the market by selling below the current market-price, he will do so, and will thereby begin a movement which gradually compels the others to introduce the cheaper mode of production, and one which reduces the socially necessary labor to a new, and lower, level. If one side has the advantage, all belonging to it gain. It is as though they exerted their common monopoly.— C. 3.

COMMON OWNERSHIP
Haxthausen discovered common ownership of land in Russia, Maurer proved it to be the social foundation from which all Teutonic races started in history.—C. M.

COMMUNE
"Commune" was the name taken in France by the nascent towns even before they had conquered from their feudal lords and masters local self-government and political rights as the "Third Estate."—C. M.

The working class did not expect miracles from the *Commune*. They have no ready-made utopias to introduce by decree of the people. They have *no ideals* to realize, but to set free the elements of the new society with which old collapsing bourgeois society is pregnant.—C. W.

COMMUNISM
Communism is the positive expression of annulled private property.—M.

Communism differs from all previous movements in that it overturns the basis of all earlier relations of production, and for the first time consciously treats all natural premises as the creatures of man and strips them of their natural character and subjugates them to the power of individuals united. Its organization is, therefore, essentially economic, the material production of the conditions of this unity.—C. 1.

The communists never cease, for a single moment, to instill into the working class the clearest possible recognition of the hostile antagonism between bourgeoisie and proletariat.—C. M.

The communists everywhere support every revolutionary movement against the existing social and political order of things.—C. M.

Communism begins from the outset with atheism; but atheism is at first far from being communism; indeed, it is still mostly an abstraction.—M.

Communism as the positive transcendence of private property, as human self-estrangement, and therefore as the real appropriation of human essence by and for man; communism therefore is the complete return of man to himself as a social (i.e., human) being—a return become conscious, and accomplished within the entire wealth of previous development.—M.

Communism is the riddle of history solved, and it knows itself to be this solution.—M.

In order to abolish the idea of private property, the idea of communism is completely sufficient. It takes actual communist action to abolish actual private property. History will come to it; and this movement, which in theory we already know to be a self-transcending movement, will constitute in actual fact a very severe and protracted process. But we must regard it as a real advance to have gained beforehand a consciousness of the limited character as well as of the goal of this historical movement—and a consciousness which reaches out beyond it.—M.

Communism is . . . the negation of the negation, and is hence the actual phase necessary for the next stage of historical development in the process of human emancipation and recovery. Communism is the necessary pattern and the dynamic principle of the *immediate* future, but communism as such is *not* the goal of human development—the structure of human society.—M.

This communism, as fully developed naturalism, equals humanism, and as fully developed humanism equals naturalism; it is the genuine resolution of the conflict between man and nature and between man and man—the true resolution of the strife between existence and essence, between objectification and self-confirmation, between freedom and necessity, between the individual and the species.—M.

COMMUNISM, ACCUSATION OF
Where is the party in opposition that has not been decried as communistic by its opponents in power? Where the opposition that has not hurled back the branding reproach of communism, against the more advanced opposition parties, as well as against its reactionary adversaries?—C. M.

COMMUNISM, CRUDE
The first positive annulment of private property—crude communism—is merely one form in which the vileness of private property, which wants to set itself up as the positive community, comes to the surface.—M.

COMMUNISM, IMMATURE
The other, still immature communism, meanwhile seeks an historical proof for itself—a proof in the realm of the existent—amongst disconnected historical phenomena opposed to private property, tearing single phases from the historical process and focusing attention on them as proofs of its historical pedigree. By so doing it simply makes clear that by far the greater part of this process contradicts its claims, and that, if it has once been, precisely its being in the past refutes its pretension to being essential.—M.

COMMUNIST AIM
The immediate aim of the communists is the same as that of all the other proletarian parties: formation of the proletariat into a class, overthrow of the bourgeois supremacy, conquest of political power by the proletariat.—C. M.

COMMUNIST CONCLUSIONS
The theoretical conclusions of the communists are in no way based on ideas or principles that have been invented, or discovered, by this or that would-be universal reformer. They merely express, in general terms, actual relations springing from an existing class struggle, from a historical movement going on under our very eyes.—C. M.

COMMUNIST MANIFESTO
It is high time that communists should openly, in the face of the whole world, publish their views, their aims, their tendencies, and meet the nursery tale of the Specter of Communism with a Manifesto of the party itself.—C. M.

COMMUNIST MOTTO
Working men of all countries, unite!—C. M.

COMMUNIST POWER
Communism is already acknowledged by all European Powers to be itself a Power.—C. M.

COMMUNIST PROGRAM
The theory of the Communists may be summed up in the single sentence: abolition of private property.—C. M.

Theoretically, the communists have over the great mass of the proletariat the advantage of clearly understanding the line of march, the conditions, and the ultimate general results of the proletarian movement.—C. M.

COMMUNIST REVOLUTION
The communists disdain to conceal their views and aims. They openly declare that their ends can be attained only by the forcible overthrow of all existing social conditions. Let the ruling classes tremble at a communist revolution. The proletarians have nothing to lose but their chains. They have a world to win.—C. M.

COMMUNIST SPECTER
A specter is haunting Europe—the specter of communism. All the powers of old Europe have entered into a holy alliance to exorcise this specter.—C. M.

COMMUNIST WORKMEN
When communist workmen associate with one another, theory, propaganda, etc., is their first end. But at the same time, as a result of this association, they acquire a new need—the need for society—and what appears as a means becomes an end.—M.

COMMUNISTS
The communists do not form a separate party opposed to other working-class parties. They have no interest separate and apart from those of the proletariat as a whole. They do not set up any sectarian principles of their own, by which to shape and mold the proletarian movement.—C. M.

COMPENSATION
Concerning the relationship between worker and capitalist one should add that the capitalist is more than compensated for the raising of wages by the reduction in the amount of labor time. —M.

The more hazardous lines pay higher insurance rates, and recover them in the prices of their commodities. In practice all this means that every circumstance, which renders one line of production—and all of them are considered equally necessary within certain limits—less profitable, and another more profitable, is taken into account once and for all as valid ground for compensation, without always requiring the renewed action of competition to justify the motives or factors for calculating this compensation.—C. 3.

COMPETITION

Competition is only possible if capitals are held in many hands. —M.

Competition is not industrial emulation, it is commercial emulation.—P. P.

Competition compels the producer to sell the product of two hours as cheaply as the product of one hour.—P. P.

Competition always tends to level the rate of profits, which can rise only temporarily above the ordinary rate.—P. P.

Since we already know that monopoly prices are as high as possible, since the interest of the capitalists, even from the point of view commonly held by political economists, stands in hostile opposition to society, and since a rise of profit operates like compound interest on the price of the commodity, it follows that the sole defense against the capitalists is competition, which according to the evidence of political economy acts beneficently by both raising wages and lowering the prices of commodities to the advantage of the consuming public.—M.

Competition can influence the rate of profit only to the extent that it affects the prices of commodities. Competition can only make the producers within the same sphere of production sell their commodities at the same prices, and make them sell their commodities in different spheres of production at prices which will give them the same profit, the same proportional addition to the price of commodities which has already been partially determined by wages. Hence competition can only equalize inequalities in the rate of profit.—C. 3.

Competition, according to an American economist, determines how many days of simple labor are contained in a day of complex labor.—P. P.

Competition lowers the prices of commodities to the advantage of the consuming public.—M.

The sole defense against the capitalists is *competition.*—M.

The side of competition which happens for the moment to be weaker is also the side in which the individual acts independently of, and often directly against, the mass of his competitors, and precisely in this manner is the dependence of one upon the other impressed upon them, while the stronger side acts always more or less as a united whole against its antagonist. If the demand for this particular kind of commodity is greater than the supply, one buyer outbids another—within certain limits—and so raises the price of the commodity for all of them above the market-value, while on the other hand the sellers unite in trying to sell at a high market-price. If, conversely, the supply exceeds the demand, one begins to dispose of his goods at a cheaper rate and the others must follow, while the buyers unite in their efforts to depress the market-price as much as possible below the market-value.—C. 3.

The battle of competition is fought by cheapening of commodities. The cheapness of commodities depends, *ceteris paribus,* on the productiveness of labor, and this again on the scale of production. Therefore, the larger capitals beat the smaller. . . . It always ends in the ruin of many small capitalists, whose capitals partly pass into the hand of their conquerors, partly vanish.—C. 1.

Competition engenders poverty, foments civil war; it disturbs families, corrupts the public conscience, "changes the natural zones," confounds nationalities, "overturns the notions of equity, of justice," of morality, and what is worse, it destroys honest and free commerce and does not even give in exchange synthetical value, fixed and honest price. It disenchants everybody, even the economists. It forces things on, even to its own destruction.—P. P. *See* Economic Relation.

COMPETITION, CAPITALISTIC
The competition among capitalists becomes more intense. The concentration of capitals increases, the big capitals ruin the small, and a section of the erstwhile capitalists sinks into the working class, which as a result of this supply again suffers to some extent a depression of wages and passes into a still greater dependence on a few big capitalists. The number of capitalists having been diminished, their competition with respect to workers scarcely exists any longer; and the number of workers having been augmented, their competition among themselves has become all the more intense, unnatural and violent. Consequently, a section of the working class falls into the ranks of beggary or starvation just as necessarily as a section of the middle capitalists falls into the working class.—M.

COMPOSITION OF CAPITAL
Political economy has never thoroughly analyzed the differences in the organic *composition of capital*.—C. 3.

CONCENTRATION
Concentration is the secret of strategy.—D. T.

CONCENTRATION, CAPITALIST
The splitting up of the total social capital into many individual capitals or the repulsion of its fractions one from another is counteracted by their attraction. This last does not mean that simple concentration of the means of production and of the command over labor, which is identical with accumulation. It is concentration of capitals already formed, destruction of their individual independence, expropriation of capitalist by capitalist, transformation of many small into few large capitals.—C. 1.

CONSCIENCE
How can I have a good conscience if I am not conscious of anything?—M.

CONSCIOUSNESS
Consciousness—self-consciousness—is at home with itself in its other-being as such.—M.

Consciousness is from the start a product of society, and it remains such as long as men exist at all. At the beginning consciousness is of course only consciousness of the *immediate* sensuous surroundings and consciousness of the limited connection with other persons and things outside the individual becoming conscious of itself; at the same time it is consciousness of nature, which at the beginning confronts man as a completely alien, almighty and unassailable power to which man's attitude is a purely animal one and to which he submits like a beast; it is therefore a purely animal consciousness of nature.—G. I.

It is not the consciousness of men that determines their being, but, on the contrary, their social being that determines their consciousness.—P. E.

It is not consciousness that determines life, but life that determines consciousness.—G. 1.

CONSPIRACY
The workers' demonstrations in London are the work of the "International." Mr. Lucraft, for instance, the captain in Trafalgar Square, is one of our Council. This proves the difference between working behind the scenes by disappearing in public and the Democrats' way of making oneself important in public and doing nothing.—Ltr. to Engels.

The pamphlet must first be published anonymously, so that the public believes that its author is a great general. In the second printing, you mention yourself in a six-line preface. This then will be a triumph for our party.—Ltr. to Engels.

CONSTANT CAPITAL
That part of capital which is represented by the means of production, by the raw material, auxiliary material and the instruments of labor, does not, in the process of production, undergo any quantitative alteration of value. I therefore call it the constant part of capital, or, more shortly, constant capital. —C. 1.

CONSUMER
It is the consumer who verifies the utility of a product.—P. P.

The consumer is not more free than the producer. His choice depends upon his means and his wants. The one and the other are determined by his social position, which itself depends upon the entire social organization.—P. P.

CONSUMER NECESSITY
For our purposes we may call this entire subdivision consumer necessities, regardless of whether such a product as tobacco is really a consumer necessity from the physiological point of view. It suffices that it is habitually such.—C. 2.

CONSUMPTION
There would be no production without consumption.—M.

The capitalist produces with absolutely no direct regard for consumption.—C. 4.

From a social point of view the working class is just as much an appendage of capital as the ordinary instruments of labor. Even its individual consumption is a mere factor in the process of production. That process, however, takes good care to prevent these self-conscious instruments from leaving it in the lurch, for it removes their product, as fast as it is made, from their pole to the opposite pole of capital. Individual consumption provides, on the one hand, the means for their maintenance and reproduction: on the other hand, it secures by the annihilation of the necessaries of life, the continued reappearance of the workman in the labor-market.—C. 1.

The individual consumption of the laborer, whether it proceed within the workshop or outside it, whether it be part of the process of production or not, forms a factor of the production and reproduction of capital; just cleaning machinery does, whether it be done while the machinery is working or while it is standing. The fact that the laborer consumes his means of subsistence for his own purposes, and not to please the capitalist, has no bearing on the matter. The consumption of food by a beast of burden is none the less a necessary factor in the process of production, because the beast enjoys what it eats.—C. 1.

The capitalist considers that part alone of the laborer's individual consumption to be productive which is requisite for the perpetuation of the class, and which therefore must take place in order that the capitalist may have labor power to consume; what the laborer consumes for his own pleasure beyond that part is unproductive consumption. If the accumulation of capital were to cause a rise of wages and an increase in the laborer's consumption, unaccompanied by increase in the consumption of labor power by capital, an additional capital would be consumed unproductively.—C. 1.

Productive consumption is distinguished from individual consumption by this, that the latter uses up products, as means of subsistence for the living individual; the former, as means whereby alone labor, the labor power of the living individual, is enabled to act. The product, therefore, of individual consumption, is the consumer himself; the result of productive consumption is a product distinct from the consumer.—C. 1.

CONSUMPTION, PRIVATE
So far as the capitalist's actions are a mere function of capital —endowed as capital is, in his person, with consciousness and a will—his own private consumption is a robbery perpetrated on accumulation, just as in bookkeeping by double entry, the private expenditure of the capitalist is placed on the debtor side of his account against his capital. To accumulate is to conquer the world of social wealth, to increase the mass of human beings exploited by him, and thus to extend both the direct and the indirect sway of the capitalist.—C. 1.

CONSUMPTION AND WEALTH
Real political economy à la Smith treats the capitalist only as personified capital. But who is to consume the products? The laborers?—but they don't. The capitalist himself? Then he is acting as a big idle consumer and not as a capitalist. The owners of land and money rents? They do not reproduce their consumption, and thereby are of disservice to wealth. Nevertheless, there are also two correct aspects in this contradictory view, which regards the capitalist only as a real amasser of wealth,

not an illusory one like the miser proper: (1) capital is treated only as an agent for the development of the productive forces and of production; (2) it expresses the standpoint of emerging capitalist society, to which what matters is exchange-value, not use-value; wealth, not enjoyment. The enjoyment of wealth seems to be a superfluous luxury, until it itself learns to combine exploitation and consumption and to subordinate itself to the enjoyment of wealth.—C. 4.

CONTRADICTION, CAPITALIST
The contradiction of the capitalist mode of production lies precisely in its tendency toward an absolute development of the productive forces, which continually come into conflict with the specific conditions of production in which capital moves, and alone can move.—C. 3.

CONTRIVED APPETITES
The extension of products and needs falls into contriving refined, unnatural and imaginary appetites.—M.

CONTROL, CAPITALIST
The control exercised by the capitalist is not only a special function, due to the nature of the social labor-process, and peculiar to that process, but it is, at the same time, a function of the exploitation of a social labor-process, and is consequently rooted in the unavoidable antagonism between the exploiter and the living and laboring raw material he exploits. —C. 1.

CONTROVERSY, ECONOMIC
Of course a controversy now arises in the field of political economy. The one side recommends luxury and execrates thrift. The other recommends thrift and execrates luxury. But the former admits that it wants luxury in order to produce labor (i.e., absolute thrift); and the latter admits that it recommends thrift in order to produce wealth (i.e., luxury).—M.

CONVERSION OF NATURE
Advancing human labor converts the product of nature into the manufactured product of nature.—M.

CONVERSION, CAPITALIST
To accumulate it is necessary to convert a portion of the surplus-product into capital. But we cannot convert into capital anything but such articles as can be employed in the labor-process (i.e., means of production), and such further articles as are suitable for the sustenance of the laborer (i.e., means of subsistence).—C. 1.

CONVICTION, RELIGIOUS
Religious and theological conviction counts in a democracy all the more for being apparently without political importance or earthly purpose, an affair of spirits in flight from the world, the expression of a limitation on reason, a product of whim and fancy, a truly other-worldly existence.—J. Q.

COOPERATION
When numerous laborers work together side by side whether in one and the same process or in different connected processes, they are said to cooperate, or to work in cooperation.—C. 1.

When the laborer cooperates systematically with others, he strips off the fetters of his individuality, and develops the capabilities of his species.—C. 1.

The cooperation of wage laborers is entirely brought about by the capital that employs them. Their union into one single productive body and the establishment of a connexion between their individual functions are matters foreign and external to them, are not their own act, but the act of the capital that brings and keeps them together.—C. 1.

Cooperation allows of the work being carried on over an extended space; it is consequently imperatively called for in certain undertakings, such as draining, constructing dikes, irrigation works, and the making of canals, roads and railways. On the other hand, while extending the scale of production, it renders possible a relative contraction of the arena. This contraction of arena simultaneously with, and arising from, extension scale, whereby a number of useless expenses are cut down, is owing to the conglomeration of laborers, to the aggregation of various processes, and to the concentration of the means of production.—C 1.

CORRUPTION
The union between the *Constitutional Monarchy* and the monopolizing moneyed interest, between the Company of East India and the "glorious" revolution of 1688 was fostered by the same force by which the liberal interests and a liberal dynasty have at all times and in all countries met and combined, by the force of corruption, that first and last moving power of Constitutional Monarchy, the guardian angel of William III and the fatal demon of Louis Philippe.—D. T.

COST OF PRODUCTION
It costs less labor to build one workshop for twenty persons than to build ten to accommodate two weavers each; thus the value of the means of production that are concentrated for use in common on a large scale does not increase in direct proportion to the expansion and to the increased useful effect of those means.—C. 1.

The costs of the product include all the elements of its value paid by the capitalist or for which he has thrown an equivalent into production. These costs must be made good to preserve the capital or to reproduce it in its original magnitude.—C. 3.

COST PRICE
The minimum limit of the selling price of a commodity is its cost price. If it is sold under its cost price, the expended constituent elements of productive capital cannot be fully replaced out of the selling price. If this process continues, the value of the advanced capital disappears. From this point of view alone, the capitalist is inclined to regard the cost price as the true inner value of the commodity.—C. 3.

What the commodity costs the capitalist and its actual production cost are two quite different magnitudes. That portion of the commodity-value making up the surplus-value does not cost the capitalist anything simply because it costs the laborer unpaid labor. Yet, on the basis of capitalist production, after the laborer enters the production process he himself constitutes an ingredient of operating productive capital, which belongs to the capitalist. Therefore, the capitalist is the actual producer of the commodity. For this reason the cost price of the commodity necessarily appears to the capitalist as the actual cost of the commodity.—C. 3.

COTTON
Without cotton you cannot have modern industry—P. P.

COUNTRY
The communists are reproached with desiring to abolish countries and nationalities. The working men have no country. We cannot take away from them what they have not got.—C. M.

COURT
Do you consider it wrong to appeal to the courts when you are cheated?—L. A.

CRASH, ECONOMIC
The manufacturer may actually sell to the exporter, and the exporter, in his turn, to his foreign customer; the importer may sell his raw materials to the manufacturer, and the latter may sell his products to the wholesale merchant, etc. But at some particular point the goods lie unsold, or else, again, all producers and middlemen may gradually become overstocked. Consumption is then generally at its highest, either because one industrial capitalist sets a succession of others in motion, or because the laborers employed by them are fully employed and have more to spend than usual. . . . This may go on undisturbed for some time. The crisis occurs when the returns of merchants who sell in distant markets become so slow and meager that the banks press for payment, or promissory notes for purchased commodities become due before the latter have been resold. Then forced sales take place, sales in order to meet payments. Then comes the crash, which brings the illusory prosperity to an abrupt end.—C. 3.

CREATION
The Creation is an idea very difficult to dislodge from popular consciousness. The self-mediated being of nature and of man is incomprehensible to it, because it contradicts everything palpable in practical life.—M.

CREDIT
The credit which a big capitalist enjoys compared with a smaller one means for him all the greater saving in fixed capital—that is, in the amount of ready money he must always have at hand.—M.

CREDIT SYSTEM
With capitalist production an altogether new force comes into play—the credit system. In its beginnings, the credit system sneaks in as a modest helper of accumulation and draws by invisible threads the money resources scattered all over the surface of society into the hands of individual or associated capitalists. But soon it becomes a new and formidable weapon in the competitive struggle, and finally it transforms itself into an immense social mechanism for the centralization of capitals. —C. 1.

Simultaneously with the development of capitalist production the credit system also develops. The money-capital which the capitalist cannot as yet employ in his own business is employed by others, who pay him interest for its use. It serves him as money-capital in its specific meaning, as a kind of capital distinguished from productive capital. But it serves as capital in another's hand.—C. 2.

The credit system appears as the main lever of overproduction and overspeculation in commerce solely because the reproduction process, which is elastic by nature, is here forced to its extreme limits, and is so forced because a large part of the social capital is employed by people who do not own it and who consequently tackle things quite differently than the owner, who anxiously weighs the limitations of his private capital in so far as he handles it himself.—C. 3.

CRIME

If man is unfree in the materialist sense, i.e., is free not through the negative power to avoid this and that, but through the positive power to assert his true individuality, crime must not be punished in the individual, but the antisocial source of crime must be destroyed, and each man must be given social scope for the vital manifestation of his being.—H. F.

The criminal produces an impression, partly moral and partly tragic, as the case may be, and in this way renders a "service" by arousing the moral and aesthetic feelings of the public. He produces not only compendia on Criminal Law, not only penal codes and along with them legislators in this field, but also art, belles-lettres, novels, and even tragedies, as not only Muellner's *Schuld* and Schiller's *Raeuber* show, but also Sophocles' *Oedipus* and Shakespeare's *Richard the Third*. The criminal breaks the monotony and everyday security of bourgeois life. In this way he keeps it from stagnation, and gives rise to that uneasy tension and agility without which even the spur of competition would get blunted. Thus he gives the stimulus to the productive forces. While crime takes a part of the superfluous population off the labor market and thus reduces competition among the laborers, the struggle against crime absorbs another part of this population. Thus the criminal comes in as one of those natural "counterweights" which bring about a correct balance and open up a whole perspective of "useful" occupations.—C. 4.

The criminal moreover, produces the whole of the police and of criminal justice, constables, judges, hangmen, juries, etc.; and all these different lines of business, which form equally many categories of the social division of labor, develop different capacities of the human spirit, create new needs and new ways of satisfying them. Torture alone has given rise to the most ingenious mechanical inventions, and employed many honorable craftsmen in the production of its instruments.—C. 4.

A philosopher produces ideas, a poet poems, a clergyman sermons, a professor compendia and so on. A criminal produces crimes. If we look a little closer at the connection between this latter branch of production and society as a whole, we shall rid ourselves of many prejudices. The criminal produces not only crimes but also criminal law and in addition to this the inevitable compendium in which this same professor throws his lectures onto the general market as "commodities." This brings with it augmentation of national wealth, quite apart from the personal enjoyment which the manuscript of the compendium brings to its originator himself.—C. 4.

The effects of the criminal on the development of productive power can be shown in detail. Would locks ever have reached their present degree of excellence had there been no thieves? Would the making of bank notes have reached its present perfection had there been no forgers? Would the microscope have found its way into the sphere of ordinary commerce but for trading frauds? Doesn't practical chemistry owe just as much to adulteration of commodities and the efforts to show it up as to the honest zeal for production? Crime, through its constantly new methods of attack on property, constantly calls into being new methods of defense, and so is as productive as strikes for the invention of machines. And if one leaves the sphere of private crime: would the world market ever have come into being but for national crime? Indeed, would even the nations have arisen? And hasn't the Tree of Sin been at the same time the Tree of Knowledge ever since the time of Adam?—C. 4.

CRISES, ECONOMIC
The ultimate reason for all real crises always remains the poverty and restricted consumption of the masses as opposed to the drive of capitalist production to develop the productive forces as though only the absolute consuming power of society constituted their limit.—C. 3.

The commercial crises by their periodical return put on trial, each time threateningly, the existence of the entire bourgeois society. In these crises a great part not only of the existing products, but also of the previously created productive forces, is periodically destroyed.—C. M.

Crises do not come to the surface, do not break out, in the retail business first, which deals with direct consumption, but in the spheres of wholesale trade, and of banking, which places the money-capital of society at the disposal of the former.—C. 3.

It is sheer tautology to say that crises are caused by the scarcity of effective consumption, or of effective consumers. The capitalist system does not know any other modes of consumption than effective ones, execpt that of *sub forma paperis* or of the swindler. That commodities are unsalable means only that no effective purchasers have been found for them, i.e., consumers. —C. 2.

CRITICISM, ABSOLUTE
The absolute critic is vexed when something which he claims as the latest scientific knowledge is proved to be generally known.—J. Q.

A main task of absolute criticism is to place all questions of the day in their appropriate form. It does not answer real questions, but substitutes others for them. It must first turn the questions of the day into "critical-critical" questions.—J. Q.

CRITICISM, POLITICAL
The criticism of the German philosophy of state and right, which attained its most consistent, richest and last formulation through Hegel, is both a critical analysis of the modern state and of the reality connected with it.—C. C.

CRITICISM, THEOLOGICAL
Criticism has plucked the imaginary flowers from the chain not so that man will wear the chain without any fantasy or consolation but so that he will shake off the chain and cull the living flower. The criticism of religion disillusions man to make him think and act and shape his reality like a man who has been disillusioned and has come to reason, so that he will revolve round himself and therefore round his true sun.—C. C.

Thus the criticism of heaven turns into the criticism of the earth, the criticism of religion into the criticism of right, the criticism of theology into the criticism of politics.—C. C.

On close inspection theological criticism—genuinely progressive though it was at the inception of the movement—is seen in the final analysis to be nothing but the culmination and consequence of the old philosophical transcendentalism, twisted into a theological caricature.—M.

CRUELTY
Cruelty, like every other thing, has its fashion, changing according to time and place. Caesar, the accomplished scholar, candidly narrates how he ordered many thousand Gallic warriors to have their right hands cut off. Napoleon would have been ashamed to do this. He preferred dispatching his own French regiments, suspected of republicanism, to Santo Domingo, there to die of the blacks and the plague.—D. T.

CULTURE, BOURGEOIS
That culture, the loss of which the bourgeois laments, is, for the enormous majority, a mere training to act as a machine.—C. M.

CYCLES, BUSINESS
Modern industry has its decennial cycles and periodic phases, which, as accumulation advances, are complicated by irregular oscillations following each other more and more quickly.—C. 1.

D

DARWIN
Darwin's book is of utmost importance and provides me with a foundation in natural science for the class struggles in history. —Ltr. to Lassalle.

Darwin has interested us in the history of nature's technology, i.e., in the formation of the organs of plants and animals, which organs serve as instruments of production for sustaining life. —C. 1.

DEATH
Death seems to be a harsh victory of the species over the definite individual and to contradict their unity. But the determinate individual is only a determinate species being, and as such mortal.—M.

DECENTRALIZING EFFECT
The process of accumulation and concentration of capital would soon bring about the collapse of capitalist production if it were not for counteracting tendencies, which have a continuous decentralizing effect alongside the centripetal one.—C. 3.

DECLINE OF PROFIT
The drop in the rate of profit is not due to an absolute, but only to a relative decrease of the variable part of the total capital, i.e., to its decrease in relation to the constant part.—C. 3.

DEFENSIVE
Kugelmann confounds a defensive war with a defensive military operation. And I become an aggressor, if I knock an assailant in the street down instead of only parrying his blow!—Ltr. to Engels.

DEGRADATION, HUMAN
Dirt—this stagnation and putrefaction of man—the sewage of civilization (speaking quite literally)—comes to be the element of life for him. Utter, unnatural neglect, putrefied nature, comes to be his life element. None of his senses exist any longer, and not only in his human fashion, but in an unhuman fashion, and therefore not even in an animal fashion.—M.

The worker no longer feels himself to be freely active in any but his animal functions—eating, drinking, procreating, or at most in his dwelling and in dressing up, etc.; and in his human functions he no longer feels himself to be anything but an animal. What is animal becomes human and what is human becomes animal.—M.

DEMAND
A thing can only be scarce or abundant according as it is in demand.—P. P.

No doubt demand also exists for him who has no money.—M.

With the development of capitalist production, the scale of production is determined less and less by the direct demand for the product and more and more by the amount of capital in the hands of the individual capitalist, by the urge for self-expansion inherent in his capital and by the need of continuity and expansion of the process of production. Thus in each particular branch of production there is a necessary increase in the mass of products available in the market in the shape of commodities, i.e., in search of buyers.—C. 2.

DEMAND, STIMULATION OF
No eunuch flatters his despot more basely or uses more

despicable means to stimulate his dulled capacity for pleasure in order to sneak a favor for himself than does the industrial eunuch—the producer—in order to sneak for himself a few pennies—in order to charm the golden birds out of the pockets of his beloved neighbors. He puts himself at the service of the other's most depraved fancies, plays the pimp between him and his need, excites in him morbid appetites, lies in wait for each of his weaknesses—all so that he can then demand the cash of this service of love.—M.

DEMOCRACY
The first step in the revolution by the working class is to raise the proletariat to the position of ruling class, to win the battle of democracy.—C. M.

There is a difference between working behind the scenes by disappearing in public and the *Democrats'* way of making oneself important in public and doing nothing.—Ltr. to Engels.

DEPENDENCE
A man who lives by the grace of another regards himself as a dependent being. But I live completely by the grace of another if I owe him not only the sustenance of my life, but if he has, moreover, *created* my life—if he is the source of my life; and if it is not of my own creation, my life has necessarily a source of this kind outside it.—M.

The Roman slave was held by fetters: the wage-laborer is bound to his owner by invisible threads. The appearance of independence is kept up by means of a constant change of employers, and by the *fictio juris* of a contract.—C. 1.

DEPRECIATION
The development of productive power is accompanied by a partial depreciation of functioning capital. So far as this depreciation makes itself acutely felt in competition, the burden falls on the laborer, in the increased exploitation of whom the capitalist looks for his indemnification.—C. 1.

DESPOTISM, BOURGEOIS
Masses of laborers, crowded into the factory, are organized like

soldiers. As privates of the industrial army they are placed under the command of a perfect hierarchy of officers and sergeants. Not only are they the slaves of the bourgeois class, and of the bourgeois state, they are daily and hourly enslaved by the machine, by the overlooker, and, above all, by the individual bourgeois manufacturer himself. The more openly this despotism proclaims gain to be its end and aim, the more petty, the more hateful and the more embittered it is.—C. M.

DESTINY
A man never realizes what he may achieve or what strange fellowship he may have to endure.—Ltr. to Engels.

DESTITUTION, PROLETARIAN
In the gravitation of market-price to natural price it is the worker who loses most of all and necessarily. And it is just the capacity of the capitalist to direct his capital into another channel which renders destitute the worker who is restricted to some particular branch of labor, or forces him to submit to every demand of this capitalist. The accidental and sudden fluctuations in market-price hit rent less than they do that part of the price which is resolved into profit and wages; but they hit profit less than they do wages. In most cases, for every wage that rises, one remains stationary and one falls.—M.

Even in the condition of society most favorable to the worker, the inevitable result for the worker is overwork and premature death, decline to a mere machine, a bond servant of capital, which piles up dangerously over against him, more competition, and for a section of the workers starvation or beggary.—M.

DESTRUCTION OF CAPITAL
Overproduction of capital is never anything more than overproduction—of means of labor and necessities of life—which may serve as capital, i.e., may serve to exploit labor at a given degree of exploitation; a fall in the intensity of exploitation below a certain point, however, calls forth disturbances, crises, and destruction of capital.—C. 3.

DESTRUCTION OF MACHINERY
The laborers direct their attacks against the instruments of production themselves; they destroy imported wares that compete with their labor, they smash to pieces machinery, they set factories ablaze.—C. M.

DETERMINATION, MANIFOLD
To this confusion—determining prices through demand and supply, and, at the same time, determining supply and demand through prices—must be added that demand determines supply, just as supply determines demand, and production determines the market, as well as the market determines production.—C. 3.

DEVALUATION
With the increasing value of the world of things proceeds in direct proportion the devaluation of the world of men.—M.

DIALECTICS
To speak Greek, we have the thesis, the antithesis and the synthesis. As to those who are not acquainted with Hegelian language, we would say to them in the sacramental formula, affirmation, negation, and negation of the negation.—P. P.

DIAMONDS
Diamonds are of very rare occurrence, and hence their mining costs, on an average, a great deal of labor time. With richer mines, the same quantity of labor would embody itself in more diamonds, and their value would fall. If we could succeed at a small expenditure of labor in converting carbon into diamonds, their value might fall below that of bricks.—C. 1.

DICTATORSHIP OF THE PROLETARIAT
The class struggle necessarily results in the dictatorship of the proletariat.—Ltr. to Weydemeyer.

The proletarian dictatorship is only transitory, leading to the abolition of all classes or to a classless society.—Ltr. to Weydemeyer.

DIFFERENTIAL RENT
Wherever rent exists at all, differential rent appears at all times, and is governed by the same laws as agricultural differential rent. Wherever natural forces can be monopolized and guarantee a surplus-profit to the industrial capitalist using them, be it waterfalls, rich mines, waters teeming with fish, or a favorably located building site, there the person who by virtue of title to a portion of the globe has become the proprietor of these natural objects will wrest this surplus-profit from functioning capital in the form of rent.—C. 3.

In the analysis of differential rent we proceeded from the assumption that the worst soil does not pay any ground-rent; or, to put it more generally, only such land pays ground-rent whose product has an individual price of production below the price of production regulating the market, so that in this manner a surplus-profit arises which is transformed into rent. It is to be noted that the law of differential rent as such is entirely independent of the correctness or incorrectness of this assumption. —C. 3.

DIFFERENTIATION
With the differentiation of the instruments of labor, the industries that produce these instruments become more and more differentiated.—C. 1.

DIMINISHING RETURN
With the increase of capitals the profits on the capitals diminish, because of competition. The first to suffer is the small capitalist.—M.

DISADVANTAGE OF WORKER
Another respect in which the worker is at a disadvantage: The labor-prices of the various kinds of workers show much wider differences than the profits in the various branches in which capital is applied. In labor all the natural, spiritual and social variety of individual activity is manifested and is variously rewarded, whilst dead capital always shows the same face and is indifferent to the real individual activity.—M.

DISPLACEMENT OF WORKMEN
So soon as machinery sets free a part of the workmen employed in a given branch of industry, the reserve men are also diverted into new channels of employment, and become absorbed in other branches; meanwhile the original victims, during the period of transition, for the most part starve and perish.—C. 1.

Machinery displaces labor and increases the net revenue; it reduces the number of laborers and increases the products. So this would be desirable. But no. In that case it must be shown that machinery does not deprive the laborers of bread. And how is this to be shown? By the fact that after a shock (to which perhaps the section of the population which is directly affected cannot offer any resistance) machinery once again employs more people than were employed before it was introduced—and therefore once again increases the number of "productive laborers" and restores the former disproportion. That is in fact what happens.—C. 4.

A whole series of bourgeois economists insists that all machinery that displaces workmen simultaneously and necessarily sets free an amount of capital adequate to employ the same identical workmen. The real facts, which are travestied by the optimism of economists, are as follows: The laborers, when driven out of the workshop by the machinery, are thrown upon the labor market, and there add to the number of workmen at the disposal of the capitalists. . . . Even should they find employment, what a poor look-out is theirs! Crippled as they are by division of labor, these poor devils are worth so little outside their old trade, that they cannot find admission into any industries, except a few of inferior kind, that are oversupplied with underpaid workmen.—C. 1.

Although machinery necessarily throws men out of work in those industries into which it is introduced, yet it may, notwithstanding this, bring about an increase of employment in other industries. This effect, however, has nothing in common with the so-called theory of compensation.—C. 1.

As the use of machinery extends in a given industry, the immediate effect is to increase production in the other industries that furnish the first with means of production. How far employment is thereby found for an increased number of men, depends, given the length of the working day and the intensity of labor, on the composition of the capital employed.—C. 1.

DISRAELI
For some time, Mr. Disraeli affects an awful solemnity of speech, an elaborate slowness of utterance and a passionless method of formality, which, however consistent they may be with his peculiar notions of the dignity becoming a Minister in expectance, are really distressing to his tortured audience. Once he succeeded in giving even commonplaces the pointed appearance of epigrams. Now he contrives to bury even epigrams in the conventional dullness of respectability. An orator who, like Mr. Disraeli, excels in handling the danger rather than in wielding the sword, should have been the last to forget Voltaire's warning, that "All styles are good save the tiresome kind."—D. T.

DISSOLUTION, INDUSTRIAL
At a certain stage of development, the petty mode of production brings forth the material agencies for its own dissolution. From that moment new forces and new passions spring up in the bosom of society; but the old social organization fetters them and keeps them down. It must be annihilated; it is annihilated. —C. 1.

DISTRIBUTION
The mode of the distribution of the social product will vary the productive organization of the community, and the degree of historical development attained by the producers.—C. 1.

DISTURBANCES, SOCIAL
In capitalist society where social reason always asserts itself only *post festum,* great disturbances may and must constantly occur. —C. 2.

DIVINE BEING

Since the real existence of man and nature has become practical, sensuous and perceptible—since man has become for man as the being of nature, and nature for man as the being of man—the question about an alien (divine) being, above nature and man—a question which implies the admission of the inessentiality of nature and of man—has become impossible in practice.—M.

DIVISION OF LABOR

Both product and producer are improved by division of labor. —C. 1.

Whilst the division of labor raises the productive power of labor and increases the wealth and refinement of society, it impoverishes the worker and reduces him to a machine.—M.

Where there is considerable division it is most difficult for the worker to direct his labor into other channels; because of his subordinate relation to the capitalist, he is the first to suffer.—M.

Division of labor in the interior of a society, and that in the interior of a workshop, differ not only in degree, but also in kind. . . . The division of labor in the workshop implies concentration of the means of production in the hands of one capitalist; the division of labor in society implies their dispersion among many independent producers of commodities.—C. 1.

Division of labor in manufacture demands that division of labor in society at large should previously have attained a certain degree of development. Inversely, the former division reacts upon and develops and multiplies the latter.—C. 1.

The accumulation of capital increases the *division of labor,* and the division of labor increases the numbers of the workers. Conversely, the workers' numbers increase the division of labor, just as the division of labor increases the accumulation of capitals.— M.

The guildmasters were pushed aside by the manufacturing middle class; division of labor between the different corporate guilds vanished in the face of division of labor in each single workshop.—C. M.

To explain exchange there must be division of labor.—P. P.

To explain the *division of labor* there must be wants which necessitate the division of labor.—P. P.

The relation between the coat and the labor that produced it is not altered by the circumstance that tailoring may have become a special trade, an independent branch of the social *division of labor.*—C. 1.

DOGMATISM
If from the outset everything which contradicts your faith is error and must be dealt with as such, what is there to distinguish your claims from those of the Mohammedans, from the claims of any other religion? Must philosophy adopt different principles for every country, according to the saying "different countries, different customs," in order not to contradict the basic truths of dogma? Must it believe in one country that $3 \times 1 = 1$, in another that women have no soul and in yet another that beer is drunk in heaven?—L. A.

DOMESTICATED ANIMALS
In the earliest period of human history domesticated animals, i.e., animals which have been bred for the purpose, and have undergone modifications by means of labor, play the chief part as instruments of labor along with specially prepared stones, wood, bones, and shells.—C. 1.

DOUBLE BONDAGE
Thus in this double respect the worker becomes a slave of his object, first, in that he receives an object of labor, i.e., in that he receives work; and secondly, in that he receives means of

subsistence. Therefore, it enables him to exist, first, as a worker; and, second, as a physical subject. The extremity of this bondage is that it is only as a worker that he continues to maintain himself as a physical subject, and that it is only as a physical subject that he is a worker.—M.

DOUBLE PROFIT
The capitalist profits doubly—first, by the division of labor; and secondly, in general, by the advance which human labor makes on the natural product. The greater the human share in a commodity, the greater the profit of dead capital.—M.

DUEHRING
At the Museum, where I did nothing but leaf through catalogues, I also realized that Duehring is a great philosopher. For he has written a *Natural Dialectic* against Hegel's "unnatural" one.—Ltr. to Engels.

DUEL
We do not believe that such an intangible affair as a duel can be labeled as good or bad. The duel certainly is irrational and a relic of a past cultural stage.—Ltr. to Lassalle.

DUNS SCOTUS
Duns Scotus wondered: "Can matter think?" In order to bring about that miracle he had recourse to God's omnipotence, i.e., he forced theology itself to preach materialism. In addition he was a nominalist.—H. F.

DURATION OF THE PRODUCTIVE ACT
The differences in the duration of the productive act can also be observed within one and the same sphere of production. An ordinary dwelling house is built in less time than a large factory and therefore requires fewer continuous labor-processes. While the building of a locomotive takes three months, that of an armored man-of-war requires one year or more. It takes nearly a year to produce grain and several years to raise cattle, while

timber-growing needs from twelve to one hundred years. A few months will suffice for a country road, while a railway is a job of years. An ordinary carpet is made in about a week, but a Goblin takes years, etc. Hence the time consumed in the performance of the productive act varies infinitely.—C. 2.

DUTCH EAST INDIA COMPANY
A purely commercial company like the old Dutch East India Company, which had a monopoly of production, could fancy that it could continue a method adapted at best to the beginnings of capitalist production, under entirely changed conditions.—C. 3.

DWELLING, HUMAN
A dwelling in the light, which Prometheus in Aeschylus designated as one of the greatest boons, by means of which he made the savage into a human being, ceases to exist for the worker. —M.

E

EARNINGS
Whilst the rent of the lazy landowner usually amounts to a third of the product of the soil, and the profit of the busy capitalist to as much as twice the interest on money, the "something more" which the worker himself earns at the best of times amounts to so little that of four children of his, two must starve and die. Whilst according to the political economists it is solely through labor that man enhances the value of the products of nature, whilst labor is man's active property, according to this same political economy the landowner and the capitalist, who *qua* landowner and capitalist are merely privileged and idle gods, are everywhere superior to the worker and lay down the law to him.—M.

EASY MONEY MARKET
An easy money market calls enterprises into being en masse.— C. 2.

ECONOMIC FORMS
Natural economy, money-economy, the credit-economy have been placed in opposition to one another as being the three characteristic economic forms of movement in social production.—C. 2.

ECONOMIC STRUCTURE
The economic structure of capitalistic society has grown out of the economic structure of feudal society. The dissolution of the latter set free the elements of the former.—C. 1.

ECONOMICS
The material of the economists is the active and busy life of men.—P. P.

ECONOMISTS, FATALIST
We have the fatalist economists, who in their theory are as indifferent to what they call the inconveniences of bourgeois production as the bourgeois themselves are, in actual practice, to the sufferings of the proletarians who assist them to acquire riches.—P. P.

ECONOMIST'S CONTRADICTION
The political economist tells us that originally and in theory the whole produce of labor belongs to the worker. But at the same time he tells us that in actual fact what the worker gets is the smallest and utterly indispensable part of the product—as much, only, as is necessary for his existence, not as a man but as a worker, and for the propagation, not of humanity, but of the slave-class of workers.—M.

Whilst according to the political economists it is solely through labor that man enhances the value of the products of nature, according to this same political economy the landowner and the capitalist are everywhere superior to the worker.—M.

The political economist tells us that everything is bought with labor and that capital is nothing but accumulated labor; but at the same time he tells us that the worker, far from being able to buy everything, must sell himself and his human identity.—M.

ECONOMY
The capitalist's fanatical insistence on economy in means of production is quite understandable. That nothing is lost or wasted and the means of production are consumed only in the manner required by production itself depends partly on the skill and intelligence of the laborers and partly on the discipline enforced by the capitalist for the combined labor. This discipline will become superfluous under a social system in which the laborers work for their own account.—C. 3.

EDUCATION, COMMUNIST
And your education! Is not that also social, and determined by the social conditions under which you educate, by the intervention, direct or indirect, of society by means of schools, etc.? The communists have not invented the intervention of society in education; they do but seek to alter the character of that intervention, and to rescue education from the influence of the ruling class.—C. M.

EDUCATION, COST OF
If I buy the service of a teacher not to develop my faculties but to acquire some skill with which I can earn money—or if others buy this teacher for me—and if I really learn something (which in itself is quite independent of the payment for the service), then these costs of education, just as the costs of my maintenance, belong to the costs of production of my labor power. —C. 4.

EDUCATOR
The educator himself needs educating.—T. F.

EGOTISTICAL MAN
The recognition of the freedom of egotistical man is the recognition of the unrestrained movement of spiritual and material elements that form its content.—J. Q.

ELASTICITY, ECONOMIC
Finally, all the springs of (capitalist) production act with greater elasticity, the more its scale extends with the mass of the capital advanced.—C. 1.

EMANCIPATION
Political emancipation is a great goal. It is not the ultimate form of human emancipation, but it is the ultimate form within the present world order. And let it be understood that we mean real, practical emancipation.—J. Q.

Human emancipation is achieved only when the individual gives up being an abstract citizen and becomes a member of his species as individual man in his daily life and work and situation, when he recognizes and organizes his *"forces propres,"* his own strength, as part of the forces of society, which are then no longer separated from him as a political power.—J. Q.

EMANCIPATION, GERMAN
As philosophy finds its material weapon in the proletariat, so the proletariat finds its spiritual weapon in philosophy. And once the lightning of thought has squarely struck this ingenious soil of the people, the emancipation of the Germans into men will be accomplished.—C. C.

EMOTION
The dominion of the objective being in me, the sensuous outburst of my essential activity, is emotion, which thus becomes here the activity of my being.—M.

EMPIRICAL WORLD
If man draws all his knowledge, sensation, etc., from the world of the senses and the experience gained in it, the empirical world must be arranged so that in it man experiences and gets used to what is really human and that he becomes aware of himself as man.—H. F.

EMPIRICISM
Empiric observation must in every single case reveal the connection of the social and political organization with production, empirically and without any mystification of speculation.—G. I.

It is hardly necessary to assure the reader conversant with political economy that my results have been won by means of a wholly empirical analysis based on a conscientious critical study of the political economy.—M.

EMPLOYMENT
As the use of machinery extends in a given industry, the immediate effect is to increase production in the other industries that furnish the first with means of production. How far employment is thereby found for an increased number of men depends on the composition of the capital employed.—C. 1.

END OF THE WORLD
The dream of the early Christians that the world was nearing its end inspired them in their struggle and gave them confidence in victory.—Ltr. to Nieuwenhuis.

ENGLAND
Being the metropolis of capital, the ruler of the world market, England is for the present time the most important country for the revolution of the workers. It therefore is the most momentous objective of the International Workingmen's Association to speed up the social revolution in England. The independence of Ireland would be a decisive impetus to such acceleration.—Ltr. to Meyer and Vogt.

ENLARGED REPRODUCTION
It does not alter matters any, if simple reproduction is replaced by reproduction on an enlarged scale, by accumulation. In the first instance the capitalist consumes the entire surplus-value, in the second he demonstrates his civic virtue by consuming only a part of it and converting the remainder into money.—C. 1.

ENRICHMENT
One of the savants of Paul de Kock may tell me that without buying trousers, just as without buying bread, I cannot live, and therefore also I cannot enrich myself; that the purchase of the trousers is therefore an indirect means, or at least a condition, for my enrichment— in the same way as the circulation of my blood or the process of breathing are conditions for my enrichment. But neither the circulation of my blood nor my breathing in themselves make me any of the richer; on the contrary, they both presuppose a costly assimilation of food; if that were not necessary, there would be no poor devils about. C. 4.

ENTREPRENEUR
An entrepreneur of theaters, concerts, brothels, etc., buys the temporary disposal over the labor power of the actors, musicians, prostitutes, etc.—in fact in a roundabout way that is only of formal economic interest; in its result the process is the same—

he buys this so-called "unproductive labor," whose "services perish in the very instant of their performance" and do not fix or realize themselves in "any permanent subject or vendible commodity" (apart from themselves).—C. 4.

EQUALITY
Certainly, the tendency to equality appertains to our century. —P. P.

Equality as the groundwork of communism is its political justification.—M.

The Constitution of 1795 determined appropriately the importance and force of equality: "Equality means that the law is the same for all, whether it protects or punishes" (Article 5).—J. Q.

EQUILIBRIUM IN PRODUCTION
The different spheres of production constantly tend to an equilibrium: for, on the one hand, while each producer of a commodity is bound to produce a use-value, to satisfy a particular social want, and while the extent of these wants differs quantitatively, still there exists an *inner* relation which settles their proportions into a regular system, and that system one of spontaneous growth; and, on the other hand, the law of the value of commodities ultimately determines how much of its disposable working time society can expend on each particular class of commodities. This constant tendency to equilibrium, of the various spheres of production, is exercised in the shape of a reaction against the constant upsetting of this equilibrium.—C. 1.

ESPIONAGE
I received this information from a close assistant of Bismarck. This man is aware of the discrediting reports, which were formerly sent to me by him, and are still in my possession. He is thus depending on my discretion, and continually wants to prove his good intentions towards me. The same person warned me of Bismarck's intention to arrest me, should I visit Kugelmann this year.—Ltr. to Breesly.

ESTRANGEMENT
The proposition that man's species nature is estranged from him means that one man is estranged from the other, as each of them is from man's essential nature. The estrangement of man, and in fact every relationship in which man stands to himself, is first realized and expressed in the relationship in which a man stands to other men.—M.

Just as the worker begets his own product as a loss, as a product not belonging to him, so he begets the dominion of the one who does not produce over production and over the product. Just as he estranges from himself his own activity, so he confers to the stranger activity which is not his own.—M.

In degrading spontaneous activity, free activity, to a means, estranged labor makes man's species life a means to his physical existence. The consciousness which man has of his species is thus transformed by *estrangement* in such a way that the species life becomes for him a means.—M.

This *estrangement* manifests itself in that it produces refinement of needs and of their means on the one hand, and a bestial barbarization, a complete, unrefined, abstract simplicity of need, on the other; or rather in that it merely resurrects itself in its opposite.—M.

ESTRANGEMENT OF LABOR
It is only because man is a species being that he is a conscious being, i.e., that his own life is an object for him. Only because of that is his activity free activity. Estranged labor reverses this relationship, so that it is just because man is a conscious being that he makes his life-activity, his essential being, a mere means to his existence.—M.

The object of labor is the objectification of man's species life: for he duplicates himself not only, as in consciousness, intellectually, but also actively, is reality, and therefore he contemplates himself in a world that he has created. In tearing away from man the object of his production, therefore, estranged labor tears from him his species life, his real species objectivity, and transforms his advantage over animals in to the disadvantage that his inorganic body, nature, is taken from him.—M.

ETHICS OF POLITICAL ECONOMY
The ethics of political economy is *acquisition*, work, thrift, sobriety—but political economy promises to satisfy my needs. The political economy of ethics is the opulence of a good conscience, of virtue, etc.; but how can I live virtuously if I do not live? And how can I have a good conscience if I am not conscious of anything?—M.

EVIL, ORIGIN OF
Theology explains the origin of evil by the fall of man.—M.

EXCESS
Excess and intemperance come to be the true norm of the modern economic system. Subjectively, this is even partly manifested in that the extension of products and needs falls into contriving and ever-calculating subservience to inhuman, refined, unnatural and imaginary appetites. Private property does not know how to change crude into human need. Its idealism is fantasy, caprice and whim.—M.

EXCHANGE
The constant repetition of exchange makes it a normal social act. In the course of time, some portion at least of the products of labor must be produced with a special view to exchange.—C. 1.

Exchange itself appears to be a fortuitous fact.—M.

EXCHANGE VALUE
The act of exchange gives to the commodity converted into money, not its value, but its specific value-form.—C. 1.

When commodities are exchanged, their exchange value manifests itself as something totally independent of their use-value. But if we abstract from their use-value, there remains their value. Therefore, the common substance that manifests itself in the exchange value of commodities, whenever they are exchanged, is their value.—C. 1.

In supposing the subdivision of labor you have exchange, and consequently exchange value.—P. P.

All commodities are non-use-values for their owners, and use-values for their non-owners. Consequently, they must all change hands. But this change of hands is what constitutes their exchange, and the latter puts them in relation with each other as values, and realizes them as values. Hence commodities must be realized as values before they can be realized as use-values.—C. 1.

The vulgar economist does not suspect that the actual everyday exchange relations need not be directly identical with the magnitudes of value.—Ltr. to Kugelmann.

Exchange value, at first sight, presents itself as a quantitative relation, as the proportion in which values in use of one sort are exchanged for those of another sort, a relation constantly changing with time and place. Hence exchange value appears to be something accidental and purely relative, and consequently an intrinsic value, i.e., an exchange value that is inseparably connected with, inherent in, commodities seems a contradiction in terms.—C. 1.

In the form of society we are about to consider, use-values are, in addition, the material depositories of exchange value.—C. 1.

The exchange value of a product falls in proportion as the supply increases; in other terms, the greater the abundance of a product relative to the demand, the lower its exchange value or its price falls.—P. P.

EXCRETIONS OF CONSUMPTION
Excretions of consumption are the natural waste matter discharged by the human body, remains of clothing in the forms of rags, etc. Excretions of consumption are of the greatest importance for agriculture. So far as their utilization is concerned, there is an enormous waste of them in the capitalist economy. In London, for instance, they find no better use for the excretion of four and a half million human beings than to contaminate the Thames with it at heavy expense.—C. 3.

EXCRETIONS OF PRODUCTION
The capitalist mode of production extends the utilization of the excretions of production and consumption. By the former we mean the waste of industry and agriculture, and by the latter partly the excretions produced by the natural exchange of matter in the human body and partly the form of objects that remains after their consumption. In the chemical industry, for instance, excretions of production are such by-products as are wasted in production on a smaller scale; iron filings accumulating in the manufacture of machinery and returning into the production of iron as raw material, etc.—C. 3.

The economy of the excretions of production is to be distinguished from economy through the prevention of waste, that is to say, the reduction of excretions of production to a minimum, and the immediate utilization to a maximum of all raw and auxiliary materials required in production.—C.3.

EXPLOITATION
General *exploitation* of communal human nature, like every imperfection in man, is a bond with heaven—an avenue giving the priest access to his heart.—M.

Every enterprise engaged in commodity production becomes at the same time an enterprise exploiting labor power. But only the capitalist production of commodities has become an epoch-making mode of *exploitation*, which, in the course of its historical development, revolutionizes, through the organization of the labor-process and the enormous improvement of technique, the entire economic structure of society in a manner eclipsing all former epochs.—C. 2.

Once discovered, the law of the deviation of the magnetic needle in the field of an electric current, or the law of magnetization of iron, around which an electric current circulates, cost never a penny. But the *exploitation* of these laws for the purposes of telegraphy, etc., necessitates a costly and expensive apparatus.— C. 1.

EXPLOITATION OF LABOR
The degree of exploitation of labor, the appropriation of surplus-value and surplus-labor, is raised notably by lengthening the working day and intensifiying labor.—C. 3.

The rate of surplus-value is an exact expression for the degree of exploitation of labor power by capital, or of the laborer by the capitalist.—C. 1.

EXPLOITATION, BOURGEOIS
No sooner is the exploitation of the laborer by the manufacturer so far at an end, that he receives his wages in cash, than he is set upon by the other portions of the bourgeoisie, the landlord, the shopkeeper, the pawnbroker, etc.—C. M.

For exploitation, veiled by religious and political illusions, the bourgeoisie has substituted naked, shameless, direct, brutal exploitation.—C. M.

EXPROPRIATION OF THE MASSES
The annihilation of the old social organization, the transformation of the individualized and scattered means of production into socially concentrated ones, of the pygmy property of the many into the huge property of the few, the expropriation of the great mass of the people from the soil, from the means of subsistence, and from the means of labor, this fearful and painful expropriation of the mass of the people forms the prelude to the history of capital.—C. 1.

EXTRACTIVE INDUSTRY
That industry in which the material for labor is provided directly by nature, such as mining, hunting, fishing, and agriculture (so far as the latter is confined to breaking up virgin soil).—C. 1.

F

FACTORY DISCIPLINE
The barrack discipline is elaborated into a complete system in the factory.—C. 1.

FACTORY SYSTEM
The factory system is the essence of industry—of labor—brought to its maturity.—M.

The revolution in the instruments of labor attains its most highly developed form in the organized system of machinery in a factory.—C. 1.

Modern industry has converted the little workshop of the patriarchal master into the great factory of the industrial capitalist.—C. M.

In the factory tools make use of the workman.—C. 1.

The increase in the class of people wholly dependent on work intensifies competition among them, thus lowering their price. In the factory system this situation of the worker reaches its climax.—M.

FACTORY WORK
At the same time that factory work exhausts the nervous system to the uttermost, it does away with the many-sided play of the muscles, and confiscates every atom of freedom, both in bodily and intellectual activity. . . . Every kind of capitalist production insofar as it is not only a labor-process, but also a process of

creating surplus-value, has this in common, that it is not the workman that employs the instruments of labor, but the instruments of labor that employ the workman.—C. 1.

FACTORY WORKER
The special skill of each individual insignificant factory operative vanishes as an infinitesimal quantity before the science, the gigantic physical forces, and the mass of labor that are embodied in the factory mechanism and, together with that mechanism, constitute the power of the "master."—C. 1.

FAITH
It is faith that brings salvation.—C. 3.

FALLING PROFIT
The capitalist mode of production produces a progressive decrease of the variable capital as compared to the constant capital, and consequently a continuously rising organic composition of the total capital. The immediate result of this is that the rate of surplus-value, at the same time, or even a rising degree of labor exploitation, is represented by a continually falling general rate of profit. The progressive tendency of the general rate of profit to fall is, therefore, just an expression peculiar to the capitalist mode of production of the progressive development of the social productivity of labor.—C. 3.

FALLING PROFIT, TENDENCY OF
Political economy, which has until now been unable to explain the law of the tendency of the rate of profit to fall, pointed self-consolingly to the increasing mass of profit, i.e., to the growth of the absolute magnitude of profit, be it for the individual capitalist or for the social capital, but this was also based on mere platitude and speculation.—C. 3.

FALLING RENT
From the relation of ground-rent to interest on money it follows that rent must fall more and more, so that eventually only the wealthiest people can live on rent. Hence the ever greater competition between landowners who do not lease their land to tenants. Ruin of some of these—further accumulation of large landed property.—M.

FALLOW CAPITAL
That part of the latent productive capital which is held in readiness only as a requisite for the productive process, such as cotton, coal, etc., in a spinning-mill, acts as creator of neither products nor value. It is fallow capital, although its fallowness is essential for the uninterrupted flow of the process of production. The buildings, apparatus, etc., necessary for the storage of the productive supply (latent capital) are conditions of the productive process and therefore constitute component parts of the advanced productive capital.—C. 2.

FAMILY
Abolition of the family! Even the most radical flare up at this infamous proposal of the communists.—C. M.

FAMILY, BOURGEOIS
The bourgeoisie has torn away from the family its sentimental veil, and has reduced the family relation to a mere money relation.—C. M.

On what foundation is the present family, the bourgeois family, based? On capital, on private gain. In its completely developed form this family exists only among the bourgeoisie. But this state of things finds its complement in the practical absence of the family among the proletarians.—C. M.

FARMER, MODERN
Compare a modern farmer of the Scotch lowlands with an old-fashioned small peasant on the Continent. The former sells his entire product and has therefore to replace all its elements, even his seed, in the market; the latter consumes the greater part of his product directly, buys and sells as little as possible, fashions tools, makes clothing, etc., so far as possible himself. C. 2.

FARMER, TENANT
The tenant farmer is the landowner's representative—the landowner's revealed secret: it is only through him that the landowner has his economic existence—his existence as a private proprietor—for the rest of his land only exists due to the competition between the farmers.—M.

FASHION
Fashion determines use.—M.

FAUSTIAN CONFLICT
Along with the growth of the capitalist, there is at the same time developed in his breast a Faustian conflict between the passion for accumulation and the desire for enjoyment.—C. 1.

FEELINGS
If man's feelings, passions, etc., are not merely anthropological phenomena, but truly ontological affirmations of essential being (of nature), and if they are only really affirmed because their object exists for them as an object of sense, then it is clear that they have by no means merely one mode of affirmation, but rather that the distinctive character of their existence, of their life, is constituted by the distinctive mode of their affirmation.—M.

FERTILITY OF SOIL
Victory goes to the proprietor of the more fertile soil.—M.

All progress in increasing the fertility of the soil for a given time is a progress toward ruining the lasting sources of that fertility.—C. 1.

FETISHISM
Fetishism is so far from raising man above the appetites that it is on the contrary "the religion of sensuous appetites." The fantasy of the appetites tricks the fetish worshiper into believing that an "inanimate object" will give up its natural character to gratify his desires. The crude appetite of the fetish worshiper therefore smashes the fetish when the latter ceases to be its most devoted servant.—L. A.

The sensuous consciousness of the fetish worshiper is different from that of the Greek, because his sensuous existence is still different. The abstract enmity between sense and spirit is necessary so long as the human feeling for nature, the human sense of nature, and therefore also the natural sense of man, are not yet produced by man's own labor.—M.

FETTERS, SOCIOLOGICAL

At a certain stage of their development, the material productive forces of society come into conflict with the existing relations of production, or—what is but a legal expression for the same thing—with the property relations within which they have been at work hitherto. From forms of development of the productive forces these relations turn into their fetters.—P. E.

FEUDAL PROPERTY

Feudal landed property gives its name to its lord, as does a kingdom to its king. His family history, the history of his house, etc.—all this individualizes the state for him and makes it literally his house, personifies it.—M.

At a certain stage in the development of the means of production and of exchange, the conditions under which feudal society produced and exchanged, the feudal organization of agriculture and manufacturing industry, in one word, the feudal relations of property became no longer compatible with the already developed productive forces; they became so many fetters. They had to be burst asunder; they were burst asunder.—C. M.

FEUDAL PROVERB

The proverb, *Nulle terre sans maître* (There is no land without its master), expresses the fusion of nobility and landed property.—M.

FEUDALISM

The feudal organization of national life did not raise work or property to the role of social elements; rather, it separated them from the state as a whole and constituted them as special societies within the total society.—J. Q.

FEUERBACH

Feuerbach's great achievement is: the proof that philosophy is nothing else but religion rendered into thoughts and thinkingly expounded, and that it has therefore likewise to be condemned as another form and manner of existence of the estrangement of the essence of man.—M.

It is only with Feuerbach that positive, humanistic and naturalistic criticism begins. The less noise they make, the more certain, profound, widespread and enduring is the effect of Feuerbach's writings, the only writings since Hegel's *Phaenomenologie* and *Logik* to contain a real theoretical revolution.—M.

Positive criticism as a whole—and therefore also German positive criticism of political economy—owes its true foundation to the discoveries of Feuerbach.—M.

Feuerbach is the only one who has a serious, critical attitude to the Hegelian dialectic and who has made genuine discoveries in this field. He is in fact the true conqueror of the old philosophy. The extent of his achievement, and the unpretentious simplicity with which he, Feuerbach, gives it to the world, stand in striking contrast to the reverse.—M.

The writings of *Feuerbach* contain a real theoretical revolution. —M.

Positive criticism as a whole owes its true foundation to the discoveries of Feuerbach, against whose *Philosophie der Zukunft* and *Thesen zur Reform der Philosophie,* despite the tacit use that is made of them, the petty envy of some and the veritable wrath of others seem to have instigated a regular conspiracy of silence.—M.

FIRST CAUSE
Who begot the first man, and nature as a whole? I can only answer you: Your question is itself a product of abstraction.—M.

FLUCTUATION OF PRICE
The accidental and sudden fluctuations in market-price hit rent less than they do that part of the price which is resolved into profit and wages; but they hit profit less than they do wages.—M.

FLUCTUATION OF PROFIT
Fluctuations in the arts of profit may occur irrespective of changes in the organic components of the capital, or of the absolute magnitude of the capital, through a rise or fall in the value of the fixed or circulating advanced capital caused by an increase or a reduction of the working time required for its reproduction, this increase or reduction taking place independently of the already existing capital.—C. 3.

FONDS
Fonds, or stock, is any accumulation of products of the soil or of manufacture.—M.

FORCE
Between equal rights force decides.—C. 1.

FOREIGN COMPETITION
As a result of foreign competition, rent of land can in most cases form no longer an independent income. A large number of landowners have to displace farmers, some of whom in this way sink into the proletariat. On the other hand, many farmers will take over landed property; for the big proprietors who with their comfortable incomes have mostly given themselves over to extravagance are, for the most part, not competent to conduct large-scale agriculture, and in some cases possess neither the capital nor the ability for the exploitation of the land. Hence a section of this class, too, is completely ruined.—M.

FOREIGN TRADE
Capitalist production does not exist at all without foreign commerce.—C. 1.

Capitals inverted in foreign trade can yield a higher rate of profit, because there is competition with commodities produced in other countries with inferior production facilities, so that the more advanced country sells its goods above their value even though cheaper than the competing countries. Insofar as the labor of the more advanced country is here realized as labor of higher specific weight, the rate of profit rises, because labor which has not been paid as being of a higher quality is sold as such.—C. 3.

Since foreign trade partly cheapens the elements of constant capital, and partly the necessities of life for which the variable capital is exchanged, it tends to raise the rate of profit by increasing the rate of surplus-value and lowering the value of constant capital. It generally acts in this direction by permitting an expansion of the scale of production. It thereby hastens the process of accumulation, on the one hand, but causes the variable capital to shrink in relation to the constant capital, on the other, and thus hastens a fall in the rate of profit. In the same way, the expansion of foreign trade, although the basis of the capitalist mode of production in its infancy, has become its own product, however, with the further progress of the capitalist mode of production, through the innate necessity of this mode of production, its need for an ever-expanding market.—C. 3.

FORESTRY
The development of culture and of industry in general has ever evinced itself in such energetic destruction of forests that everything done by it conversely for their preservation and restoration appears infinitesimal.—C. 2.

The long production time (which comprises a relatively small period of working time) and the great length of the periods of turnover entailed make forestry an industry of little attraction to private and therefore capitalist enterprise.—C. 2.

FORMULAE, ECONOMIC
Political economy expresses in abstract formulae the material process through which private property actually passes, and these formulae it then takes for laws.—M.

FREE COMPETITION
Free competition brings out the inherent laws of capitalist production, in the shape of external coercive laws having power over every individual capitalist.—C. 1.

In the place of the feudal relations of property stepped free competition, accompanied by a social and political constitution adapted to it, and by the economical and political sway of the bourgeois class.—C. M.

FREE TRADE
The bourgeoisie has resolved personal worth into exchange value, and in place of the numberless indefeasible chartered freedoms, has set up that single, unconscionable freedom—Free Trade.—C. M.

FREEDMEN
The historical movement which changes the producers into wageworkers appears, on the one hand, as their emancipation from

serfdom and from the fetters of the guilds, and this side alone exists for our bourgeois historians. But, on the other hand, these new *freedmen* became sellers of themselves only after they had been robbed of all their own means of production, and of all the guarantee of existence afforded by the old feudal arrangements. And the history of this, their expropriation, is written in the annals of mankind in letters of blood and fire.—C. 1.

FREEDOM
By freedom is meant, under the present bourgeois conditions of production, free trade, free selling and buying.—C. M.

The realm of freedom actually begins only where labor which is determined by necessity and mundane considerations ceases; thus in the very nature of things it lies beyond the sphere of actual material production. Just as the savage must wrestle with nature to satisfy his wants, to maintain and reproduce life, so must civilized man, and he must do so in all social formations and under all possible modes of production. With his development this realm of physical necessity expands as a result of his wants; but, at the same time, the forces of production which satisfy these wants also increase.——C. 3.

FREEDOM, ECONOMIC
Freedom in the economic field can only consist in socialized men, the associated producers, rationally regulating their interchange with nature, bringing it under their common control, instead of being ruled by it as by the blind forces of nature; and achieving this with the least expenditure of energy and under conditions most favorable to, and worthy of, their human nature. Beyond it begins that development of human energy which is an end in itself, the true realm of freedom, which, however, can blossom forth only with this realm of necessity as its basis.—C. 3.

FREEDOM OF CONSCIENCE
Among the human rights is freedom of conscience, the right to practice the religion of one's choice. The privilege of belief is implicitly recognized either as a human right or as a consequence of human rights (freedom).—J. Q.

"Freedom of conscience!" If one had desired at the time of the *Kulturkampf* to remind liberalism of its old catchwords, it surely could have been done only in the following form: Everyone should be able to attend to his religious as well as his bodily needs without the police sticking their noses in. But the workers' party ought at any rate in this connection to have expressed its awareness of the fact that bourgeois "freedom of conscience" is nothing but the toleration of all possible kinds of religious freedom of science, and that for its part it endeavors rather to liberate the conscience from the witchery of religion. But one chooses not to overstep the "bourgeois" level.—G. P.

FREEMASON SOCIETY
Here, then, we have a mathematically precise proof why capitalists form a veritable Freemason society vis-à-vis the whole working class, while there is little love lost between them in competition among themselves.—C. 3.

G

GEOGENY
The creation of the earth has received a mighty blow from *geogeny*—i.e., from the science which presents the formation of the earth, the coming-to-be of the earth, as a process, as self-generation.—M.

GEOLOGY
Geological revolutions have created the surface of the earth.—D. T.

GERMAN BOURGEOISIE
In Germany the petty bourgeois class, a relic of the sixteenth century, and since then constantly cropping up again under various forms, is the real social basis of the existing state of things. To preserve this class is to preserve the existing state of things in Germany.—C. M.

GERMAN INDUSTRY
In German industry, [the] maxim is: People will surely appreciate if we send them good samples first, and then inferior goods afterward.—C. 3.

GERMAN PHILOSOPHY
To the German philosophers of the eighteenth century, the demands of the first French Revolution were nothing more than the demands of "Practical Reason" in general, and the utterance of the will of the revolutionary French bourgeoisie signified in their eyes the laws of pure Will, of Will as it was bound to be, of true human Will generally.—C. M.

GERMAN RESURRECTION
When all inner requisites are fulfilled, the day of German resurrection will be proclaimed by the crowing of the cock of Gaul. —C. C.

GERMAN SOCIALISM
German Socialism forgot, in the nick of time, that the French criticism, whose silly echo it was, presupposed the existence of modern bourgeois society, with its corresponding economic conditions, and the political constitution adapted thereto, the very things whose attainment was the object of the pending struggle in Germany.—C. M.

GERMANS
Being Germans, they have heads on their shoulders capable of generalizing.—Ltr. to Engels.

GOD
The more man puts into God, the less he retains in himself.—M.

GODS OF GREECE
The gods of Greece, already tragically wounded to death in Aeschylus' *Prometheus Bound,* had to re-die a comic death in Lucian's *Dialogues.* Why this course of history? So that humanity should part with its past cheerfully.—C. C.

GOLD
Only by virtue of serving as a universal measure of value does gold, the equivalent commodity par excellence, become money. —C. 1.

Gold and silver become of themselves social expressions for superfluity of wealth.—C. 1.

The capitalists producing gold possess their entire product in gold—that portion which replaces constant capital as well as that which replaces variable capital.—C. 2.

GOLD, DRAIN OF
A drain, a continued and heavy export of precious metal (gold), takes place as soon as returns no longer flow, markets are overstocked, and an illusory prosperity is maintained only by means of credit; in other words, as soon as a greatly increased demand

for loan capital exists and the interest rate, therefore, has reached at least its average level. Under such circumstances, which are reflected precisely in a drain of precious metal, the effect of continued withdrawal of capital, in a form in which it exists directly as loanable money-capital, is considerably intensified.—C. 3.

GOLD RESERVE
The metal (gold) reserve is the pivot of the bank.—C. 3.

GOLD STANDARD
In order to make gold a standard of price, a certain weight must be fixed upon as the unit.—C. 1.

A change in the value of gold does not, in any way, affect its function as a standard of price. No matter how this value varies, the proportion between the values of different quantities of the metal remain constant.—C. 1.

GOSPEL
The distinction between "the letter of the Gospel" and "the spirit of the Gospel" is an irreligious act. The state that lets the Gospel speak in political terms or, for that matter, in any other terms than those of the Holy Ghost, commits an act of sacrilege, if not in the eyes of men, then in its own religious eyes.—J. Q.

GOVERNING POWER
Capital is the governing power over labor.—M.

The capitalist, by means of capital, exercises his governing power of capital over the capitalist himself.—M.

GOVERNMENT
Aristotle says that supremacy in the political and economic fields imposes the functions of government upon the ruling powers.—C. 3.

GOVERNMENT SECURITIES
Government securities, like stocks and other securities of all kinds, are spheres of investment for loanable capital—capital

intended for bearing interest. They are forms of loaning such capital. But they themselves are not the loan capital, which is invested in them.—C. 3.

GRAPES
Grapes after being pressed must ferment a while and then rest for some time in order to reach a certain degree of perfection.—C. 2.

GRATIFICATION
In what manner the object exists for man's feelings is the characteristic mode of their gratification.—M.

GREECE
Greece and Rome are certainly the countries of the highest "historical culture" among the peoples of antiquity. The peak of Greece's greatest internal progress coincides with the time of Pericles, its external zenith with the time of Alexander.—L. A.

Greek society was founded upon slavery, and had, therefore, for its natural basis, the inequality of men and of their labor powers.—C. 1.

GROUND RENT
Ground rent may in another form be confused with interest and thereby its specific character overlooked. Ground rent assumes the form of a certain sum of money, which the landlords draws annually by leasing a certain plot on our planet.—C. 3.

We have already learnt that the size of the rent depends on the degree of fertility of the land. Another factor in its determination is situation.—M.

The relation between increasing house rent and increasing poverty is an example of the landlord's interest in society, for the ground rent, the interest obtained from the land on which the house stands, goes up with the rent of the house.—M.

In theory, ground rent and profit on capital are deductions suffered by wages.—M.

Ground rent cannot be paid on all commodities. For instance, in many districts no rent is paid for stones.—M.

GROWTH, ECONOMIC
The state of economic growth must sooner or later reach its peak.—M.

GUERRILLA
They fail from limiting themselves to a guerrilla war.—C.M.

H

HABITATION, HUMAN
Man returns to living in a cave, which is now, however, contaminated with the mephitic breath of plague given off by civilization, and which he continues to occupy only precariously, it being for him an alien habitation which can be withdrawn from him any day—a place from which, if he does not pay, he can be thrown out any day. For this mortuary he has to pay.—M.

HANDICRAFT SKILL
Handicraft skill is the foundation of manufacture.—C. 1.

HEGEL
I would like to explain to the ordinary human understanding what is rational in the method which Hegel discovered but also wrapped up in mysticism.—Ltr. to Engels.

Hegel has no problems to put. He has only dialectic.—P. P.

One must begin with Hegel's *Phaenomenologie*, the true point of origin and the secret of the Hegelian philosophy.—M.

The outstanding thing in Hegel's *Phaenomenologie* is that Hegel conceives the self-genesis of man as a process, conceives objectification as loss of the object, as alienation and as transcendence of this alienation; that he thus grasps the essence of labor and comprehends objective man—true, because real man—as the outcome of man's own labor.—M.

For Hegel the essence of man—man—equals self-consciousness. All estrangement of the human essence is therefore nothing but estrangement of self-consciousness. The estrangement of self-consciousness is not regarded as an expression of the real estrangement of the human being—its expression reflected in the realm of knowledge and thought. Instead, the real estrangement—that which appears real—is from its innermost, hidden nature (a nature only brought to light by philosophy) nothing but the manifestation of the estrangement of the real essence of man, of self-consciousness. The science which comprehends this is therefore called *Phenomenology*.—M.

Hegel's *Encyclopaedia*, beginning as it does with Logic, with pure speculative thought, and ending with Absolute Knowledge—with the self-consciousness, self-comprehending, philosophic or absolute (i.e., superhuman) abstract mind—is in its entirety nothing but the display, the self-objectification, of the essence of the philosophic mind, and the philosophic mind is nothing but the estranged mind of the world thinking its self-estrangement—i.e., comprehending itself abstractly.—M.

Because Hegel has conceived the negation of the negation from the point of view of the positive relation inherent in it as the true and only positive, and from the point of view of the negative relation inherent in it as the only true act and self-realizing act of all being, he has only found the abstract, logical, speculative expression for the movement of history; and this historical process is not yet the real history of man—of man as a given subject, but only man's act of genesis—the story of man's origin.—M.

Speculative philosophy, that is, Hegel's philosophy, first had to translate all questions from the language of every sound common sense into the language of the speculative intellect and turn every real question into a speculative question before it could answer it.—J. Q.

HEIRS
The heirs are quarreling among themselves over the inheritance even before the obituary notice has been printed and the testament read.—H. P.

HEROISM
Bourgeois society is lacking in heroism.—E. B.

HISTORIC REVERSION
At the very time when men appear engaged in revolutionizing things and themselves, in bringing about what never was before, precisely at such epochs of revolutionary crisis do they anxiously conjure up into their service the spirits of the past, assume their names, their battle cries, their costumes, to enact a new historic scene in such time-honored disguise and with such borrowed language.—E. B.

HISTORICAL FORM
In order to examine the connection between spiritual production and material production it is above all necessary to grasp the latter itself not as a general category but in definite historical form.—C. 4.

HISTORICAL MATERIALISM
The social organization and the state constantly arise from the life-process of definite individuals, of those individuals not as they or other people imagine them to be, but as they are really, i.e., as they act, as they materially produce, consequently as they are active under definite material limitations, provisions and conditions which do not depend on their free will.—G. I.

What avails lamentation in the face of *historical necessity?*—C. 1.

HISTORICAL RECURRENCE
All great historic facts and personages recur twice—once as tragedy, and once as farce.—E. B.

HISTORICAL RETRIBUTION
There is something in human history like retribution; and it is a rule of *historical retribution* that its instrument be forged not by the offended, but by the offender himself. D. T.

HISTORY
History resembles paleontology. Owing to certain prejudices even the best scientists do not notice facts which lie in front of their noses. Later, they are surprised to discover traces everywhere of what they failed to realize.—Ltr. to Engels.

Human history differs from natural history in this, that we have made the former, but not the latter.—C. I.

Man makes his own history, but he does not make it out of whole cloth; he does not make it out of conditions chosen by himself, but out of such as he finds close at hand.—E. B.

All history is the preparation for "man" to become the object of sensuous consciousness, and for the needs of "man as man" to become (natural, sensuous) needs. History itself is a real part of natural history—of nature's coming to be man. Natural science will in time subsume under itself the science of man, just as the science of man will subsume under itself natural science.—M.

After philosophy comes history. This is no longer either descriptive history or dialectic history, it is comparative history.—P. P.

All preceding conception of history has either completely ignored the real basis of history or has considered it only as incidental and in no way connected with the course of history. That is why history had always to be written according to a standing lying outside it; real life-production appeared as prehistoric while what was historical appeared as separated from common life and extra-supra-mundane. Man's relation to nature was thus excluded from history, as a result of which the antithesis of nature and history was produced. Hence this conception of history saw in history only the main official actions of the state and the religious and generally theoretical struggles.—G. I.

The entire movement of history is both its actual act of genesis (the birth act of its empirical existence) and also for its thinking consciousness the comprehended and known process of its coming-to-be.—M.

HISTORY, BOURGEOIS
The bourgeois period of history has to create the material basis of the new world—on the one hand the universal intercourse founded upon the mutual dependency of mankind, and the means of that intercourse; on the other hand the development of the productive powers of man and the transformation of material production into a scientific domination of natural agencies. Bourgeois industry and commerce create these material conditions of a new world in the same way as geological revolutions have created the surface of the earth.—D. T.

HISTORY, MATERIALISTIC CONCEPTION OF
This conception of history has not to seek a category in every epoch like the idealistic conception of history, but it remains constantly on the real ground of history; it does not explain practice by the idea but explains the formation of ideas by material practice. Accordingly it comes to the result that all forms and products of consciousness can be dissolved not by spiritual criticism, but by the practical overthrow of the real social relations; that not criticism but revolution is the motive force of history as well as of religion, philosophy and all other forms of theory.—G. I.

HISTORY, TASK OF
The task of history, once the world beyond the truth has disappeared, is to establish the truth of this world. The immediate task of philosophy, which is at the service of history, once the saintly form of human self-alienation has been unmasked, is to unmask self-alienation in its unholy forms. Thus the criticism of heaven turns into the criticism of the earth, the criticism of religion into the criticism of right and the criticism of theology into the criticism of politics.—C. C.

HOARDING
The simplest form in which the additional latent money-capital may be represented is that of a hoard. It may be that this hoard is additional gold or silver secured directly or indirectly in exchange with countries producing precious metals. And only in this manner does the hoarded money in a country grow absolutely. On the other hand, it may be—and is so in the majority of cases—that this hoard is nothing but money which has been withdrawn from circulation at home and has assumed the form of a hoard in the hands of individual capitalists.—C. 2.

HOBBES
According to Hobbes science, not operative labor, is the mother of the arts. The product of mental labor—science—always stands far below its value, because the labor-time needed to reproduce it has no relation at all to the labor-time for its original production. For example, a schoolboy can learn the binominal theorem in an hour.—C. 4.

For Hobbes labor is the sole source of all wealth, apart from those gifts of nature which are to be found already in a consumable state.—C. 4.

HOME INDUSTRY
The home and petty form of industry is intended for self-consumption, not producing commodities.—C. 4.

HONOR
Honor attaches to great historic struggles.—E. B.

HOSPITALITY
It is a custom in the north to treat guests to exquisite liqueurs before meager meals.—L. A.

HOSTILITY, CAPITALIST
Capitalist production is hostile to certain branches of spiritual production, for example, art and poetry.—C. 4.

The interest of the capitalists, even from the point of view commonly held by political economists, stands in hostile opposition to society.—M.

HOSTILITY, INTERNATIONAL
In proportion as the exploitation of one individual by another is put an end to, the exploitation of one nation by another will also be put an end to. In proportion as the antagonism between classes within the nation vanishes, the hostility of one nation to another will come to an end.—C.M.

HOUSE RENT
House rent stands in inverse proportion to industrial poverty. The lower the standard of living, the higher the house rent.—M.

HUCKSTERING
Feudal landed property is already by its very nature huckstered land.—M.

HUMAN
Assume man to be man and his relationship to the world to be a human one: then you can exchange love only for love, trust for trust, etc.—M.

HUMAN ACTIVITIES
Certainly eating, drinking, procreating, etc., are also genuinely human functions. But in the abstraction which separates them from the sphere of all other human activity and turns them into sole and ultimate ends, they are animal.—M.

The animal is immediately identical with its life activity. It does not distinguish itself from it. It is its life activity. Man makes his life activity itself the object of his will and of his consciousness. He has conscious life activity.—M.

HUMAN IDENTITY
The worker must sell his human identity.—M.

Is there not a universal *human nature* just as there is a universal nature of plants and heavenly bodies?—L. A.

HUMAN NATURE
The relation of man to woman is the most natural relation of human being to human being. It therefore reveals the extent to which man's natural behavior has become human, or the extent to which the human essence in him has become a natural essence—the extent to which his human nature has come to be nature to him.—M.

Not only the five senses but also the so-called mental senses—the practical senses (will, love, etc.)—in a word, human sense—the humanness of the senses—comes to be by virtue of its object, by virtue of humanized nature.—M.

HUMAN RIGHTS
Let us consider for a moment these so-called human rights in their authentic expression, the expression they were given by their discoverers, the Americans and the French. These human rights are partly political rights, rights that can be exercised only in community with others. Participation in the community, the political community of state, provides their content.—J. Q.

HUMAN THOUGHT
The humanness of nature and of the nature begotten by history—the humanness of man's products—appears in the form that they are products of abstract mind and as such, therefore, phases of mind—thought entities.—M.

HUMANITY

It is obvious that the human eye gratifies itself in a way different from the crude, nonhuman eye; the human ear different from the crude ear, etc.—M.

HUNGER

Hunger is a natural need; it therefore needs a nature outside itself, an object outside itself, in order to satisfy itself, to be stilled. Hunger is an acknowledged need of my body for an object existing outside it, indispensable to its integration and to the expression of its essential being.—M.

HYPOTHESES

Hypotheses are only made in view of some end.—P. P.

Each new thesis which reason discovers in absolute reason, and which is the negation of the first thesis, becomes for it a synthesis, which it naively accepts as the solution of the problem in question. It is thus that this reason strives with ever new contradictions, until finding itself at the end of contradictions it perceives that all theses and syntheses are not contradictory hypotheses.—P. P.

I

IDEAL SOCIETY
Society in a state of maximum wealth—an ideal.—M.

IDEALISM
Idealism does not know real, sensuous activity as such.—T. F.

IDEOLOGY
Ideology is a process achieved by a so-called thinker, consciously, it is true, but with a false consciousness. He is not aware of his real driving motives—only for this reason it is an ideological process.—Ltr. to Mehring.

Morals, religion, metaphysics and other forms of ideology and the forms of consciousness corresponding to them no longer retain their apparent independence. They have no history, they have no development, but men, developing their material production and their material intercourse, with this, their reality, their thinking and the products of their thinking also change.—G. I.

IDOLATRY
Man debases himself by idolatry.—H. F.

IMPORT TRADE
The volume of import trade is determined and stimulated by the export trade.—C. 2.

IMPOVERISHMENT
The accumulation of wealth at one pole is at the same time accumulation of slavery, ignorance, brutality, mental degradation at the opposite pole, that is, on the side of the class that produces its product.—C. 1.

IMPOVERISHMENT OF THE WORKER
When society is in a state of decline, the worker suffers most severely. The specific severity of his burden he owes to his position as a worker, but the burden as such to the position of society. But when society is in a state of progress, the ruin and impoverishment of the worker is the product of his labor and of the wealth produced by him. The misery results, therefore, from the essence of present-day labor itself.—M.

IMPROVEMENT OF MACHINERY
Improved construction of the machinery is necessary, partly because without it greater pressure cannot be put on the workman, and partly because the shortened hours of labor force the capitalist to exercise the strictest watch over the cost of production. The improvements in the steam-engine have increased the piston speed. . . . The improvements in the transmitting mechanism have lessened friction.—C. 1.

IMPULSES
As a living natural being man is furnished with natural powers of life—he is an active natural being. These forces exist in him as tendencies and abilities—as impulses.—M.

INCREASE IN PRODUCTION
As the use of machinery extends in a given industry, the immediate effect is to increase production in the other industries that furnish the first with means of production.—C. 1.

INDEPENDENCE
A being only considers himself independent when he stands on his own feet; and he only stands on his own feet when he owes his existence to himself.—M.

In bourgeois society capital is independent and has individuality, while the living person is dependent and has no individuality. —C. M.

INDIA

However changing the political aspect of India's past must appear, its social condition has remained unaltered since its remotest antiquity, until the first decennium of the nineteenth century. The hand-loom and the spinning-wheel, producing their regular myriads of spinners and weavers, were the pivots of the structure of that society. From immemorial times, Europe received the admirable textiles of Indian labor, sending in return for them her precious metals, and furnishing thereby his material to the goldsmith, that indispensable member of Indian society, whose love of finery is so great that even the lowest class, those who go about nearly naked, have commonly a pair of gold earrings and a gold ornament of some kind round their necks.—D. T.

England has to fulfil a double mission in India: one destructive, the other regenerating—the annihilation of old Asiatic society, and the laying of the material foundations of Western society in Asia.—D. T.

The day is not far distant when, by a combination of railways and steam vessels, the distance between England and India, measured by time, will be shortened to eight days, and when that once fabulous country will thus be actually annexed to the Western world.—D. T.

The Indians will not reap the fruits of the new elements of society scattered among them by the British bourgeoisie, till in Great Britain itself the new ruling classes shall have been supplanted by the industrial proletariat, or till the Hindus themselves shall have grown strong enough to throw off the English yoke altogether.—D. T.

INDIA, CONQUEST OF

How came it that English supremacy was established in India? The paramount power of the Great Mogul was broken by the Mogul Viceroy. The power of the Viceroys was broken by the Mahrattas. The power of the Mahrattas was broken by the Afghans, and while all were struggling against all, the Briton rushed in and was enabled to subdue them all. A country not only divided between Mohammedan and Hindu, but between tribe and tribe, between caste and caste; a society whose framework was based on a sort of equilibrium, resulting from a general repulsion and constitutional exclusiveness between all its members. Such a country and such a society, were they not the predestined prey of conquest? If we knew nothing of the past history of Hindustan, would there not be the one great and incontestable fact, that even at this moment India is held in English thralldom by an Indian army maintained at the cost of India?—D. T.

The antagonism of the various races, tribes, castes, creeds and sovereignties the aggregate of which forms the geographical unity of what is called India, continued to be the vital principle of British supremacy.—D. T.

INDIA, PROPERTY IN
It is agreed that in India, as in most Asiatic countries, the ultimate property in the soil vests in the government; but while one party to this controversy insists that the government is to be looked upon as a soil proprietor, letting out the land on shares to the cultivators, the other side maintains that in substance the land in India is just as much private property as in any other country whatever—this alleged property in the government being nothing more than the derivation of title from the sovereign, theoretically acknowledged in all countries, the codes of which are based on the feudal law and substantially acknowledged in all countries whatever in the power of the government to levy taxes on the land to the extent of the needs of the government, quite independent of all considerations, except as mere matter of policy, of the convenience of the owners.—D. T.

INDIAN CASTE SYSTEM
Modern industry, resulting from the railway system, will dissolve the hereditary divisions of labor, upon which rest the Indian castes, those decisive impediments to Indian progress and Indian power.—D. T.

INDIAN CIVIL SERVICE
For service in India, at least in the civil line, some knowledge of the languages spoken there is necessary, and to prepare young ment to enter their civil service, the East India Company has a college at Haileybury. A corresponding college for the military

service, in which, however, the rudiments of military science are the principal branches taught, has been established at Addiscombe, near London.—D. T.

INDIAN DOMINION
The present state of affairs in Asia suggests the inquiry, What is the real value of their Indian dominion to the British nation and people? Directly, that is in the shape of tribute, or surplus of Indian receipts over Indian expenditures, nothing whatever reaches the British Treasury. On the contrary, the annual outgo is very large. From the moment that the East India Company entered extensively on the career of conquest, their finances fell into an embarrassed condition, and they were repeatedly compelled to apply to Parliament, not only for military aid to assist them in holding the conquered territories, but for financial aid to save them from bankruptcy. Such being the case, it is evident that the advantage to Great Britain from her Indian Empire must be limited to the profits and benefits which accrue to individual British subjects. These profits and benefits, it must be confessed, are very considerable.—D. T.

INDIAN INDUSTRY
The small stereotype forms of social organism in India have been in the greater part dissolved, and are disappearing, not so much through the brutal interference of the British tax-gatherer and the British soldier, as to the working of English steam and English Free Trade. Those family communities were based on domestic industry, in that peculiar combination of hand-weaving, hand-spinning and hand-tilling agriculture which gave them self-supporting power.—D. T.

I continued the concealed warfare in a first article concerning India, characterizing the destruction of its native industry as a revolutionary development.—Ltr. to Engels.

INDIAN MISERY
England has broken down the entire framework of Indian society, without any symptoms of reconstitution yet appearing. This loss of his old world, with no gain of a new one, imparts a particular kind of melancholy to the present misery of the Hindu, and separates Hindustan, ruled by Britain, from all its ancient traditions, and from the whole of its past history.—D. T.

INDIAN REVOLT
The first blow to the French monarchy proceeded from the nobility, not from the peasants. The Indian revolt does not commence with the riots, tortured, dishonored and stripped naked by the British, but with the sepoys, clad, fed, petted, fatted and pampered by them.—D. T.

INDIAN TAXATION
On the one hand, we must admit the nominal amount of Indian taxation to be relatively small; but on the other, we might heap evidence upon evidence from parliamentary documents, as well as from the writings of the greatest authorities on Indian affairs, all proving beyond doubt that this apparently light taxation crushes the mass of the Indian people to the dust, and that its exaction necessitates a resort to such infamies as torture.—D. T.

INDIVIDUALITY, BOURGEOIS
You must confess that by "individual" you mean no other person than the bourgeois, than the middle-class owner of property. This person must, indeed, be swept out of the way, and made impossible.—C. M.

The abolition of the bourgeois state of things is called by the bourgeois, abolition of individuality and freedom! And rightly so. The abolition of bourgeois individuality, bourgeois freedom, is undoubtedly aimed at.—C. M.

INDUSTRIAL ARMY
An industrial army of workmen, under the command of a capitalist, requires, like a real army, officers (managers), and sergeants (foremen, overlookers), who, while the work is being done, command in the name of the capitalist. The work of supervision becomes their established and exclusive function.—C. 1.

INDUSTRIAL RESERVE ARMY
Capitalist production can by no means content itself with the quantity of disposable labor power which the natural increase of population yields. It requires for its free play an industrial reserve army independent of these natural limits.—C. 1.

The industrial reserve army, during the periods of stagnation and average prosperity, weighs down the active labor army; during the periods of overproduction and paroxysm, it holds its pretensions in check.—C. 1.

If a surplus laboring population is a necessary product of accumulation or of the development of wealth on a capitalist basis, this surplus population becomes, conversely, the lever of capitalistic accumulation, nay, a condition of existence of the capitalist mode of production. It forms a disposable industrial reserve army, that belongs to capital quite as absolutely as if the latter has bred it at its own cost.—C. 1.

INDUSTRIALIST
The working, sober, economical, and prosaic industrialist is quite enlightened about the nature of wealth.—M.

The *industrial capitalists,* these new potentates, had on their part not only to displace the guild masters of handicrafts, but also the feudal lords, the possessors of the sources of wealth. In this respect their conquest of social power appears as the fruit of a victorious struggle both against feudal lordship and its revolting prerogatives, and against the guilds and the fetters they laid on the free development of production and the free exploitation of man by man.— C. 1.

INDUSTRY
Gigantic *industrial enterprises* depend for their realization on a previous centralization of capitals.—C. 1.

Industry speculates on the refinement of needs, but it speculates just as much on their crudeness.—M.

It will be seen how the history of industry and the established objective existence of industry are the open book of man's essential powers.—M.

INDUSTRY, MODERN
The place of manufacture was taken by the giant, modern industry, the place of the industrial middle class, by industrial millionaires, the leaders of whole industrial armies, the modern bourgeoisie.—C. M.

INFLATION
In those branches of industry in which production can be rapidly expanded (manufacture proper, mining, etc.), climbing prices give rise to sudden expansion soon followed by collapse. The same effect is produced in the labor market, attracting great numbers of the latent relative surplus-population to the new lines of business. . . . A general rise in wages ensues, even in the hitherto well-employed sections of the labor market. This lasts until the inevitable crash again releases the reserve army of labor and wages are once more depressed to their minimum, and lower.—C. 2.

INFLUENCE
If you want to exercise influence over other people, you must be a person with a stimulating and encouraging effect on other people.—M.

INSOMNIA
My terrible insomnia makes me very restless, but has psychological motives.—Ltr. to Engels.

INSTRUMENTS OF LABOR
The use and fabrication of instruments of labor, although existing in the germ among certain species of animals, is specifically characteristic of the human labor-process.—C. 1.

An instrument of labor is a thing, or a complex of things, which the laborer interposes between himself and the subject of his labor, and which serves as the conducter of his activity. He makes use of the mechanical, physical, and chemical properties of some substances in order to make other substances subservient to his aims.—C. 1.

Instruments of labor not only supply a standard of the degree of developmnt to which human labor has attained, but they are also indicators of the social conditions under which that labor is carried on.—C. 1.

INSURANCE
Entirely different from the replacement of wear and tear and from the work of maintenance and repair is insurance, which relates to destruction caused by extraordinary phenomena of nature, fire, flood, etc.—C. 2.

Investments of capital in lines exposed to greater hazards, for instance in shipping, are compensated by higher prices. As soon as capitalist production, and with it the *insurance* business, are developed, the hazards are, in effect, made equal for all spheres of production; but the more hazardous lines pay higher insurance rates, and recover them in the prices of their commodities.—C. 3.

INTELLECTUAL CREATION
The intellectual creations of individual nations become common property—C. M.

INTELLIGENCE IN PRODUCTION
Intelligence in production expands in one direction, because it vanishes in many others.—C. 1.

INTENSIFICATION OF LABOR
We now come to the question: How is labor intensified? This is effected in two ways: by increasing the speed of the machinery, and by giving the workman more machinery to tend.—C. 1.

INTENTIONS
I told him that I did not give a farthing for "good intentions" which had the effect of bad intentions.—Ltr. to Engels.

INTEREST
If correctly understood interest is the principle of all morale, man's private interest must be made to coincide with the interest of humanity.—H. F.

Interest-bearing capital is a very old form of capital.—C. 3.

The fall in the interest on money is a necessary consequence and result of industrial development. The extravagant rentier's means therefore dwindle day by day in inverse proportion to the increasing possibilities and pitfalls of pleasure.—M.

In an increasingly prosperous society it is only the very richest people who can go on living on money interest. Everyone else has to carry on a business with his capital, or venture it in trade.—M.

The raising of wages and the raising of interest on capital operate on the price of commodities like simple and compound interest respectively.—M.

INTERNATIONAL TRADE
The bourgeoisie has through its exploitation of the world market given a cosmopolitan character to production and consumption in every country. To the great chagrin of reactionists, it has drawn from under the feet of industry the national ground on which it stood. All old-established national industries have been destroyed or are daily being destroyed. They are dislodged by new industries, whose introduction becomes a life-and-death question for all civilized nations, by industries that no longer work up indigenous raw material, but raw material drawn from the remotest zones; industries whose products are consumed, not only at home, but in every quarter of the globe.—C. M.

Transoceanic steamships and the railways of North and South America enabled some very singular tracts of land to compete in European grain markets. These were the North American prairies and the Argentine pampas—plains cleared for the plough by nature itself, and virgin soil which offered rich harvests for years to come even with primitive cultivation and without fertilizers.—C. 3.

INTERNATIONALISM
In place of the old local and national seclusion and self-sufficiency, we have intercourse in every direction, universal interdependence of nations. And as in material, so also in intellectual production.—C. M.

INTUITION
The abstract idea, which without mediation becomes intuiting, is nothing else through-and-through but abstract thinking that gives itself up and resolves on intuition. This entire transition from logic to natural philosophy is nothing else but the transition—so difficult to effect for the abstract thinker and therefore so queer in his description of it—from abstracting to intuiting. —M.

INVENTION
Inventions reduce the necessary labor-time.—C. 3.

Every new invention, every new application in manufacture of a previously unused or little-used raw material, augments the rent of the land. Thus, for example, there was a tremendous rise in the rent of coal mines with the advent of the railways, steamships, etc.—M.

A manufacturer who employs a new invention before it becomes generally used undersells his competitors and yet sells his commodity above its individual value, that is, realizes the specifically higher productiveness of the labor he employs as surplus-labor. He thus secures a surplus-profit.—C. 3.

A critical history of technology would show how little any of the inventions of the eighteenth century are the work of a single individual.—C. 1.

INVERSE INCREASE
The increase of wealth is identical with the increase of poverty and slavery.—M.

INVERSE INTEREST
In the economic system, under the rule of private property, the interest which an individual has in society is in precisely inverse proportion to the interest the society has in him—just as the interest of the money-lender in the spendthrift is by no means identical with the interest of the spendthrift.—M. *See* Mutual Interest.

INVERTED REPRESENTATION
That in their appearance things often represent themselves in inverted form is pretty well known in every science except political economy.—C. 1.

INVESTMENT
Whether a man buys his house ready built or gets it built for him, in neither case will the mode of acquisition increase the amount of money laid out on the house.—C. 1.

INVESTMENT, LONG-TERM
If we conceive society as being not capitalistic but communistic, there will be no money-capital at all in the first place, nor the disguises cloaking the transactions arising on account of it. The question then comes down to the need of society to calculate

beforehand how much labor, means of production, and means of subsistence it can invest, without detriment, in such lines of business as for instance the building of railways, which do not furnish any means of production or subsistence, nor produce any useful effect for a long time, a year or more, while they extract labor, means of production and means of subsistence from the total annual production.—C. 2.

IRELAND
I earlier considered the separation of Ireland from England as impossible; I now believe it inevitable, although there may follow a federation after the separation.—Ltr. to Engels.

Ireland represents the bulwark of the landed aristocracy in England. That exploited land not only supplies much of their material wealth, but also constitutes their main moral strength. By means of Ireland, therefore, the English aristocracy maintains its rule over England itself.—Ltr. to Meyer and Vogt.

IRISH HUNGER
The Irishman no longer knows any need now but the need to eat, and indeed only the need to eat potatoes—and scabby potatoes at that, the worst kind of potatoes.—M.

ITALIAN BOOKKEEPING
In Italian bookkeeping the role of the capitalist as a capitalist, as personified capital, is even always contrasted with him as a mere person, in which capacity he appears only as a personal consumer and debtor of his own capital.—C. 4.

J

JEW
Let us look at the real Jew of our time; not the Jew of the Sabbath, but the Jew of everyday life. What is the Jew's foundation in our world? Material necessity, private advantage. What is the object of the Jew's worship in this world? Usury. What is his worldly god? Money. Very well then; emancipation from usury and money, that is, from practical, real Judaism, would constitute the emancipation of our time.—J. Q.

JEWISH QUESTION
It is only in the free States of North America—or at least in some of them—that the Jewish question loses its theological character and becomes a truly secular one.—J. Q.

JEWRY
The social emancipation of Jewry is the emancipation of society from Jewry.—J. Q. *See* Jew, Anti-Semitism.

JEWS AND CHRISTIANS
The relation between Jews and Christians is as follows: The Christian's only interest in Jewish emancipation is a general, humanitarian, theoretical one. Judaism is a fact offensive to the Christian's religious eye. As soon as his eye ceases to be religious, however, the fact ceases to offend him. And so Jewish emancipation in itself involves no work for the Christian.—J. Q.

The stiffest form of opposition between Jew and Christian is religious. How is this to be resolved? By making it impossible. How can this be achieved? By abolishing religion.—J. Q.

Christianity sprang from Judaism; it has now dissolved itself back into Judaism. The Christian was from the start the theorizing Jew; the Jew therefore the practical Christian, and the practical Christian has once more become Jew.—J. Q.

JOBBING TAILOR
The jobbing tailor (who works for me at my home) is not a productive laborer, although his labor provides me with the product, the trousers, and him with the price of his labor, the money. It may be that the quantity of labor performed by the jobbing tailor is greater than that contained in the price which he gets from me. And this is even probable. This however is all the same so far as I am concerned. Once the price has been fixed, it is a matter of complete indifference to me whether he works eight or ten hours. What I am concerned with is only the use-value, the trousers; and naturally, whether I buy them one way or the other, I am interested in paying as little as possible for them, but in one case neither less nor more than in the other; in other words, I am interested in paying only the normal price for them.—C. 4.

JOHN BULL
As Delhi has not, like the walls of Jericho, fallen before mere puffs of wind, John Bull is to be steeped in cries of revenge up to his very ears, to make him forget that this government is responsible for the mischief hatched and the colossal dimensions it had been allowed to assume. —D. T.

It is certain that these obstinate John Bulls, whose skulls appear to have been manufactured for the bludgeons of the constables, will never accomplish anything without a truly bloody struggle with the ruling powers.—Ltr. to Engels.

JUDAISM
Judaism has maintained itself not in spite of, but because of, history.—J. Q.

JUNE INSURRECTION
The Paris proletariat answered with the June Insurrection, the most colossal event in the history of European civil wars.—E. B.

JURIDICAL RELATION
The juridical relation which expresses itself in a contract, whether such contract be part of a developed legal system or not, is a relation between two wills, and is but the reflex of the real economical relation between the two. It is this economical relation that determines the subject-matter comprised in each such juridical act.—C. 1.

JURISPRUDENCE
Your jurisprudence is but the will of your class made into a law for all, a will whose essential character and direction are determined by the economic conditions of existence of your class.—C. M. *See* Bourgeois superstructure.

JUSTIFICATION, BOURGEOIS
When the spiritual labors themselves are more and more performed in its service and enter into the service of capitalist production—then things take a new turn, and the bourgeoisie tries to justify "economically," from its own standpoint, what at an earlier stage it had criticized and fought against. Its spokesmen and conscience-salvers in this line are the Garniers, etc. In addition to this, these economists, who themselves are priests, professors, etc., are eager to prove their "productive" usefulness, to justify their wages "economically."—C. 4.

K

KANT
Kant considers the solution of the antinomies as something "beyond" the human understanding.—Ltr. to Schweitzer.

KNELL OF CAPITALISM
The monopoly of capital becomes a fetter upon the mode of production, which has sprung up and flourished along with it, and under it. Centralization of the means of production and socialization of labor at last reach a point where they become incompatible with their capitalist integument. This integument is burst asunder. The knell of capitalist private property sounds. The expropriators are expropriated.—C. 1.

KOSCIUSKO
Why does the popular dictator Kosciusko tolerate a king beside himself?—Ltr. to Engels.

KUGELMANN
Kugelmann is a fanatical advocate of our doctrine and of us both. He sometimes annoys me with his enthusiasm, which is at variance with his detachment as a medical man. However, he understands, and is very honest. He also is resolute, self-sacrificing, and, what is the most important, convinced.—Ltr. to Engels.

L

LABOR
Labor is man's active property.—M.

Labor is the source of value.—P. P.

Man enhances through labor the value of the products of nature. —M.

Labor, is in the first place, a process in which both man and nature participate, and in which man of his own accord starts, regulates, and controls the material reactions between himself and nature. He opposes himself to nature as one of her own forces, setting in motion arms and legs, head and hands, the natural forces of his body, in order to appropriate nature's productions in a form adapted to his own wants.—C. 1.

That which determines the magnitude of the value of any article is the amount of labor socially necessary, or the labor-time socially necessary for its production. Each individual commodity, in this connection, is to be considered as an average sample of its class.—C. 1.

LABOR, ABSTRACT
A use-value, or useful article, has value only because human labor in the abstract has been embodied or materialized in it. —C. 1.

LABOR, CAPITALIST
The labor of a capitalist stands altogether in inverse proportion to the size of his capital.—C. 3.

LABOR, CHILD
The capitalist buys children and young persons under age.—C. 1.

LABOR, COMMUNIST
In bourgeois society, living labor is but a means to increase accumulated labor. In communist society, accumulated labor is but a means to widen, to enrich, to promote the existence of the laborer.—C. M.

LABOR, COST OF
The constant tendency of capital is to force the cost of labor back toward zero.—C. 1.

LABOR, ESTRANGEMENT OF
Political economy starts from labor as the real soul of production; yet to labor it gives nothing, and to private property everything. From this contradiction Proudhon has concluded in favor of labor and against private property. We understand, however, that this apparent contradiction is the contradiction of estranged labor with itself, and that political economy has merely formulated the laws of estranged labor.—M.

The laws of political economy express the estrangement of the worker in his object thus: the more the worker produces, the less he has to consume; the more values he creates, the more valueless, the more unworthy he becomes; the better formed his product, the more deformed becomes the worker; the more civilized his object, the more barbarous becomes the worker; the mightier labor becomes, the more powerless becomes the worker; the more ingenious labor becomes, the duller becomes the worker and the more he becomes nature's bondsman.—M.

LABOR, INSTRUMENTS OF
It is not the workman that employs the instruments of labor, but the instruments of labor that employ the workman.—C. 1.

All other circumstances being equal, the degree of fixity increases with the durability of the instrument of labor. It is this durability that determines the magnitude of the difference between the capital-value fixed in instruments of labor and that part of its value which it yields to the product in repeated labor-processes.—C. 2.

LABOR, MEANS OF
The unity (of labor) in cooperation, the combination (of labor) through the division of labor, the use for productive purposes in machine industry of the forces of nature and science alongside the products of labor—all this confronts the individual laborers themselves as something extraneous and objective, as a mere form of existence of the means of labor that are independent of them and control them.—C. 4.

LABOR, MEASUREMENT OF
The quantity of labor is measured by its duration.—C. 1.

LABOR, ORGANIZATION OF
The organization of labor is determined by the means of production.—Ltr. to Engels.

LABOR, PRICE OF
The cost of production of a workman is restricted, almost entirely, to the means of subsistence that he requires for his maintenance, and for the propagation of his race.—C. M.

The price of labor, at the moment when demand and supply are in equilibrium, is its natural price, determined independently of the relation of demand and supply.—C. 1.

LABOR, PRODUCTS OF
It is true that labor produces for the rich wonderful things—but for the worker it produces privation. It produces palaces—but for the worker, hovels. It produces beauty—but for the worker, deformity. It replaces labor by machines—but some of the workers it throws back to a barbarous type of labor, and the other workers it turns into machines. It produces intelligence—but for the worker idiocy, cretinism.—M.

LABOR POWER
By labor power or capacity for labor is to be understood the aggregate of those mental and physical capabilities existing in a human being, which he exercises whenever he produces a use-value of any description.—C. 1.

Human labor power is by nature no more capital than are the means of production.—C. 2.

Simple labor power, on an average, apart from any special development, exists in the organism of every ordinary individual.—C. 1.

The value of labor power is determined by the labor-time necessary for the reproduction of this special article.—C. 1.

LABOR POWER, CONSUMPTION OF
The consumption of labor power is at one and the same time the production of commodities and of surplus-value. The consumption of labor power is completed, as in the case of every other commodity, outside the limits of the market or of the sphere of circulation.—C. 1.

LABOR POWER, EXHAUSTION OF
The capitalistic mode of production (essentially the production of surplus-value, the absorption of surplus-labor), produces thus, with the extension of the working day, not only the deterioration of human labor power by robbing it of its normal, moral and physical conditions of development and function. It produces also the premature exhaustion and death of this labor power itself. It extends the laborer's time of production during a given period by shortening his actual lifetime.—C. 1.

LABOR POWER, PURCHASE OF
By the purchase of labor power, the capitalist incorporates labor, as a living ferment, with the lifeless constituents of the product. From his point of view, the labor-process is nothing more than the consumption of the commodity purchased, i.e., of labor power.—C. 1.

The capitalist buys labor power in order to use it; and labor power in use is labor itself. The purchaser of labor power consumes it by setting the seller of it to work. By working, the latter becomes actually, what before he only was potentially, labor power in action, a laborer.—C. 1.

LABOR POWER, SALE OF
The alienation of labor power and its actual appropriation by the buyer, its employment as a use-value, are separated by an interval of time. But in those cases in which the formal alienation by sale of the use-value of a commodity is not simultaneous with its actual delivery to the buyer, the money of the latter usually functions as means of payment.—C. 1.

LABOR POWER, VALUE OF
The value of labor power is determined, as in the case of every other commodity, by the labor-time necessary for the production, and consequently also the reproduction, of this special article. —C. 1.

The *labor prices* of the various kinds of workers show much wider differences than the profits in the various branches in which capital is applied.—M.

LABOR PROCESS
The labor process is a process between things that the capitalist has purchased, things that have become his property. The product of this process also belongs, therefore, to him.—C. 1.

The fabrication of instruments of labor is specifically characteristic of the human labor process.—C. 1.

LABOR THEORY OF VALUE
The product is nothing more than a measure of the labor absorbed by (the raw materials).—C. 1.

In the finished product the labor by means of which it has acquired its useful qualities is not palpable, has apparently vanished.—C. 1.

LABOR TIME
Labor time finds its standard in weeks, days, and hours.—C. 1.

The labor time socially necessary is that required to produce an article under the normal conditions of production, and with the average degree of skill and intensity prevalent at the time.—C. 1.

LABORER, EXPLOITATION OF
It is evident that the laborer is nothing else, his whole life through, than labor power, that therefore all his disposable time is by nature and law labor time, to be devoted to the self-expansion of capital. Time for education, for intellectual development, for the fulfilling of social functions and for social intercourse, for the free play of his bodily and mental activity, even the rest time of Sunday—moonshine!—C. 1.

Stripped of the conditions of production, the laborers are compelled by need to labor to increase the wealth of others in order themselves to live.—C. 4.

LABORER, MODERN
The modern laborers, who must sell themselves piecemeal, are a commodity, like every other article of commerce, and are consequently exposed to all vicissitudes of competition, to all fluctuations of the market.—C. M.

LADIES
Ladies cannot complain of the *International,* which has elected a lady to be a member of the General Council.—Ltr. to Kugelmann.

LAISSEZ FAIRE, LAISSEZ PASSER
The reason why the physiocrats preached *laissez faire, laissez passer*—in short, free competition—is correctly stated in the following passage from Adam Smith: "The trade which is carried on between these two sets of people (country and town) consists ultimately in a certain quantity of rude produce exchanged for a certain quantity of manufactured produce. The dearer the latter, therefore, the cheaper the former; and whatever tends in any country to raise the price of manufactured produce tends to lower that of the rude produce of the land, and thereby to discourage agriculture."—C. 4.

LAND
As capital, land is not more eternal than any other capital.—P. P.

LANDED PROPERTY
Landed property is the root of private property.—M.

It is essential that that which is the root of landed property—filthy self-interest—make its appearance in its cynical form. It is essential that the immovable monopoly turn into the mobile and restless monopoly, into competition; and that the idle enjoyment of the other people's blood and toil turn into a bustling commerce in the same commodity.—M.

Landed property is based on the monopoly by certain persons over definite portions of the globe, as exclusive spheres of their private will to the exclusion of all others. With this in mind, the problem is to ascertain the economic value, that is, the realization of this monopoly on the basis of capitalist production. With the legal power of these persons to use or misuse certain portions of the globe, nothing is decided. The use of this power depends wholly upon economic conditions, which are independent of their will.—C. 3.

In general the relationship of large and small landed property is like that of big and small capital. But in addition, there are special circumstances which lead inevitably to the accumulation of large landed property and to the absorption of small property by it.—M.

Landed property in its distinction from capital is private property—capital—still afflicted with local and political prejudices: it is capital which has not yet regained itself from its entanglement with the world—capital not yet fully developed. It must in the course of its world-wide development achieve its abstract, that is, its pure expression.—M.

Where industry has attained to great power, as in England at the present time, it progressively forces large landed property to discard its monopolies against foreign countries and throws them into competition with landed property abroad. For under the sway of industry landed property could keep its feudal grandeur secure only by means of monopolies against foreign countries, thereby protecting itself against the general laws of trade, which are incompatible with its feudal character. Once thrown into competition, landed property obeys the laws of competition, like every other commodity subjected to competition. It begins thus to fluctuate, to decrease and to increase, to fly from one hand to another; and no law can keep it any longer in a few predestined hands.—M.

133

Landed property had to develop in each of those two ways so as to experience in both its necessary eclipse, just as industry both in the form of monopoly and in that of competition had to ruin itself so as to learn to believe in man.—M.

LANDED PROPERTY, LARGE
Large landed property, as in England, drives the overwhelming majority of the population into the arms of industry and reduces its own workers to utter wretchedness. Thus, it engenders and enlarges the power of its enemy, capital, industry, by throwing poor people and an entire activity of the country on to the other side. It makes the majority of the people of the country industrial, and thus opponents of large landed property.—M.

Large landed property, as we see in England, has already cast off its feudal character and adopted an industrial character insofar as it is aiming to make as much money as possible. To the owner it yields the utmost possible rent, to the tenant farmer the utmost possible profit on his capital. The workers on the land, in consequence, have already been reduced to the minimum, and the class of tenant farmers already represent within landed property the power of industry and capital.—M. *See* Nobility.

LANDLORDS
The landlords of houses make enormous profit out of poverty. —M.

The landlord being interested in the welfare of society means, according to the principles of political economy, that he is interested in the growth of its population, production, in the expansion of its needs—in short, in the increase of wealth; and the increase of wealth is identical with the increase of poverty and slavery.—M.

It is absurd to conclude, as Smith does, that since the landlord exploits every benefit which comes to society, the interest of the landlord is *always* identical with that of society.—M.

LANDLORDS, AGRARIAN
The vitality of the class of big landlords is amazing. No social class lives so sumptuously, no other class claims the right it does to traditional luxury in keeping with its "estate," regardless

of where the money for this purpose may be derived, and no other class piles debt upon debt so lightheartedly. And yet it always lands again on its feet—thanks to the capital invested by other people in the land, which yields a rent, completely out of proportion to the profits reaped therefrom by the capitalist.—C. 3.

LANDOWNERS
The competition has the further consequence that a large part of landed property falls into the hands of the capitalists and that capitalists thus become simultaneously landowners, just as the smaller landowners are on the whole already nothing more than capitalists. Similarly, a section of large landowners become simultaneously industrialists.—M.

LANDOWNERS' PROFITS
We have already learnt that with equal fertility and equally efficient exploitation of lands, mines and fisheries, the produce is proportionate to the size of the capital. Hence the victory of the big landowner.—M.

LANGUAGE
The element of thought itself—the element of thought's living expression—language—is of a sensuous nature.—M.

A foreign language is appropriated by translation.—C.M.

The beginner, who has acquired a new language, keeps on translating it back into his own mother tongue; only then has he grasped the spirit of the new language and is able freely to express himself therewith when he moves in it without recollection of the old, and has forgotten in its use his own hereditary tongue.—E. B.

LARGE CAPITAL
If large capital is opposed by small capitalists with small profits, as it is under the presupposed condition of intense competition, it crushes them completely. The necessary result of this competition is a general deterioration of commodities, adulteration, fake-production and universal poisoning, evident in large towns.—M.

LASSALLE
It is the immortal achievement of Lassalle to have reawakened the German workers' movement after its fifteen years of slumber. He however committed serious mistakes; he allowed himself to be too much guided by the nearest circumstances of his time. —Ltr. to Schweitzer.

Lassalle went astray because he was a "Realpolitiker."—Ltr. to Kugelmann.

Lassalle, dazzled by the reputation he enjoys in certain scholarly circles by his *Heraclitus* and in a certain group of parasites by his excellent wine and cookery, is unaware of his discredit among the community at large. There also is his mania to be always right, his adherence to Hegel's "speculative conception," his infection with old French liberalism, his inflated writing, his importunity, tactlessness, etc.—Ltr. to Engels.

The moment Lassalle was convinced that he could not play his games with me, he decided to establish himself as the "workers'" dictator against me.—Ltr. to Kugelmann.

Heraclitus the Dark by *Lassalle* the Bright basically is a very silly bungling work.—Ltr. to Engels.

Lassalle's misfortune has been damnably in my head these days. After all he was still one of the old guard and the adversary of our adversaries. And then the thing happened so surprisingly that it is hard to believe such a noisy, stirring, pushing man is now as dead as a mouse and has got to keep his mouth shut altogether.—Ltr. to Engels.

LAW, CIVIL
Are not the majority of civil laws concerned with property? —L. A.

LAW OF CAPITALIST PRODUCTION
The law of capitalist production, that is at the bottom of the pretended "natural law of population," reduces itself simply to this: The correlation between accumulation of capital and rate of wages is nothing else than the correlation between the

unpaid labor transformed into capital, and the additional paid labor necessary for the setting in motion of this additional capital. It is therefore in no way a relation between two magnitudes, independent one of the other: on the one hand, the magnitude of the capital; on the other, the number of the laboring population; it is rather, at bottom, only the relation between unpaid and the paid labor of the same laboring population. —C. 1.

LAW OF CAPITALISTIC ACCUMULATION
The law of capitalistic accumulation, metamorphosed by economists into a pretended law of nature, in reality merely states that the very nature of accumulation excludes every diminution in the degree of exploitation of labor, and every rise in the price of labor, which could seriously imperil the continual reproduction, on an ever enlarging scale, of the capitalistic relation.—C. 1.

LAW OF CIRCULATION OF COMMODITIES
According to the law of the circulation of commodities, the quantity of money must be equal to the amount of money required for circulation plus a certain amount held in the form of a hoard, which increases or decreases as the circulation contracts or expands.—C. 1.

LAW OF FALLING PROFIT
The law of the falling rate of profit, which expresses the same, or even a higher, rate of surplus-value, states that any quantity of the average social capital, say, a capital of 100, comprises an ever larger portion of means of labor, and an ever smaller portion of living labor.—C. 3.

LAW OF INCREASING PROLETARIAN MISERY
Along with the constantly diminishing number of the magnates of capital grows the mass of misery.—C. 1. See Law of Static Misery.

LAW OF POPULATION
Every historic mode of (human) production has its own special laws of population. An abstract law of population exists for plants and animals only insofar as man has not interfered with them.—C. 1.

LAW OF STATIC MISERY
Society in a state of maximum wealth means for the workers static misery.—M. *See* Law of Increasing Proletarian Misery.

LAZINESS
It has been objected, that upon the abolition of private property all work will cease, and universal laziness will overtake us.—C. M.

LEADER OF INDUSTRY
It is not because he is a leader of industry that a man is a capitalist; on the contrary, he is a leader of industry because he is a capitalist. The leadership of industry is an attribute of capital, just as in feudal times the functions of general and judge were attributes of landed property.—C. 1.

LEGAL RELATIONS
My investigation led to the result that legal relations as well as forms of state are to be grasped neither from themselves nor from the so-called general development of the human mind, but rather have their roots in the material conditions of life.—P.E.

LEGISLATIVE RECOGNITION OF WORKERS
The organization of the proletarians into a class, and consequently into a political party, compels legislative recognition of particular interests of the workers, by taking advantage of the divisions among the bourgeoisie itself.—C. M.

LENDING
The lender expends his money as capital; the amount of value which he relinquishes to another is capital, and consequently returns to him. But the mere return of it would not be the reflux of the loaned sum of value as capital, but merely the return of a loaned sum of value. To return as capital, the advanced sum of value must not only be preserved in the movement but must also expand, must increase in value.—C. 3.

LENGTHENING THE WORKING DAY
If machinery is the most powerful means for shortening the working time required in the production of a commodity, it becomes in the hands of capital the most powerful means, in those industries first invaded by it, for lengthening the working

day beyond all bounds set by human nature. It creates, on the one hand, new conditions by which capital is enabled to give free scope to this its constant tendency, and on the other hand, new motives with which to whet capital's appetite for the labor of others.—C. 1.

LEVELING OF PROFIT
It has been said that competition levels the rates of profit of the different spheres of production into an average rate of profit and thereby turns the values of the products of these different spheres into prices of production. This occurs through the continual transfer of capital from the sphere to another, in which, for the moment, the profit happens to lie above average. This incessant outflow and inflow of capital between the different spheres of production creates trends of rise and fall in the rate of profit, which equalize one another more or less and thus have a tendency to reduce the rate of profit everywhere to the same common and general level.—C. 3.

LIBERATION
Liberated industry, industry constituted for itself as such, and liberated capital, are a necessary development of labor.—M.

LIBERTY
Are you not furious at the slightest infringement of your personal liberty?—L. A.

Liberty is the right to do anything that does not harm others. The limit within which each can move without harming others is determined by the law, just as the boundary between two fields is determined by a fence. It is the liberty of man conceived as an isolated man referring only to itself.—J. Q.

The human right of liberty is not based on the link between man and man, but rather on the separation of man from man. It is the right to this separation, the right to the individual limited to himself.—J. Q.

LIBERTY, RELIGIOUS
The idea of religious liberty and freedom of conscience merely gave expression to the sway of free competition within the domain of knowledge.—C. M.

LICENSE
The license of shamelessness is sometimes called "free."—L. A.

LIFE
It is not consciousness that determines life, but life that determines consciousness.—G. I.

LIFE, LENGTH OF LABORER'S
Capital cares nothing for the length of life of labor power. All that concerns it is simply and solely the maximum of labor power, that can be rendered fluent in a working day. It attains this end by shortening the extent of the laborer's life, as a greedy farmer snatches increased product from the soil by robbing it of its fertility.—C. 1.

LIFE PROCESS
Consciousness can never be anything else than conscious being, and the being of men is their real *life process*. If in the whole of ideology men and their relations appear upside down as in a *camera obscura*, this is due as much to their historical life-process.—G. I.

LIFE SPAN
The shortening of their life span is a favorable circumstance for the working class as a whole, for as a result of it an ever-fresh supply of labor becomes necessary.—M.

LIMITED COMPETITION
The capitalist may exploit all the advantages of limited competition.—M.

LIVING, CAPITALIST
The more capital increases by means of successive accumulations, the more does the sum of the value increase that is divided into consumption-fund and accumulation-fund. The capitalist can therefore, live a more jolly life, and at the same time show more "abstinence."—C. 1.

LOCKE
[In this passage] Locke has in part the polemical interest of showing landed property that its rent is in no way different from usury. Locke's view is all the more important because it was the classical expression of bourgeois society's ideas of right as

against feudal society, and moreover his philosophy served as the basis for all the ideas of the whole of subsequent English political economy.—C. 4.

Taking Locke's general doctrine of labor together with his doctrine of the origin of interest and rent—for he considers surplus-value only in these specific forms—surplus-value is nothing but another person's labor, surplus-labor, which land and capital —the conditions of labor—enable their owners to appropriate. And ownership of a greater quantity of conditions of labor than one person can himself put to use with his own labor is, according to Locke, a *political* invention that contradicts the law of nature on which private property is founded.—C. 4.

LOGIC
Logic (mind's coin of the realm, the speculative or thought-value of man and nature—their essence grown totally indifferent to all real determinateness, and hence their unreal essence) is alienated thinking, and therefore thinking which abstracts from nature and from real man: abstract thinking.—M.

LOSS OF REALITY
So much does labor's realization appear as loss of reality that the worker loses reality to the point of starving to death. So much does objectification appear as loss of the object that the worker is robbed of the objects most necessary not only for his life but for his work. Indeed, labor itself becomes an object which he can get hold of only with the greatest effort and with the most irregular interruptions. So much does the appropriation of the object appear as estrangement that the more objects the worker produces, the fewer can he possess and the more he falls under the dominion of his product, capital.—M.

LOVE
You can exchange love only for love.—M.

It is delightful to be at a distance during this first stage of love's young dawn.—Ltr. to Engels.
LOVE, UNREQUITED

If you love without evoking love in return—that is, if your loving as loving does not produce reciprocal love; if through a living expression of yourself as a loving person you do not make yourself a loved person, then your love is impotent—a misfortune. —M.

LUTHER
Luther, we grant, overcame bondage out of devotion by replacing it by bondage out of conviction. He shattered faith in authority because he restored the authority of faith. He turned priests into laymen because he turned laymen into priests. He freed man from outer religiosity because he made religiosity the inner man. He freed the body from chains because he enchained the heart.—C. C.

Luther recognized religion—faith—as the substance of the external world and in consequence stood opposed to Catholic paganism—he superseded external religiosity by making religiosity the inner substance of man—he negated the priests outside the layman because he transplanted the priest into laymen's hearts.—M.

LUXURY
The quarrel between the political economists about luxury and thrift is only the quarrel between that economy which has achieved clarity about the nature of wealth, and that political economy which is still afflicted with romantic, anti-industrial memories. Neither side, however, knows how to reduce the subject of the controversy to its simple terms, and neither therefore can make short work of the other.—M.

M

MACHINE AND TOOL
There is a great dispute as to what distinguishes a machine from a tool. The English merchants, in their crude manner, denote a tool a simple machine and a machine a complicated tool. The English technologists, however, base the distinction between the two on the fact that in one case the motive power originates from a human being, in the other from a natural force. The German asses, who are great at these small affairs, have therefore concluded that, for instance, a plough is a machine, while the most complicated spinning-jenny, etc., insofar as it is worked by hand, is not.—Ltr. to Engels.

MACHINE COMPETITION
Every article produced by a machine is cheaper than a similar article by hand.—C. 1.

The division of labor brings with it the competition not only of men but of machines. Since the worker has sunk to the level of a machine, he can be confronted by the machine as a competitor. —M.

MACHINE LABOR
As long as the labor spent on a machine, and consequently the portion of its value added to the product, remains smaller than the value added by the workman to the product with his tool, there is always a difference of labor saved in favor of the machine. The productiveness of a machine is therefore measured by the human labor power it replaces.—C. 1.

Machine labor is simplified in order to make a worker out of the human being still in the making, the completely immature human being, the child—whilst the worker has become a neglected child. The machine accommodates itself to the weakness of the human being in order to make the weak human being into a machine.—M.

MACHINERY
The starting point of modern industry is . . . the revolution in the instruments of labor, and this revolution attains its most highly developed form in the organized system of machinery in a factory.—C. 1.

In the form of *machinery*, the implements of labor become automatic.—C. 1.

Machinery is intended to cheapen commodities.—C. 1.

The machines are not wage-workers.—P. P.

MACHINERY AND CLASS CONFLICT
The unceasing improvement of machinery, ever more rapidly developing, makes the livelihood of the workers more and more precarious, the collisions between individual workmen and individual bourgeois take more and more the character of collision between two classes.—C. M.

MACHINERY AND COST
It is possible for the difference between the price of the machinery to vary very much, although the difference between the quantity of labor requisite to produce the machine and the total quantity replaced by it remains constant. But it is the former difference alone that determines the cost, to the capitalist, of producing a commodity, and, through the pressure of competition, influences his action. Hence the invention nowadays of machines in England that are employed only in North America; just as in the sixteenth and seventeenth centuries, machines were invented in Germany to be used only in Holland, and just as many a French invention of the eighteenth century was exploited in England alone.—C. 1.

MACHINERY AND LABOR
A machine which does not serve the purposes of labor is useless. In addition, it falls a prey to the destructive influence of natural forces. . . . Living labor must seize upon these things and rouse them from their death-sleep, change them from mere possible use-values into real and effective ones.—C. 1.

Machinery is the most powerful means for increasing the productiveness of labor, i.e., for shortening the working time required in the production of a commodity.—C. 1.

Machinery obliterates all distinction of labor, and nearly everywhere reduces wages to the same low level.—C. M.

However much the use of machinery may increase the surplus-labor at the expense of the necessary labor by heightening the productiveness of labor, it is clear that it attains this result only by diminishing the number of workmen employed by a given amount of capital.—C. 1.

Nothing could be more absurd than to see in machinery the antithesis of the division of labor, the synthesis giving unity again to divided labor.—P. P.

Machinery, by annexing the labor of women and children, augments the number of the human beings who form the material for capitalistic exploitation.—C. 1.

MACHINES, IMPROVEMENT OF
The improvements in the operative machines have, while reducing their size, increased their speed and efficiency.—C. 1.

MAINTENANCE COSTS
Fixed capital entails special maintenance costs. A part of this maintenance is provided by the labor-process itself. . . . The fixed capital, however, requires also a positive expenditure of labor for its maintenance in good repair.—C. 2.

MALTHUS
Malthus, hugely astonished at his success, gave himself to stuffing into his book materials superficially compiled, and adding to it new matter, not discovered but annexed by him.—C. 1.

MAN
Man, as much as he may be a particular individual, is just as much the totality.—M.

Man in general belongs to no class, has no reality, exists only in the misty realm of philosophical fantasy.—C. M.

Man is no abstract being squatting outside the world. Man is the world of man, the state, society.—L.A.

Man can be distinguished by consciousness, religion, or anything else you like. They themselves begin to distinguish themselves from animals as soon as they begin to produce their means of subsistence.—G. I.

MAN AND ANIMAL
An animal produces only itself, whilst man reproduces the whole of nature. An animal's product belongs immediately to its physical body, whilst man freely confronts his product. An animal forms things in accordance with the standard and the need of the species to which it belongs, whilst man knows how to produce in accordance with the standard of every species, and knows how to apply everywhere the inherent standard to the object.—M.

MAN AS CREATOR
It is clear as noonday that man, by his industry, changes the forms of the materials furnished by nature in such a way as to make them useful to him. The form of wood, for instance, is altered, by making a table out of it. Yet, for all that the table continues to be that common, everyday thing, wood.—C. 1.

MAN AS LABORER
Man himself, viewed as the impersonation of labor power, is a natural object, a thing, although a living conscious thing, and labor is the manifestation of this power residing in him.—C. 1.

MAN AS NATURAL BEING
Man is not a natural being; he is a human natural being.—M.

Man is directly a natural being. As a natural being and as a living natural being he is on the one hand furnished with natural powers of life—he is an active natural being. These forces exist in him as tendencies and abilities—as impulses. On the other hand, as a natural, corporeal, sensuous, objective being being he is a suffering, conditioned and limited creature, like animals and plants.—M.

Man lives on nature—means that nature is his body, with which he must remain in continuous intercourse if he is not to die. That man's physical and spiritual life is linked to nature means simply that nature is linked to itself, for man is a part of nature.—M.

MAN AS PRODUCER
Man himself is the basis of his material production, as of my other production that he carries on. All circumstances, therefore, which affect man, the *subject* of production, more or less modify all his functions and activities, and therefore too his functions and activities as the creator of material wealth, of commodities. In this respect, it can in fact be shown that *all* human relations and functions, however and in whatever form they may appear. influence material production and have a more or less decisive influence on it.—C. 4.

MANAGEMENT
The labor of supervision and management, arising as it does out of an antithesis, out of the supremacy of capital over labor, and being therefore common to all modes of production based on class contradictions like the capitalist mode, is directly and inseparably connected, also under the capitalist system, with productive functions which all combined social labor assigns to individuals as their special tasks.—C. 3.

The work of management and supervision—so far as it is not a special function determined by the nature of all combined social labor, but rather by the antithesis between the owner of means of production and the owner of mere labor power, regardless of whether this labor power is purchased by buying the laborer himself, as it is under the slave system, or whether the laborer himself sells his labor power, so that the production process also appears as a process by which capital consumes his labor—this function arising out of the servitude of the direct producers has all too often been quoted to justify this relationship.—C. 3.

MANDEVILLE
In his *Fable of the Bees* Mandeville had already shown that every possible kind of occupation is productive, and had given expression to the line of this whole argument: "That what we call evil in this world, moral as well as natural, is the grand principle that makes us sociable creatures, the solid basis, the life and support of all trades and employments without exception . . . there we must look for the true origin of all arts and sciences; and . . . the moment evil ceases, the society must be spoiled if not totally dissolved." Only Mandeville was of course infinitely bolder and more honest than the philistine apologists of bourgeois society.—C. 4. *See* Theodicy.

MANIA, CAPITALIST
The raising of wages excites in the worker the capitalist's mania to get rich, which he, however, can only satisfy by the sacrifice of his mind and body.—M.

MAN'S POWER OVER MAN
If the product of labor does not belong to the worker, if it confronts him as an alien power, this can only be because it belongs to some other man than the worker. If the worker's activity is a torment to him, to another it must be a delight and his life's joy. Not the gods, not nature, but only man himself can be this alien power over man.—M.

MAN'S REAL NATURE
One basis for life and another basis for science is a priori a lie. The nature which comes to be in human history—the genesis of human society—is *man's real nature;* hence nature as it comes to be through industry, even though in an estranged form, is true anthropological nature.—M.

MANUAL LABOR
Where industrial labor has reached a high level, almost all manual labor has become factory labor.—M.

MANUFACTURE

The feudal system of industry, under which industrial production was monopolized by closed guilds, no longer sufficed for the growing wants of the markets. The manufacturing system took its place.—C. M.

Manufacture either introduces division of labor into a process of production, or further develops that division; on the other hand, it unites together handicrafts that were formerly separate. But whatever may have been its particular starting point, its final form is invariably the same—a productive mechanism whose parts are human beings.—C. 1.

Manufacture is characterized by the differentiation of the instruments of labor—a differentiation whereby implements of a given sort acquire fixed shapes, adapted to each particular application, and by the specialization of those instruments, giving to each special instrument its full play only in the hands of a specific detail laborer.—C. 1.

With regard to the mode of production itself, manufacture, in its strict meaning, is hardly to be distinguished, in its earliest stages, from the handicraft trades of the guilds, otherwise than by the greater number of workmen simultaneously employed by one and the same individual capital. The workshop of the medieval master handicraftsman is simply enlarged.—C. 1.

While simple cooperation leaves the mode of working by the individual for the most part unchanged, manufacture thoroughly revolutionizes it, and seizes labor power by its roots. It converts the laborer into a crippled monstrosity, by forcing his detail dexterity at the expense of a world of productive capabilities and instincts.—C. 1.

The advance made by human labor in converting the product of nature into the manufactured product of nature increases, not the wages of labor, but in part the number of profitable capitals, and in part the size of every subsequent capital in comparison with the foregoing.—M.

MANUFACTURING PERIOD

The manufacturing period simplifies, improves, and multiplies the implements of labor, by adapting them to the exclusively special functions of each detail laborer. It thus creates at the same time one of the material conditions for the existence of machinery, which consists of a combination of simple instruments.—C. 1.

MANUFACTURING SECRETS
The capitalist gains by virtue of some manufacturing or trading secret.—M.

The worker need not necessarily gain when the capitalist does, but he necessarily loses when the latter loses. Thus the worker does not gain if the capitalist keeps the market-price above the natural price by virtue of some manufacturing or trading secret, or by virtue of monopoly or the favorable situation of his property.—M.

MANUFACTORY
A manufactory consists in the union of a large number of workpeople and many varied trades in a single place, in one apartment, under the control of one capital, than in the analysis of the different operations and the adaptation of each worker to one simple task.—P. P.

MARGINAL DETERMINATION
If the supply is too small, the market-value is always regulated by the commodities produced under the least favorable circumstances and, if the supply is too large, always by the commodities produced under the most favorable conditions; it is one of the extremes which determines the market-value.—C. 3.

MARKET
The transaction in the market effectuates only the interchange of the individual components of the annual product, transfers them from one hand to another, but can neither augment the total annual production nor alter the nature of the objects produced. —C. 1.

MARKET, INTERNATIONAL
The need of a constantly expanding market for its products chases the bourgeoisie over the whole surface of the globe. It must nestle everywhere, settle everywhere, establish connections everywhere.—C. M.

MARKET PRICE
The market price signifies that the same price is paid for commodities of the same kind, although they may have been produced under very different individual conditions and hence may have considerably different cost prices.—C. 3.

MARRIAGE
Bourgeois marriage is in reality a system of wives in common and thus, at the most, what the communists might possibly be reproached with is that they desire to introduce, in substitution for a hypocritically concealed, an openly legalized community of women.—C. M.

MARX AT WORK
I am now working like a horse, because I must use the time in which it is possible to work and the carbuncles are still there, though now they only disturb me locally and not in the cranium. Between whiles, since one cannot always be writing, I am doing some Differential Calculus. I have no patience to read anything else. Any other reading drives me back to my writing desk.— Ltr. to Engels.

Because of its gigantic shape the manuscript, although finished, cannot be completed for publication by anyone but me, not even by you. The thing progressed very quickly, since it naturally is intriguing to lick the baby smooth after so many birth pangs. However, the carbuncle again interfered, so that I could not really proceed. And to finish the work, I must at least be able to sit down.–Ltr. to Engels.

Dear Fred: I have just finished correcting the last sheet of the book. Preface ditto corrected and returned yesterday. So this volume is finished. This has been possible thanks to *you* alone. Without your self-sacrifice for me I could never possibly have accomplished the enormous preparations of the three volumes. I embrace you, full of thanks!
    Enclosed two sheets of corrected proofs.
    The £ 15 received with best thanks.
    Greetings, my dear, beloved friend!
Yours,
K. Marx (to Engels)

MARX'S DIPLOMACY
At the next Congress in Brussels I shall personally put an end to these fools of Proudhonists. I have managed the whole thing diplomatically and did not want to come out personally until my book was published and our Association had struck root. I will also use the rod on them in the official report of the General Council.—Ltr. to Engels.

It was very difficult to compose the thing so that our view should appear in a form acceptable from the present standpoint of the workers' movement. It will take time before the reawakened movement permits the old boldness of speech. It will be necessary to be *fortiter in re, suaviter in modo* (bold in matter, mild in manner). As soon as the stuff is printed you will receive it.— Ltr. to Engels.

MARX'S FAMILY
The days are dull since you left—you and Johnny and Harra! Forgetting that you now live across the Channel, I often hurry to the window when I hear the sound of children's voices that resemble those of our children.—Ltr. to his daughter Jenny.

The house is totally deserted and orphaned since the death of the dear child, who was its animating soul. It is indescribable how we everywhere miss the child. I have suffered all kinds of mishaps, but now I know what a real disaster is.—Ltr. to Engels.

I feel sorry for my wife, who bears the main burden, and at bottom she is right. *Il faut que l'industrie soit plus productive que le marriage.* (It is necessary that the industry should be more productive than the marriage.) I am by nature very little patient and even a little rough, so that from time to time I lose my equanimity.—Ltr. to Engels.

I myself overcome our misery through deep indulgence in general affairs, but my wife of course has not these resources available.—Ltr. to Engels.

Today I received very sad news concerning the death of my uncle who was an excellent man. But he died nicely, speedily, surrounded by all his children, in his full senses, and watering the priest with fine Voltairean irony.—Ltr. to Engels.

MARX'S FINANCES
I have exacted £160 from my uncle, so that I could pay most of my debts. My mother who has not cash, but fast approaches her disintegration, has destroyed some older notes which I had previously signed. This was a very pleasant result of the two days I resided with her. I myself did not mention money matters; she herself took the initiative in this respect.—Ltr. to Engels.

MARX'S HEALTH
Your satisfaction is more important to me than anything the rest of the world may say of it. At any rate I hope the bourgeoisie will think of my carbuncles all the rest of their lives.—Ltr. to Engels.

It is necessary to stoop while writing, but it pains me. As you see, I am plagued like Job, though not so God-fearing.—Ltr. to Engels.

I was afraid that the examining doctor would discover my infirmities. However, seeing my athletic chest, he did not check up further on me.—Ltr. to Engels.

MARX'S LEARNING
I do not fare better with mechanics than with languages. I comprehend the mechanical laws, but the simplest technical reality requiring sensual perception is to me more difficult than to the most stupid persons.—Ltr. to Engels.

MARX'S MOTHER
Yesterday I received an answer from my old lady. Only "tender" phrases, but no cash. She also informs me, what I already know, that she is 75 years of age, and suffers under some infirmities of old age.—Ltr. to Engels.

Two hours ago I received a telegram that my mother has died. Fate wanted one member of the family. I myself stood already with one foot in the grave. Under present circumstances I (am) at any rate still more needed than the old lady.—Ltr. to Engels.

MARX'S SELF-ASSURANCE
Precisely because political economy does not grasp the connections within the movement ... we have to grasp the essential connection between private property, avarice, and the separation of labor, capital and landed property; between exchange and competition, value and the devaluation of men, monopoly and competition, etc.; the connection between this whole estrangement and the money system.—M.

MARX'S STYLE OF LIFE
It is truly depressing to be dependent half of one's life. My sole consolation is that we both carry on a partnership, in which I take care of the theorizing and part work. To be sure, I live too expensively. But only this practice will give my children a chance to engage in contacts and relations which will secure them a brighter future. Even from the commercial standpoint, proletarian furniture would be here improper, and would suffice only if my wife and I lived here alone, or if I had boys instead of girls.—Ltr. to Engels.

My circumstances are terrible—I have been unable to earn additional money, but certain standards must be maintained for the children's sake. If I did not have to produce these two cursed books (and also to find an English publisher) in London, I would reside in Geneva, where I could live comfortably on my present means.—Ltr. to Kugelmann.

My wife tells me daily she wishes to lay with the children in the grave. I truly do not blame her. The humiliations, vexations, and horrors of our situation are intolerable.—Ltr. to Engels.

MARX'S WORK
Whatever shortcomings my writings have, the worth of them lies in that they form an artistic whole, and that can be accomplished only by my manner of never having them printed until they lie before me completely.—Ltr. to Engels.

As to myself, I do not claim credit for discovering the existence of classes in modern society or of the struggle between them. Long before me bourgeois historians have analyzed the historical development of this class war and bourgeois economists the economic fiber of the classes.—Ltr. to Weydemeyer.

Why I never answered you? Because I constantly hovered on the verge of the grave. I had to use *every* moment in which I was capable of work in order that I might reach the goal to which I have sacrificed my health, my happiness in life and my family. I hope this explanation must not be further supplemented. I laugh at the so-called "practical" men and their wisdom. If one chose to be an ox, one could naturally turn one's back on the agonies of mankind and look after one's own skin. But I should really have regarded myself as unpractical if I had passed away without completely finishing my book.—Ltr. to S. Meyer.

MASS OF PROFIT
The *rate* of profit must be calculated by measuring the mass of produced and realized surplus-value not only in relation to the consumed portion of capital reappearing in the commodities, but also to this part plus that portion of unconsumed but applied capital which continues to operate in production. However, the *mass* of profit cannot be equal to anything but the mass of profit or surplus-value, contained in the commodities themselves, and to be realized by their sale.—C. 3.

MASS PRODUCTION
Capitalist production is mass production from the very outset. —C. 3.

MATERIAL PRODUCTION
From the specific form of *material production* arises in the first place a specific structure of society, in the second place a specific relation of men to nature. Their state and their spiritual outlook is determined by both.—C. 4.

If *material production* itself is not conceived in its specific historical form, it is impossible to understand what is specific in the spiritual production corresponding to it.—C. 4.

MATERIALISM
The materialist doctrine that men are products of circumstances and upbringing, and that, therefore, changed men are products of other circumstances and changed upbringing, forgets that it is men that change circumstances and that the educator himself needs educating.—T. F.

The chief defect of all hitherto existing materialism is that the thing, reality, sensuousness, is conceived only in the form of the object or of sensuous perception, but not as human sensuous activity, practice, not subjectively.—H. F.

The standpoint of the old materialism is "civil" society; the standpoint of the new is human society, or socialized humanity.—T. F.

MATERIALISM, BRITISH
Materialism is the native son of Great Britain. Even Britain's scholastic Duns Scotus wondered: "Can matter think?"—H. F.

MATERIALISM, DIALECTICAL
In direct opposition to German philosophy, which come down from heaven to earth, here there is ascension from earth to heaven. That means that we proceed not from what men say, fancy or imagine, nor from men as they are spoken of, thought, fancied, imagined in order to arrive from them at men of flesh and blood; we proceed from the really active men and see the development of the ideological reflexes and echoes of their real life-process as proceeding from that life-process. Even the nebulous images in the brain of men are necessary sublimates of their material, empirically observable, materially preconditioned life-process.—G. I.

MATERIALISM, FRENCH
Mechanical French materialism followed Descartes's physics, in opposition to his metaphysics. His followers were by profession antimetaphysicists, i.e., physicists.—H. F.

MATERIALISM, HISTORICAL
The production of notions, ideas and consciousness is from the beginning directly interwoven with the material activity and the material intercourse of human beings, the language of real life. The production of men's ideas, thinking, their spiritual intercourse, here appear as the direct efflux of their material condition. The same applies to spiritual production as represented in the language of politics, laws, morals, religion, metaphysics, etc. of a people. The producers of men's ideas, notions, etc., are men, but real active men as determined by a definite development of the productive forces and the intercourse corresponding to those productive forces up to its remotest form.—G. I.

What else does the history of ideas prove than that intellectual production changes in character in proportion as material production is changed? The ruling ideas of each age have ever been the ideas of the ruling class.—C. M.

Does it require deep intuition to comprehend that man's ideas, views, and conceptions, in one word, man's consciousness, change with every change in the condition of his material existence, in his social relations and in his social life?—C. M.

Different kinds of spiritual production correspond to the capitalist mode of production and to the mode of production of the Middle Ages. If material production itself is not conceived in its specific historical form, it is impossible to understand what is specific in the spiritual production corresponding to it.—C. 4.

MATERIALISM AND COMMUNISM
There is no need of any great penetration to see from the teaching of materialism on the original goodness and equal intellectual endowment of men, the omnipotence of experience, habit and education, and the influence of environment on man, the great significance of industry, the justification of enjoyment, etc., how necessarily materialism is connected with communism and socialism.—H. F.

MATERIALISTIC DETERMINISM
It is not consciousness that determines life, but life that determines consciousness. In the first view one proceeds from consciousness as from the living individual; in the second, in conformity with real life, from the real living individuals themselves, considering consciousness only as *their* consciousness. —G. I.

MATERIALISTIC UNDERSTRUCTURE (Unterbau)
The sum of productive forces, capitals and forms of social intercourse which every individual and every generation finds already in existence is the real basis of what the philosophers imagined to be the "substance" and "essence of man," what they apotheosized and fought against, a real basis which is not in the least disturbed in its action and influence on the development of man by those philosophers, as "self-consciousness" and "ego," rebelling against it.—G. I.

MEANS OF LIFE
Nature provides labor with the means of life in the sense that labor cannot live without objects on which to operate.—M.

MEANS OF PRODUCTION
In a capitalist society, the laborer does not employ the means of production, but the means of production employ the laborer. —C. 1.

MEANS OF SUBSISTENCE
Some of the means of subsistence, such as food and fuel, are consumed daily, and a fresh supply must be provided daily. Others such as clothes and furniture last for longer periods and require to be replaced only at longer intervals. . . . But in whatever way the sum total of these outlays may be spread over the year, they must be covered by the average income, taking one day with another.—C. 1.

MECHANISM OF MANUFACTURE
By decomposition of handicrafts, by specialization of the instruments of labor, by the formation of detail laborers, and by grouping and combining the latter into a single mechanism, division of labor in manufacture creates a qualitative graduation, and a quantitative proportion in the social process of production; it consequently creates a definite organization of the labor of society, and thereby develops at the same time new productive forces in the society.—C. 1.

MERCANTILE SYSTEM
Production and consumption are essentially inseparable. From this it follows that since in the system of capitalist production they are in fact separated, their unity is restored through their opposition—that if A must produce for B, B must consume for A. Just as we find with every individual capitalist that he favors prodigality on the part of those who are co-partners with him in his revenue, so the older mercantile system as a whole depends on the idea that a nation must be frugal as regards itself, but must produce luxuries for foreign nations to enjoy. The idea here is always: on the one side, production for production, therefore on the other side consumption of foreign production. —C. 4.

MERCENARY TROOPS
Mercenary troops on a large scale appeared first among the Carthaginians.—Ltr. to Engels.

MERCHANT'S CAPITAL
Merchant's, or trading, capital breaks up into two forms or subdivisions, namely, commercial capital and money-dealing capital, which we shall now define more closely, insofar as this is necessary for our analysis of capital in its basic structure. This is all the more necessary because modern political economy, even in the persons of its best exponents, throws trading capital and industrial capital indiscriminately together and, in effect, wholly overlooks the characteristic peculiarities of the former. —C. 3.

The turnover of merchant's capital is not identical with the turnover, or a single reproduction, of an industrial capital of equal size; it is rather equal to the sum of the turnovers of a number of such capitals, whether in the same or in different spheres of production. The more quickly merchant's capital is turned over, the smaller the portion of total money-capital serving as merchant's capital; and conversely, the more slowly it is turned over, the larger this portion.—C. 3.

The great economists are perplexed over mercantile capital being a special variety, since they consider the basic form of capital, capital as industrial capital, and circulation capital (commodity-capital and money-capital) solely because it is a phase in the reproduction process of every capital. The rules concerning the formation of value, profit, etc., immediately deduced by them from their study of industrial capital, do not extend directly to merchant's capital. For this reason, they leave merchant's capital entirely aside and mention it only as a kind of industrial capital. Wherever they make a special analysis of it, they seek to demonstrate that it creates no value.—C. 3. See Modern Economics.

MERGER
It is concentration of capitals already formed, destruction of their individual independence, expropriation of capitalist by capitalist, transformation of many small into few large capitals. —C. 1.

METAPHYSICS
Metaphysics of the seventeenth century, represented in France by Descartes, has materialism as its antagonist from its very birth.—H. F.

METAPHYSICS, GERMAN
Now we are quite in Germany! We have now to talk metaphysics while speaking of political economy.—P. P.

METHODS, IMPROVED
Every introduction of improved methods works almost simultaneously on the new capital and on that already in action.—C. 1.

METHODS, NEW, OF PRODUCTION
New methods of production may secure an extra profit.—C. 3.

MIDDLE AGES
In the Middle Ages a social class is emancipated as soon as it is allowed to carry the sword.—M.

From the serfs of the Middle Ages sprang the chartered burghers of the earliest towns.—C. M.

MIDDLE CLASS
The low strata of the middle class—the small tradespeople, shopkeepers, and retired tradesmen generally, the handicraftsmen and peasants—all these sink gradually into the proletariat, partly because their diminutive capital does not suffice for the scale on which modern industry is carried on, and is swamped in the competition with the large capitalists, partly because their specialized skill is rendered worthless by new methods of production.—C. M.

MILL, JOHN STUART
Mr. John Stuart Mill also struggled with the problem of productive and unproductive labor; but in so doing he in fact added nothing to Smith's definition except that labors which produce labor power itself are also productive.—C. 4.

MINE SAFETY
Very often they had only one shaft sunk, so that apart from the lack of effective ventilation there was no escape were this shaft to become obstructed.—C. 3.

MINERALS
The dealer in *minerals* sees only the mercantile value but not the beauty and the unique nature of the mineral: he has no mineralogical sense.—M.

MINIMUM WAGE
The natural price of labor is nothing but the minimum wage. —P. P.

Eventually wages, which have already been reduced to a minimum, must be reduced yet further.—M.

MINING
The same labor extracts from rich mines more metal than from poor mines. Diamonds are of very rare occurrence on the earth's surface, and hence their discovery costs, on an average, a great deal of labor-time.—C. L.

MISER
The miser is only an illusory amasser of wealth.—C. 4.

MISER, CAPITALIST
The capitalist shares with the miser the passion for wealth as wealth. But that which in the miser is a mere idiosyncrasy is, in the capitalist, the effect of the social mechanism, of which he is but one of the wheels.—C. 1.

MISERY
Thus in a declining state of society—increasing misery of the worker; in an advancing state—misery with complications; and in a fully developed state of society—static misery.—M.

MISSION OF THE BOURGEOISIE
Accumulation for accumulation's sake, production for production's sake: by this formula classical economy expressed the historical mission of the bourgeoisie, and did not for a single instant deceive itself over the birth throes of wealth. But what

avails lamentation in the face of historical necessity? If to classical economy, the proletarian is but a machine for the production of surplus-value; on the other hand, the capitalist, is in its eyes only a machine for the conversion of this surplus-value into additional capital.—C. 1.

MODERN ECONOMICS
The real science of modern economy only begins when the theoretical analysis passes from the process of circulation to the process of production.—C. 3.

MODERN INDUSTRY
By incorporating both stupendous physical forces and the natural sciences with the process of production, modern industry raises the productiveness of labor to an extraordinary degree. —C. 1.

MONETARY SYSTEM
The monetary system is essentially a Catholic institution, the credit system essentially Protestant. "The Scotch hate gold." In the form of paper the monetary existence of commodities is only a social one. It is faith that brings salvation. Faith in money-value as the immanent spirit of commodities, faith in the mode of production and its predestined order, faith in the individual agents of production as mere personifications of self-expanding capital. But the credit system does not emancipate itself from the basis of the monetary system any more than Protestantism has emancipaed itself from the foundations of Catholicism.—C. 3.

MONEY
Money itself has no price.—C. 1.

Man becomes ever poorer as man; his need for money becomes ever greater if he wants to overpower hostile beings; and the power of his money declines exactly in inverse proportion to the increase in the volume of production.—M.

Money is the alienated ability of mankind. That which I am unable to do as man, and of which therefore all my individual essential powers are incapable, I am able to do by means of money. Money thus turns each of these powers into something which in itself it is not—turns it, that is, into its contrary.—M.

Since money, as the existing and active concept of value, confounds and exchanges all things, it is the general confounding and compounding of all things—the world upside-down—the confounding and compounding of all natural and human qualities.—M.

Money, like every other commodity, cannot express the magnitude of its value except relatively in other commodities.—C. 1.

Money is a crystal formed of necessity in the course of exchanges, whereby different products of labor are practically equated to one another and thus by practice converted into commodities. —C. 1.

The capitalist mode of production—its basis being wage-labor, the payment of the laborer in money, and in general the transformation of payments in kind into money payments—can assume greater dimensions and achieve greater perfection only where there is available in the country a quantity of money sufficient for circulation and the formation of a hoard (reserve fund, etc.) promoted by it.—C. 2.

The first chief function of money is to supply commodities with the material for the expression of their values, or to represent their values as magnitudes of the same denominations, qualitatively equal, and quantitatively comparable. It thus serves as a universal measure of value.—C. 1.

The currency of money is the constant and monotonous repetition of the same process. The commodity is always in the hands of the seller; the money, as a means of purchase, always in the hands of the buyer. And money serves as a means of purchase by realizing the price of the commodity. This realization transfers the commodity from the seller to the buyer, and removes the money from the hands of the buyer into those of the seller, where it again goes through the same process with another commodity.—C. 1.

Money is the measure of value inasmuch as it is the socially recognized incarnation of human labor.—C. 1.

Money degrades all the gods of mankind and turns them into commodities. Money is the universal and self-constituted value set upon all things. It has therefore robbed the whole world, of both nature and man, of its original value. Money is the essence of man's life and work, which have become alienated from him. This alien monster rules him and he worships it.—J. Q.

As money is not exchanged for any specific quality, for any specific thing, or for any particular human essential power, but for the entire objective world of man and nature, from the standpoint of its possessor it therefore serves to exchange every property for every other, even contradictory, property and object: it is the fraternization of impossibilities. It makes contradictions embrace.—M.

MONEY CAPITAL
Capital in the form of money must always be available, particularly for the payment of wages, before production can be carried on capitalistically—C. 2.

If we conceive society as being not capitalistic but communistic, there will be no money capital at all in the first place, nor the disguises cloaking the transactions arising on account of it.—C. 2.

MONEY-LENDER
The interest of the money-lender in the spendthrift is by no means identical with the interest of the spendthrift.—M.

MONOPOLY
The necessary result of competition is the accumulation of capital in a few hands, and thus the restoration of monopoly in a more terrible form.—M.

The capitalist gains by virtue of monopoly.—M.

Monopoly in all its dreary monotony invades the world of commodities, as, in the sight and to the knowledge of everybody, monopoly invades the world of the instruments of production. —P. P.

The first abolition of monopoly is always its generalization, the broadening of its existence. The abolition of monopoly once it has come to exist in its utmost breadth and inclusiveness is its total annihilation.—M.

Modern monopoly, bourgeois monopoly, is synthetic monopoly, the negation of the negation, the unity of contraries. It is monopoly in its pure, normal, rational state.—P. P.

MONOPOLY PRICES
Monopoly prices are as high as possible.—M.

MORALE, GERMAN
The main stem of German morale and honesty, of the classes as well as of individuals, is rather that modest egoism which asserts its limitedness and allows it to be asserted against itself.—C. C.

MULTILATERAL ACCUMULATION
The formation of many capitals is only possible as a result of multilateral accumulation, since capital comes into being only by accumulation; and multilateral accumulation necessarily turns into unilateral accumulation. Competition among capitals increases accumulation of capitals.—M.

MUTILATION
The infamous mutilations committed by the sepoys remind one of the practices of the Christian Byzantine Empire, or the prescriptions of Emperor Charles V's criminal law, or the English punishments for high treason, as still recorded by Judge Blackstone.—D. T.

MUTINY
A motley crew of mutineering soldiers who have murdered their own officers, torn asunder the ties of discipline, and not succeeded in discovering a man upon whom to bestow the supreme command are certainly the body least likely to organize a serious and protracted resistance.—D. T.

MYTHOLOGY

I employ the term "modern mythology" in reference to the goddesses of "Justice, Freedom, Equality, etc."—Ltr. to Engels. *See* Socialism.

The ancient peoples went through their prehistory in imagination, in mythology.—C. C.

N

NAPOLEON
Napoleon brought about, within France, the conditions under which alone free competition could develop, the partitioned lands be exploited, the nation's unshackled powers of industrial production be utilized; while, beyond the French frontier, he swept away everywhere the establishments of feudality, so far as requisite, to furnish the bourgeois social system of France with fit surroundings of the European continent.—E. B.

NASSAU, WILLIAM, SR.
According to Nassau, doctors should only be paid insofar as they cure, and lawyers insofar as they win lawsuits, and soldiers insofar as they are victorious.—C. 4.

NATIONALISM
In proportion as capitalist production is developed in a country, in the same proportion do the national intensity and productivity of labor there rise above the international level—C. 1.

NATIONALITY
National differences, and antagonisms between peoples, are daily more and more vanishing, owing to the development of the bourgeoisie, to freedom of commerce, to the world market, to uniformity in the mode of production and in the conditions of life corresponding thereto.—C. M.

In the national struggles of the different countries, the communists point out and bring to the front the common interests of the entire proletariat independently of all nationality.—C. M.

NATURAL FORCES
Apart from the natural substances, it is possible to incorporate in the productive process natural forces, which do not cost anything, to act as agents with more or less heightened effect. The degree of their effectiveness depends on methods and scientific developments which cost the capitalist nothing.—C. 2.

NATURAL LAWS
Natural laws cannot be set aside.—Ltr. to Kugelmann.

NATURAL NECESSITY
The true realm of freedom can blossom forth only with the natural realm of necessity as its basis.—C. 3.

NATURAL SCIENCE
The natural sciences have developed an enormous activity and have accumulated a constantly growing mass of material. Philosophy, however, has remained just as alien to them as they remain to philosophy.—M.

NATURE
Nature is man's inorganic body—nature, that is, insofar as it is not itself the human body.—M.

Nature is only the form of the idea's other-being.—M.

The worker can create nothing without nature, without the sensuous external world. It is the material on which his labor is manifested, in which it is active, from which and by means of which it produces.—M.

From the specific form of material production arises a specific relation of men to nature.—C. 4.

Just as plants, animals, stones, the air, etc., constitute a part of human consciousness in the realm of theory, partly as objects of natural science, partly as objects of art—his spiritual inorganic nature, spiritual nourishment which he must first prepare to make it palatable and digestible—so too in the realm of practice they constitute a part of human life and human activity. —M.

NECESSARY LABOR TIME
That portion of the working day, during which the reproduction takes place, I call "necessary" labor time, and the labor expended during that time I call "necessary" labor.—C. 1.

NECESSARY WAGE-RATE
The lowest and the only necessary wage-rate is that providing for the subsistence of the worker for the duration of his work and as much more as is necessary for him to support a family and for the race of laborers not to die out. The ordinary wage, according to Smith, is the lowest compatible with common humanity (that is a cattle-like existence).—M.

NECESSITIES OF LIFE
There are not too many necessities of life produced in proportion to the existing population. Quite the reverse. Too little is produced to decently and humanly satisfy the wants of the great mass. . . . On the other hand, too many means of labor and necessities of life are produced at times to permit of their serving as means for the exploitation of laborers at a certain rate of profit.—C. 3.

The theoretical assumption of a permanent *necessity* of existing conditions disintegrates before their practical breakdown when the inner connection is understood.—Ltr. to Kugelmann.

NEED
Every real and possible need is a weakness which will lead the fly to the gluepot.—M.

It is not only that man has no human needs—even his animal needs are ceasing to exist.—M.

Private property does not know how to change crude need into human need.—M.

The multiplication of needs and of the means of their satisfaction breeds the absence of needs and of means.—M.

Every need is an opportunity to approach one's neighbor under the guise of the utmost amiability and to say to him: Dear friend, I give you what you need, but you know the *condition sine qua non;* you know the ink in which you have to sign yourself over to me; in providing for your pleasure, I fleece you.—M.

NEEDINESS
Man's neediness grows as the power of money increases.—M.

NEGATION OF THE NEGATION
The capitalist mode of appropriation, the result of the capitalist mode of production, produces capitalist private property. This is the first negation of individual private property, as founded on the labor of the proprietor. But capitalist production begets, with the inexorability of a law of nature, its own negation. It is the negation of the negation.—C. 1.

NEGRO LABOR
The Negro labor in the Southern states of the American Union preserved something of patriarchal character so long as production was chiefly directed to immediate local consumption. But in proportion as the export of cotton became of vital interest to these states, the overworking of the Negro and sometimes the using up of his life in 7 years' of labor became a factor in a calculated and calculating system.—C. 1.

NEWSPAPERS
Information is the only delight of the newspapers.—L. A.

Philosophy speaks differently of religious and philosophical objects than you (newspapers) have. You speak without having studied them, it speaks after study; you appeal to the emotions, it appeals to reason; you curse, it teaches; you promise heaven and earth, it promises nothing but truth; you demand faith in your faith, it demands not faith in its results but the test of doubt; you frighten, it calms.—L. A.

NEW YEAR'S CONGRATULATION
Prosit New Year! May the Russians, Prussia, Bonaparte, and the British Juryman go to the devil next year!—Ltr. to Engels.

NIGHT LABOR
Furnaces and workshops that stand idle by night, and absorb no living labor, are "a mere loss" to the capitalist. Hence furnaces and workshops constitute lawful claims upon the night labor of the workpeople.—C. 1.

NINETEENTH-CENTURY REVOLUTION
The social revolution of the nineteenth century cannot draw its poetry from the past, it can draw that only from the future. It cannot start upon its work before it has stricken off all superstition concerning the past. Former revolutions required historic reminiscences in order to intoxicate themselves with their own content. The revolution of the nineteenth century must let the dead bury their dead in order to achieve its proper content. With the former, the phrase surpasses the content; with the latter, the content surpasses the phrase.—E. B.

NOBILITY AND PROPERTY
The feudal lord does not try to extract the utmost advantage from his land. Rather, he consumes what is there and calmly leaves the worry of producing to the serfs and the tenants. Such is nobility's relationship to landed property, which casts a romantic glory on its lords.—M.

It is necessary that the romantic glory of nobility be abolished— that landed property, the root of private property, be dragged completely into the movement of private property and that it become a commodity; that the rule of the proprietor appear as the undisguised rule of private property, of capital, freed of all political tincture; that the relationship between proprietor and worker be reduced to the economic relationship of exploiter and exploited; that all personal relationship between the proprietor and his property cease, property becoming merely objective, material wealth; that the marriage of convenience should take the place of the marriage of honor with the land; and that the land should likewise sink to the status of a commercial value, like man.—M.

NOMAD RACES
Nomad races are the first to develop the money form, because all their worldly goods consist of movable objects and are therefore directly alienable; and because their mode of life, by continually bringing them into contact with foreign communities, solicits the exchange of products.—C .1

Amongst nomadic peoples it is the horse which makes me a free man and a participant in the life of the community.—M.

NOMINAL WAGES

The sum of money which the laborer receives for his daily or weekly labor forms the amount of his nominal wages, or of his wages estimated in value.—C. 1.

NOMINALISM

Nominalism is a main component of English materialism and is in general the first expression of materialism.—H. F.

NORTH AMERICA

Efface North America from the map of the world and you have the anarchy, the complete decadence, of modern commerce and civilization.—P. P.

Without slavery, North America, the most progressive country, would have been transformed into a patriarchal country.—P. P.

O

OBJECTIFICATION
The product of labor is labor which has been congealed in an object: it is the objectification of labor. Labor's realization is its objectification.—M.

OBJECTIVISM, SOCIOLOGICAL
The object as being for man, as the objective being of man for other men, is at the same time the existence of man for other men, his human relation to other men, the social behavior of man in relation to man.—H. F.

OBSERVATION
Observation must reveal the connection of the social and political organization with production.—G. I.

OBSOLETE SOCIAL FORCES
It is an old and historically established maxim that obsolete social forces, nominally still in possession of all the attributes of power and continuing to vegetate long after the basis of their existence has rotted away, inasmuch as the heirs are quarreling among themselves over the inheritance even before the obituary notice has been printed and the testament read that those forces once more summon all their strength before their agony of death, pass from the defensive to the offensive, challenge instead of giving way, and seek to draw the most extreme conclusions from premises which have not only been put in question but already condemned.—H. P.

OCCUPATION
All these illustrative and time-honored occupations—sovereign, judge, officer, priest, etc.,—with all the old ideological professions to which they give rise, their men of letters, their teachers and priests, are from an economical standpoint put on the same level as the swarm of their own lackeys and jesters maintained by the bourgeoisie and by idle wealth—the landed nobility and idle capitalists. They are mere servants of the public, just as the others are their servants. They live on the produce of other people's industry, therefore, they must be reduced to the smallest number.—C. 4.

OFFER
A demand is at the same time an offer, an offer is at the same time a demand.—P. P.

OPINION
Our opinion of an individual is not based on what he thinks of himself.—P. E.

OPPOSITION OF INTEREST
Whilst the interest of the worker never stands opposed to the interest of society, society always and necessarily stands opposed to the interest of the worker.—M.

OPPRESSION
Hitherto, every form of society has been based on the antagonism of oppressing and oppressed classes.—C. M.

OPTIMISM, BOURGEOIS
The bourgeoisie naturally conceives the world in which it is supreme to be the best; and bourgeois socialism develops this comfortable conception into various more or less complete systems. In requiring the proletariat to carry out such a system, and thereby to march into the social New Jerusalem, it but requires in reality that the proletariat should remain within the bounds of existing society, but should cast away all its hateful ideas concerning the bourgeoisie.—C. M.

ORATOR
It is true that in our modern parliaments, a part lacking neither

dignity nor interest might be imagined of an independent orator who, while despairing of influencing the actual course of events, should content himself to assume a position of ironical neutrality. —D. T.

ORGANIZATION OF LABOR
It is very characteristic that the enthusiastic apologists of the factory system have nothing more damning to urge against a general organization of the labor of society than that it would turn all society into one immense factory.—C. 1.

ORGANS
The organs of plants and animals serve as instruments of production for sustaining life.—C. 1.

ORIENTAL AGRICULTURE
Climate and territorial conditions, especially the vast tracts of desert, extending from the Sahara, through Arabia, Persia, India and Tartary, to the most elevated Asiatic highlands, constituted artificial irrigation by canals and waterworks the basis of Oriental agriculture.—D. T.

ORIGINAL SIN
Original sin is at work everywhere. As the capitalist production, accumulation, and wealth become developed, the capitalist ceases to be the mere incarnation of capital. He has a fellow-feeling for his own Adam, and his education gradually enables him to smile at the rage for asceticism, as a mere prejudice of the old-fashioned miser.—C. 1.

OUTBIDDING
If the demand for a particular kind of commodity is greater than the supply, one buyer outbids another—within certain limits—and so raises the price of the commodity for all of them above the market-value, while on the other hand the sellers unite in trying to sell at a high market-price.—C. 3.

OUTRAGES, HUMAN
The outrages committed by the revolting sepoys in India are indeed appalling, hideous, ineffable—such as one is prepared

to meet only in wars of insurrection, of nationalities, of races, and above all of religions; in one word, such as respectable England used to applaud when perpetrated by the Vendeans on the "Blues," by the Spanish guerrillas on the infidel Frenchmen, by Serbians on their German and Hungarian neighbors, by Croats on Viennese rebels, by Cavaignac's Garde Mobile or Bonaparte's Decembrists on the sons and daughters of proletarian France.—D. T.

OVERPOPULATION

It is no contradiction that overproduction of capital is accompanied by more or less overpopulation. The circumstances which increased the productiveness of labor augmented the mass of produced commodities, expanded markets, accelerated accumulation of capital both in terms of its mass and its value, and lowered the rate of profit—these same circumstances have also created, and continuously create, a relative overpopulation, an overpopulation of laborers not employed by the surplus-capital owing to the low degree of exploitation at which alone they could be employed, or at least owing to the low rate of profit which they would yield at the given degree of exploitation.—C. 3.

Needlessness as the principle of political economy is most brilliantly shown in its theory of population. There are too many people. Even the existence of men is a pure luxury; and if the worker is "ethical," he will be sparing in procreation.—M.

OVERPRODUCTION

In the commercial crises there breaks out an epidemic that, in all earlier epochs, would have seemed an absurdity—the epidemic of overproduction. Society suddenly finds itself put back into a state of momentary barbarism; it appears as if a famine, a universal war of devastation, had cut off the supply of every means of subsistence; industry and commerce seem to be destroyed; and why? Because there is too much civilization, too much means of subsistence, too much industry, too much commerce.—C. M.

As the amassing of capital increases the amount of industry and therefore the number of workers, it causes the same amount of industry to manufacture a greater amount of product, which leads to overproduction and thus either ends by throwing a large section of workers out of work or by reducing their wages to the most miserable minimum. Such are the consequences of a condition of society most favorable to the worker—namely, of a condition of growing, advancing wealth.—M.

There would be absolute overproduction of capital as soon as additional capital for purposes of capitalist production $= 0$. The purpose of capitalist production, however, is self-expansion of capital, i.e., appropriation of surplus-labor, production of surplus-value, of profit.—C. 3.

OVERWORK
The raising of wages gives rise to overwork among the workers. —M.

P

PAPER MONEY
The state puts in circulation bits of paper on which their various denominations are printed. Insofar as they actually take the place of gold to the same amount, their movement is subject to the laws that regulate the currency of money itself. A law peculiar to the circulation of paper money can spring up only from the proportion in which that paper money represents gold.—C. 1.

PARISIANS
The Parisians manifest adaptability, remarkable initiative, and willingness to sacrifice. After nearly six months of starvation, they revolt. This heroism is unparalleled in history. Only their "good nature" is to be blamed for possible defeat.—Ltr. to Kugelmann.

PARLIAMENTARY ELOQUENCE
Mr. Disraeli's speeches are not intended to carry his motions, but his motions are intended to prepare for his speeches. They might be called self-denying motions, since they are so constructed as neither to harm the adversary, if carried, nor to damage the proposer, if lost. They mean, in fact, to be neither carried nor lost, but simply to be dropped. They belong neither to the acids nor to the alkalis, but are born neutrals. The speech is not the vehicle of action, but the hypocrisy of action affords the opportunity for a speech. Such, indeed, may be the classical and final form of parliamentary eloquence; but then, at all events, the final form of parliamentary eloquence must not demur to sharing the fate of all final forms of parliamentarism—that of being ranged under the category of nuisances.—D. T.

PARTIAL TURNOVER OF CAPITAL
A part of the herd (supply of cattle) remains in the process of production, while another part is sold annually as a product. In this case only a part of the capital is turned over every year.—C. 2.

PARTICULARITY
It is precisely the particularity of man which makes him an individual, and a real individual social being.—M.

PARTY DISCIPLINE
We must absolutely insist on party discipline, or everything will deteriorate.—Ltr. to Engels.

PASSION
To be sensuous is to suffer. Man as an objective, sensuous being is therefore a suffering being—and because he feels what he suffers, a passionate being. *Passion* is the essential force of man energetically bent on its object.—M.

PAST AND PRESENT
In bourgeois society, the past dominates the present; in communist society, the present dominates the past.—C. M.

PAUPERISM
Pauperism is the hospital of the active labor army and the dead weight of the industrial reserve army. . . . Pauperism forms a condition of capitalist production, and of the capitalist development of wealth. It enters into the *faux frais* of capitalist production; but capital knows how to throw these, for the most part, from its own shoulders on to those of the working class and the lower middle class.—C. 1.

The modern laborer, instead of rising with the progress of industry, sinks deeper and deeper below the conditions of existence of his own class. He becomes a pauper, and pauperism develops more rapidly than population and wealth.—C. M.
The lowest sediment of the relative surplus population dwells in the sphere of pauperism. Exclusive of vagabonds, criminals, prostitutes, in a word, the "dangerous" classes, this layer of society consists of three categories. First, those able to work. . . .

Second, orphans and pauper children. . . . Third, the demoralized and ragged, and those unable to work, chiefly people who succumb to their incapacity for adaptation, due to the division of labor.—C. 1.

PEACE
The dogs of democrats and liberal scoundrels will realize that we are the only fellows who have not been stupefied by this terrible period of peace.—Ltr. to Engels.

PEASANT
The peasant is the bulwark of the old society.—C. 1.

The independent peasant or handicraftsman is cut up into two persons. As owner of the means of production he is capitalist; as laborer he is his own wage-laborer. As capitalist he therefore pays himself his wages and draws his profit on his capital; that is to say, he exploits himself as wage-laborer, and pays himself, in the surplus-value, the tribute that labor owes to capital. Perhaps he also pays himself a third portion as landowner (rent). —C. 4.

PERNICIOUS LABOR
That labor itself is harmful and pernicious, follows, without his being aware of it, from the political economist's line or argument.—M.

PERPETUUM MOBILE, INDUSTRIAL
In the form of machinery, the implements of labor become automatic, things moving and working independent of the workman. There are thenceforth an industrial perpetuum mobile, that would go on producing forever, did it not meet with certain natural obstructions in the weak bodies and the strong wills of its human attendants.—C. 1.

PETITIO PRINCIPII
Political economy takes for granted what it is supposed to evolve.—M.
The political economist assumes in the form of fact, of an event, what he is supposed to deduce.—M.

PETTY BOURGEOISIE
In countries where modern civilization has become fully developed, a new class of petty bourgeois has been formed, fluctuating between proletariat and bourgeoisie, and ever renewing itself as a supplementary part of bourgeois society. The individual members of this class, however, are being constantly hurled down into the proletariat by the action of competition, and, as modern industry develops, they can see the moment approaching when they will completely disappear as an independent section of modern society, to be replaced, in manufacture, agriculture and commerce, by overlookers, bailiffs and shopmen.—C. M.

PETTY INDUSTRY
The private property of the laborer in his means of production is the foundation of petty industry, whether agricultural, manufacturing or both; petty industry, again, is an essential condition for the development of social production and of the free individuality of the laborer himself.—C. 1.

PHILANTHROPISTS
The philanthropists wish to conserve the categories which express bourgeois relations, without having the antagonism which is inseparable from these relations. They fancy they are seriously combating the bourgeois system, and they are more bourgeois than the others.—P. P.

PHILANTHROPY
The philanthropy of atheism is at first only philosophical, abstract philanthropy, and that of communism is at once real and directly bent on action.—M.

PHILOSOPHER
A true philosopher takes the things inside out.—P. P.

PHILOSOPHIC MIND
The philosophic mind is nothing but the estranged mind of the world thinking within its self-estrangement.—M.

PHILOSOPHICAL INDIGESTION
If occasional individuals cannot digest modern philosophy and die of philosophical indigestion, that proves no more against philosophy than the occasional blowing up of a few passengers by the bursting of a boiler proves against mechanics.—L. A.

PHILOSOPHIZING
The "action of free reason" is what we call philosophizing.—L. A.

PHILOSOPHY
Philosophers do not grow out of the soil like mushrooms, they are the product of their time and of their people, whose most subtle, precious and invisible sap circulates in philosophical ideas. The same spirit that builds railways by the hands of the workers builds philosophical systems in the brain of the philosophers. Philosophy does not stand outside the world any more than man's brain is outside of him because it is not in his stomach; but, of course, philosophy is in the world with its brain before it stands on the earth with its feet, whereas many another human sphere has long been rooted in the earth by its feet and plucks the fruits of the world with its hands before it has any idea that the "head" also belongs to the world or that this world is the world of the head.—L. A.

The philosopher sets up himself (that is, one who is himself an abstract form of estranged man) as the measuring rod of the estranged world. The whole history of the alienation process and the whole process of the retraction of the alienation is therefore nothing but the history of the production of abstract (i.e., absolute) thought—of logical, speculative thought.—M.

Philosophy asks what is true, not what is acknowledged as such, what is true for all men, not what is true for individuals.—L. A.

Because every true philosophy is the spiritual quintessence of its time, the time must come when philosophy not only internally by its content but externally by its appearance comes into contact and mutual reaction with the real contemporary world. Philosophy then ceases to be a definitive system in presence of other definitive systems, it becomes philosophy generally, in presence of the world, it becomes the philosophy of the world of the present. The formal features which attest that philosophy has achieved that importance, that it is the living soul of the culture, that philosophy is becoming worldly, and the world philosophical, were the same in all times.—L. A.

Philosophy is world-wise enough to know that its results flatter the desire for pleasure or the egoism neither of the heavenly nor of the earthly world; but the public that loves truth and knowledge for their own sakes will be able to measure itself in judgment and morality with ignorant, servile, inconsistent and mercenary scribes.—L. A.

Philosophy, above all German philosophy, has a propensity to solitude, to systematical seclusion, to dispassionate self-contemplation which opposes it from the outset in its estrangement to the quick-witted and alive-to-events newspapers whose only delight is in information. Philosophy, taken in its systematic development, is unpopular; its secret weaving within itself seems to the layman to be an occupation as overstrained as it is unpractical; it is considered as a professor of magic whose incantations sound pompous because they are unintelligible.—L. A.

Philosophy is introduced into the world by the clamor of its enemies who betray their internal infection by their desperate appeals for help against the blaze of ideas. These cries of its enemies mean as much for philosophy as the first cry of a child for the anxious ear of the mother, they are the cry of life of the ideas which have burst open the orderly hieroglyphic husk of the system and become citizens of the world.—L. A.

Philosophy cannot be made a reality without the abolition of the proletariat, the proletariat cannot be abolished without philosophy being made a reality.—C. C.

PHILOSOPHY, MODERN
Modern philosophy has only continued a work already started by Heraclitus and Aristotle.—L. A.

PHILOSOPHY AND RELIGION
If you presume to stand so high above religion as to have the right to separate the general spirit of religion from its positive

definitions, what reproach have you to make to the philosophers if they want to make the separation complete and not a halfway one, if they claim not the Christian, but the human spirit, the universal spirit of religion?—L. A.

PHYSIOCRATIC ILLUSION
How long is it since economy discarded the physiocratic illusion, that rents grow out of the soil and not out of society?—C. 1.

PHYSIOCRATIC SYSTEM
The physiocratic system is in fact the first system which analyzes capitalist production, and presents the conditions within which capital is produced, and within which capital produces, as eternal natural laws of production. On the other hand, it has rather the character of a bourgeois reproduction of the feudal system, of the dominion of landed property; and the industrial spheres within which capital first develops independently are presented as "unproductive" branches of labor, mere appendages of agriculture.—C. 4.

PHYSIOCRATS
The analysis of capital, within the bourgeois horizon, is essentially the work of the physiocrats. It is this service that makes them the true fathers of modern political economy.—C. 4.

For the physiocrats argicultural labor is the only productive labor, because it is the only labor that produces a surplus-value, and rent is the only form of surplus-value which they know.—C. 4.

The physiocrats transferred the inquiry into the origin of surplus-value from the sphere of circulation into the sphere of direct production, and thereby laid the foundation for the analysis of capitalist production.—C. 4.

PIECE WAGES
Wages by the piece are nothing else than a converted form of wages by time, just as wages by time are a converted form of the value or price of labor power.—C. 1.

Piece wage is the form of wages most in harmony with the capitalist mode of production.—C. 1.

PLANT
The plant is an object of the sun, being an expression of the life-awakening power of the sun.—M.

PLAY
The care-burdened man in need has no sense for the finest play. —M.

PLEASURE
Pleasure is subsumed under capital, and the pleasure-taking individual under the capital-accumulating individual, whilst formerly the contrary was the case.—M.

PLETHORA, DOUBLE
The plethora of capital arises from the same causes as those which call forth relative overpopulation, and is, therefore, a phenomenon supplementing the latter, although they stand at opposite poles—unemployed capital at one pole, and unemployed worker population at the other.—C. 3.

PLUNDERING
Every new product represents a new potency of mutual swindling and mutual plundering.—M.

POLAND
Poland is the "foreign" thermometer of the intensity and vitality of all revolutions since 1789.—Ltr. to Engels.

POLEMIC
Your article is excellent, both brutal and subtle—a combination which should characterize any polemic worth its salt.—Ltr. to Weydemeyer.

POLITICAL ADVANCE OF THE BOURGEOISIE
Each step in the development of the bourgeoisie was accompanied by a corresponding political advance of that class. An oppressed class under the sway of the feudal nobility, it became an armed and self-governing association in the medieval commune; here an independent urban republic (as in Italy and Germany), there a taxable "third estate" of the monarchy (as in

France), afterward, in the period of manufacturing proper, serving either the semi-feudal or the absolute monarchy as a counterpoise against the nobility, and in fact, cornerstone of the great monarchies in general, the bourgeoisie has at last, since the establishment of modern industry and of the world market, conquered for itself, in the modern representative state, exclusive political sway.—C. M.

POLITICAL ECONOMIST
The political economist is an ideological representative of the capitalist.—C. 1.

POLITICAL ECONOMY
Political economy is an independent science.—C. 1.

Political economy—despite its worldly and wanton appearance—is a true *moral* science, the most moral of all sciences. Self-denial, the denial of life and of all human needs, is its cardinal doctrine. The less you eat, drink and read books—the greater becomes your treasure.—M.

One can transform political economy into a positive science only by substituting real contradictions for conflicting dogmas and conflicting facts whose concealed background they are.—Ltr. to Engels.

Political economy, this science of wealth, is simultaneously the science of denial, of want, of thrift, of saving—and it actually reaches the point where it spares man the need of either fresh air or physical exercise. This science of marvelous industry is simultaneously the science of asceticism, and its true ideal is the ascetic but extortionate miser and the ascetic but productive slave. Its moral ideal is the worker who takes part of his wages to the savings-bank.—M.

Political economy knows the worker only as a working-animal—as a beast reduced to the strictest bodily needs.—M.

Originally, political economy was studied by philosophers like Hobbes, Locke, Hume; by businessmen and statesmen; and especially, and with the greatest success, by medical men. Even in the middle of the eighteenth century, the Rev. Mr. Tucker, a notable economist of his time, excused himself for meddling with the things of mammon. Later on, struck the hour of the Protestant parsons.—C. 1.

Political economy has analyzed, however incompletely, value and its magnitude, and has discovered what lies beneath these forms. But it has never once asked the question why labor is represented by the value of its product and labor-time by the magnitude of that value.—C. 1.

Political economy does not disclose the source of the division between labor and capital, and between capital and land. When, for example, it defines the relationship of wages to profit, it takes the interest of the capitalists to be the ultimate cause; i.e., it takes for granted what it is supposed to evolve.—M.

As to how far external and apparently fortuitous circumstances are but the expression of a necessary course of development, political economy teaches us nothing.—M.

The foundation of modern political economy, whose business is the analysis of capitalist production, is the conception of the value of labor power as something fixed, as a given magnitude—as indeed it is in practice in each particular case.—C. 4.

Political economy proceeds from the fact of private property, but it does not explain it to us. It expresses in general, abstract formulae the material process through which private property actually passes, and these formulae it then takes for laws. It does not comprehend these laws—i.e., it does not demonstrate how they arise from the very nature of private property.—M.

POLITICAL MOVEMENT
A political movement is that in which the proletarians as a class exert pressure against the ruling classes. For example, the attempt of the workers of a factory to shorten the working day by a strike simply is an economic movement. However, their attempt at the legislation of an eight-hour day is a political movement.—Ltr. to Bolte.

POLITICAL TRAINING
When the proletariat is not organized enough to conduct a successful struggle against the political power of the ruling class, it must be trained for such a purpose by steady and hostile instigation. Or else, it shall be only a toy in the hands of the bourgeoisie.—Ltr. to Bolte.

POPULATION
Needlessness as the principle of political economy is most brilliantly shown in its theory of population. There are too many people. Even the existence of men is a pure luxury.—M.
Capitalist production collects the population in great centers, and causes an ever-increasing preponderance of the town population.—C. 1.

POPULATION DENSITY
The bourgeoisie keeps more and more doing away with the scattered state of the population.—C. M.

POPULATION, LABORING
The laboring population produces, along with the accumulation of capital produced by it, the means by which it is made relatively superfluous, is turned into a relative surplus population; and it does this to an always increasing extent. This is a law of population peculiar to the capitalist mode of production; and in fact every special historic mode of production has its own special laws of population, historically valid within its limits alone.—C. 1.

POSSESSION
Private property has made us so stupid and one-sided that an object is only ours when we have it—when it exists for us as capital, or when it is directly possessed, eaten, drunk, worn, inhabited, etc.—in short, when it is used by us. M.

POVERTY
Poverty is the passive bond which causes the human being to experience the need of the greatest wealth—the other human being.—M.

In a society based upon poverty, the poorest products have the fatal prerogative of serving the use of the greatest number.—P. P.

POWER, CAPITALIST
The capitalist possesses power, not on account of his personal qualities, but inasmuch as he is an owner of capital.—M.

POWER, PERSONAL
Each person tries to establish over the other an alien power, so as thereby to find satisfaction of his own selfish need. The increase in the quantity of objects is accompanied by an extension of the realm of the alien powers to which man is subjected. —M.

POWER, POLITICAL
Political power, properly so called, is merely the organized power of one class for suppressing another.—C. M.

PRACTICAL SOLUTIONS
It will be seen how subjectivism and objectivism, spiritualism and materialism, activity and suffering, only lose their antithetical character, and thus their existence, as such antitheses in the social condition; it will be seen how the resolution of the theoretical antitheses is only possible in a practical way, by virtue of the practical energy of men. Their resolution is therefore by no means merely a problem of knowledge, but a real problem of life, which philosophy could not solve precisely because it conceived this problem as merely a theoretical one.—M.

PRACTICE, HUMAN
Social life is essentially practical. All mysteries which mislead theory to mysticism find their rational solution in human practice and in the comprehension of this practice.—T. F.

PREJUDICES, BOURGEOIS
Law, morality, religion, are to the proletarian so many bourgeois prejudices, behind which lurk in ambush just as many bourgeois interests.—C. M.

PRESS, FREEDOM OF THE
The point is whether what lives in reality belongs to the realm of the press; it is no longer a question of a particular content

of the press, the question is the general one whether the press must be really the press, i.e., a free press.—L. A.

While the Constitution of 1793 guaranteed *"la liberté indefinie de la presse"* ("unabridged freedom of the press") as a consequence of the right of individual freedom, in reality freedom of the press was completely abolished, for "freedom of the press must not be permitted when it compromises public liberty" (Robespierre).—J. Q.

PRICE
Price is the monetary expression of the relative value of a product.—P. P.

Price is the money-name of the labor realized in a commodity. —C. 1.

The price of a commodity, and also of labor, is equal to its cost of production.—C. M.

PRICE, GRAVITATION OF
The market-price gravitates toward the natural price as the center-point.—M.

PRICE INCREASE
A price increase cuts the demand.—C. 3.

PRICE OF LABOR
Classical political economy borrowed from everyday life the category "price of labor" without further criticism, and then simply asked the question, How is this price determined? It soon recognized that the change in the relations of demand and supply explained in regard to the price of labor, as of all other commodities, nothing except its changes, i.e., the oscillations of the market price above or below a certain mean.—C. 1.

PRIESTS
The priests are the most clever people.—Ltr. to Engels.

PRIMITIVE ACCUMULATION
The so-called primitive accumulation is nothing else than the

historical process of divorcing the producer from the means of production. It appears as primitive, because it forms the prehistoric stage of capital and of the mode of production corresponding with it.—C. 1.

PRIMITIVE SOCIETY
Village communities were found to have been the primitive form of society.—C. M.

PRIMORDIAL CONDITION
Do not let us go back to a fictitious primordial condition as the political economist does, when he tries to explain. Such a primordial condition explains nothing. He merely pushes the question away into a gray nebulous distance. He assumes in the form of fact, of an event, what he is supposed to deduce—namely, the necessary relationship between two things—between, for example, division of labor and exchange.—M.

PRINCIPLE
Each principle has had its century in which to manifest itself.—P. P.

PRIVATE PROPERTY
(Private) property relations are the condition for the existence of the bourgeoisie and of its rule.—C. M.

Private property rests altogether on partitioning.—M.

You are horrified at our intending to do away with private property. But in your existing society, private property is already done away with for nine-tenths of the population; its existence for the few is solely due to its non-existence in the hands of those nine-tenths. You reproach us, therefore, with intending to do away with a form of property, the necessary condition for whose existence is, the non-existence of any property for the immense majority of society.—C. M.

The serf is the adjunct of the land. Likewise, the lord of an entailed estate, the first-born son, belongs to the land. It inherits him. Indeed, the dominion of private property begins with property in land—that is its basis.—M.

PROCREATION
Even physically, man owes his existence to man. Therefore you must not only keep sight of the *one* aspect—the infinite progression which leads you further to inquire: "Who begot my father? Who his grandfather?," etc. You must also hold on to the circular movement sensuously perceptible in that progression, by which man repeats himself in procreation, thus always remaining the subject.—M.

PRODIGALITY
Although the prodigality of the capitalist never possesses the bona-fide character of the open-handed feudal lord's prodigality, but, on the contrary, has always lurking behind it the most sordid avarice and the most anxious calculation, yet his expenditure grows with his accumulation, without the one necessarily restricting the other.—C. 1.

The progress of capitalist production not only creates a world of delights; it lays open, in speculation and the credit system, a thousand sources of sudden enrichment. When a certain stage of development has been reached, a conventional degree of prodigality, which is also an exhibition of wealth, and consequently a source of credit, becomes a business necessity to the "unfortunate" capitalist. Luxury enters into capital's expenses of representation.—C. 1.

The capitalist mode of production is generally, despite all its niggardliness, altogether too prodigal with its human material, just as, conversely, thanks to its method of distribution of products through commerce and manner of competition, it is very prodigal with its material means, and loses for society what it gains for the individual capitalist.—C. 3.

PRODUCERS
The producer, from the moment that he has produced in a society based on the division of labor and the exchange of commodities—and that is the hypothesis of M. Proudhon—is forced to sell. M. Proudhon makes the producer master of the means of production; but he will agree with us that it is not upon his free will that his means of production depend. The actual degree

of development of productive forces obliges him to produce on such and such a scale.—P. P.

Every service is productive for its seller. To swear false oaths is productive for the person who does it for cash. Forging documents is productive for anyone paid to do it. A murder is productive for a man who gets paid for doing it. The trade of sycophant, informer, toady, parasite, lickspittle, is productive for people who do not perform these "services" gratis. Hence they are "productive laborers," producers not only of wealth but of capital. The thief, too, who pays himself—just as the law courts and the state do—"employs his energy, uses it in a particular way, produces a result which satisfies a human need," i.e., the need of the thief and perhaps also that of his wife and children. —C. 4.

PRODUCTION
There are no products without production.—P. P.

Whatever the form of the process of production in a society, it must be a continuous process, must continue to go periodically through the same phases. A society can no more cease to produce than it can cease to consume. When viewed, therefore, as a connected whole, and as flowing on with incessant renewal, every social process of production is, at the same time, a process of reproduction.—C. 1.

In order to examine the connection between spiritual production and material production it is above all necessary to grasp the latter itself not as a general category but in definite historical form. Thus, for example, different kinds of spiritual production correspond to the capitalist mode of production and to the mode of production of the Middle Ages. If material production itself is not conceived in its specific historical form, it is impossible to understand what is specific in the spiritual production corresponding to it and the reciprocal influence of one on the other. Otherwise one cannot get beyond inanities. This because of the talk about "civilization."—C. 4.

The mode of production of material life conditions the social, political and intellectual life process in general.—P. E.

PRODUCTION, AIM OF
The directing motive, the end and aim of capitalist production, is to extract the greatest possible amount of surplus-value, and consequently to exploit labor-power to the greatest possible extent.—C. 1.

PRODUCTION, REVOLUTIONIZING OF
Suppose a shoemaker, with given tools, makes in one working day of twelve hours one pair of boots. If he must make two pairs in the same time, the productiveness of his labor must be doubled; and this cannot be done, except by an alteration in his tools or in his mode of working, or in both. Hence, the conditions of production, i.e., his mode of production, and the labor-process itself, must be revolutionized.—C. 1.

PRODUCTION, SPHERES OF
One sphere of production is, in fact, just as good or just as bad as another. Every one of them yields the same profit, and every one of them would be useless if the commodities it produced did not satisfy some social need.—C. 3.

PRODUCTION TIME
It is important to insist upon the point, that what determines value is not the time in which a thing has been produced, but the minimum time in which it is susceptible of being produced, and this minimum is demonstrated by competition.—P. P.

PRODUCTIVE ACTIVITY
Productive activity is nothing but the expenditure of human labor power. Tailoring and weaving, though qualitatively different productive activities, are each a productive expenditure of human brains, nerves, and muscles, and in this sense are human labor. They are but two different modes of expending human labor power. Of course, this labor power, which remains the same under all its modifications, must have attained a certain pitch of development before it can be expended in a multiplicity of modes.—C. 1.

PRODUCTIVE CAPITAL
Productive capital, in performing its functions, consumes its own

component parts for the purpose of transforming them into a mass of products of a higher value.—C. 2.

PRODUCTIVE CONSUMPTION

In reality, the individual consumption of the laborer is unproductive as regards himself, for it produces nothing but the needy individual; it is productive to the capitalist and the state, since it is the production of the power that creates their wealth.—C. 1.

PRODUCTIVE LABOR

When we speak of productive labor, we speak of socially determined labor, labor which implies a quite specific relation between the buyer and the seller of the labor.—C. 4.

The first reason why Adam Smith calls this kind of labor "productive" is that the physiocrats call it "unproductive" and "nonproductive."—C. 4.

A productive laborer is one whose labor produces commodities; and indeed such a laborer does not consume more commodities than he produces, than his labor costs. His labor fixes and realizes itself "in some such vendible commodity," "in any vendible commodity which can replace the value of their wages and maintenance."—C. 4.

The aim of the capitalist production process is the accumulation of wealth, the self-expansion of value, its increase; that is to say, the maintenance of the old value and the creation of surplus-value. And it achieves this specific product of the capitalist production process only in exchange with labor, which for that reason is called *productive labor.*—C. 4.

Only bourgeois narrow-mindedness, which regards the capitalist forms of production as absolute forms—hence as eternal, natural forms of production—can confuse the question of what is productive labor from the standpoint of capital with the question of what labor is productive in general, or what is *productive labor* in general; and consequently fancy itself very wise in giving the answer that all labor which produces anything at all, which has any kind of result, is by that very fact productive labor.—C. 4.

PRODUCTIVE LABORERS

Productive laborers may themselves in relation to me be **unproductive** laborers. For example, if I have my house repapered and the paper-hangers are wage-workers of a master who sells me the job, it is just the same for me as if I had bought a house already papered; as if I had expended money for a commodity for my consumption. But for the master who gets these laborers to hang the paper, they are productive laborers, for they produce surplus-value for him.—C. 4.

The productive power developed by the laborer when working in cooperation, is the productive power of capital. This power is developed gratuitously, whenever the workmen are placed under given conditions, and it is capital that places them under such conditions.—C. 1.

PRODUCTIVE POWER

In manufacture, in order to make the collective laborer, and through him capital, rich in social productive power, each laborer must be made poor in individual productive powers. —C. 1.

PRODUCTIVITY

The capitalist declares roundly that the *productiveness of labor* does not concern the laborer at all.—C. 1.

By increase in the productiveness of labor, we mean, generally, an alternation in the labor-process, of such a kind as to shorten the labor-time socially necessary for the production of a commodity, and to endow a given quantity of labor with the power of producing a greater quantity of use-value.—C. 1.

The productivity of capital consists in the first instance—even if one only considers the formal subsumption of labor under capital—in the compulsion to perform surplus-labor, labor beyond the immediate need; a compulsion which the capitalist mode of production shares with earlier modes of production, but which it exercises and carries into effect in a manner more favorable to production.—C. 4.

PRODUCTIVITY, BOURGEOIS

Modern bourgeois society with its relations of production, of exchange and of property, is a society that has conjured up gigantic means of production and of exchange.—C. M.

The bourgeoisie, during its rule of scarce one hundred years, has created more massive and more colossal productive forces than have all preceding generations together. Subjection of nature's forces to man, machinery, application of chemistry to industry and agriculture, steam-navigation, railways, electric telegraphs, clearing of whole continents for cultivation, canalization of rivers, whole populations conjured out of the ground—what earlier century had even a presentiment that such productive forces slumbered in the lap of social labor?—C. M.

PRODUCTIVITY, CAPITALIST
The stupendous productivity developing under the capitalist mode of production contradicts the basis, which constantly narrows in relation to the expanding wealth.—C. 3.

PRODUCTS
Products are not only results, but also essential conditions of labor.—C. 1.

A large number of products are not found in nature, they are found at the end of industry.—P. P.

Where equal capitals are employed the product is proportionate to the size of the capital.—M.

PROFESSIONAL WORKERS
The great mass of so-called "higher grade" workers—such as state officials, military people, artists, doctors, priests, judges, lawyers, etc.—some of whom are not only not productive but in essence destructive, but who know how to appropriate to themselves a very great part of the "material" wealth partly through the sale of their "immaterial" commodities and partly by forcibly imposing the latter on other people—found it not at all pleasant to be relegated economically to the same class as clowns and menial servants and to appear merely as people partaking in the consumption.—C. 4.

PROFIT
So far as profits are concerned, the various capitalists are just so many stockholders in a stock company in which the shares of profit are uniformly divided per 100, so that profits differ in the

case of the individual capitalists only in accordance with the amount of capital invested by each in the aggregate enterprise, i.e., according to his investment in social production as a whole, according to the number of his shares.—C. 3.

It goes without saying that profits also rise if the means of circulation become less expensive or easier available (e.g., paper money).—M.

The capitalist makes a profit, first, on the wages, and secondly, on the raw materials advanced by him.—M.

The greater the human share in a commodity, the greater the *profit* of dead capital.—M.

In its assumed capacity of offspring of the aggregate advanced capital, surplus-value takes the converted form of profit. Hence, a certain value is capital when it is invested with a view to producing profit, or there is profit because a certain value was employed as capital.—C. 3.

PROFIT, EXTRA
Recourse to frenzied ventures with new methods of production, new investments of capital, new adventures, may secure a shred of extra profit which is independent of the general average and rises above it.—C. 3.

PROFIT, FALLING RATE OF
If it is assumed that the gradual change in the composition of capital is not confined only to individual spheres of production, but that it occurs more or less in all, or at least in the average, organic composition of the total capital of a certain society, then the gradual growth of constant capital in relation to variable capital must necessarily lead to a gradual fall of the general rate of profit, so long as the rate of surplus-value, or the intensity of exploitation of labor by capital, remain the same.—C. 3.

PROFIT, INCREASE OF
The law that a fall in the rate of profit due to the development of productiveness is accompanied by an increase in the mass of profit also expresses itself in the fact that a fall in the price

of commodities produced by a capital is accompanied by a relative increase of the masses of profit contained in them and realized by their sale.—C. 3.

PROFIT, RATE AND MASS OF
With the development of the capitalist mode of production, the rate of profit falls, while its mass increases with the growing mass of the capital employed. Given the rate, the absolute increase in the mass of capital depends on its existing magnitude, but, on the other hand, if its magnitude is given, the proportion of its growth, i.e., the rate of its increment, depends on the rate of profit.—C. 3.

PROGRESSIVE REPRODUCTION
In economic forms of society of the most different kinds, there occurs, not only simple reproduction, but, in varying degrees, reproduction on a progressively increasing scale. By degrees more is produced and more consumed, and consequently more products have to be converted into means of production. This process, however, does not present itself as accumulation of capital, nor as the function of a capitalist, so long as the laborer's means of production, and with them his product and means of subsistence, do not confront him in the shape of capital.—C. 1.

PROLETARIAN
Political economy advances the proposition that the proletarian, the same as any horse, must get as much as will enable him to work. It does not consider him when he is not working, as a human being; but leaves such consideration to criminal law, to doctors, to religion, to the statistical tables, to politics and to the workhouse beadle.—M.

PROLETARIAN MAJORITY
All previous historical movements were movements of minorities, or in the interest of minorities. The proletarian movement is the self-conscious, independent movement of the immense majority, in the interest of the immense majority.—C. M.

PROLETARIAN MISSION
The proletarians have nothing of their own to secure and to fortify; their mission is to destroy all previous securities for, and insurances of, individual property.—C. M.

PROLETARIAT

The proletariat will use its political supremacy to wrest, by degrees, all capital from the bourgeoisie, to centralize all instruments of production in the hands of the state, i.e., of the proletariat organized as the ruling class; and to increase the total of productive forces as rapidly as possible.—C. M.

Since the *proletariat* must first of all acquire political supremacy, must rise to be the leading class of the nation, must constitute itself the nation, it is, so far, itself national, though not in the bourgeois sense of the word.—C. M.

By proletariat is meant the class of modern wage-laborers who, having no means of production of their own, are reduced to selling their labor power in order to live.—C. M.

Accumulation of capital is increase of the proletariat.—C. 1.

With the development of industry the proletariat not only increases in number, it becomes concentrated in great masses, its strength grows, and it feels that strength more. The various interests and conditions of life within the ranks of the proletariat are more and more equalized.—C. M.

The proletariat is recruited from all classes of the population. —C. M.

Not only has the bourgeoisie forged the weapons that bring death to itself; it has also called into existence the men who are to wield those weapons—the modern working class—the proletarians. In proportion as the bourgeoisie, i.e., capital, is developed, in the same proportion is the proletariat, the modern working class, developed, a class of laborers, who live only so long as they find work, and who find work only so long as their labor increases capital.—C. M.

The proletarian is without property; his relation to his wife and children has no longer anything in common with the bourgeois family-relations; modern industrial labor, modern subjugation to capital, the same in England as in France, in America as in Germany, has stripped him of every trace of national character. —C. M.

By heralding the dissolution of the hereto existing world order the proletariat merely proclaims the secret of its own existence, for it is the factual dissolution of that world order. By demanding the negation of private property, the proletariat merely raises to the rank of a principle of society what society has raised to the rank of its principle, what is already incorporated in it as the negative result of society without its own participation.—C. C.

The proletariat cannot be abolished without philosophy being made a reality.—C. C.

PROLETARIAT, GERMAN
The proletariat is beginning to appear in Germany as a result of the rising industrial movement. For it is not the naturally arising poor but the artificially impoverished, not the human masses mechanically oppressed by the gravity of society but the masses resulting from the drastic dissolution of society, mainly of the middle class, that form the proletariat.—C. C.

PROMETHEUS
Prometheus is the noblest of saints and martyrs in the calendar of philosophy.—D. E.

PROOF
Any anticipation of results still to be proved appears to me to be disturbing.—P. E.

PROPERTY
Society itself is the root of property.—C. 4.

Are not most of your court proceedings concerned with property?—L. A.

The capitalist gains by virtue of the favorable situation of his *property.*—M.

The separation of property from labor has become the necessary consequence of a law that apparently originated in their identity.—C. 1.

Does wage-labor create any property for the laborer? Not a bit. It creates capital, i.e., that kind of property which exploits wage-labor, and which cannot increase except upon condition of getting a new supply of wage-labor for fresh exploitation. Property, in its present form, is based on the antagonism of capital and wage-labor.—C. M.

PROPERTY, DEFINITION OF
To pretend to give a definition of property as of an independent relation, a separate category, an abstract and eternal idea, can only be an illusion of metaphysics or of jurisprudence.—P. P.

Property turns out to be the right, on the part of the capitalist, to appropriate the unpaid labor of others or its product and to be the impossibility, on the part of the laborer, of appropriating his own product. The separation of property from labor has become the necessary consequence of a law that apparently originated in their identity.—C. 1.

PROPERTY, MOVABLE
Moveable property for its part points to the miracles of industry and progress. It is the child of the modern time and its legitimate, native-born son.—M.

PROPERTY OWNERS
The distinction between capitalist and land-rentier, like that between the tiller of the soil and the factory worker, disappears and the whole society falls apart into the two classes—the property owners and the propertyless workers.—M. See Class Consolidation.

PROPERTY TITLES
Titles to property, for instance railway shares, may change hands every day, and their owner may make a profit by their sale even in foreign countries, so that titles to property are exportable, although the railway itself is not.—C. 2.

PROPERTYLESSNESS
The antithesis of propertylessness and property, so long as it is not comprehended as the antithesis of labor and capital, still remains an antithesis of indifference, not grasped in its active

connection, its internal relation—an antithesis not yet grasped as a contradiction.—M.

PROPORTIONALITY, LAW OF
Within the workshop, the iron law of proportionality subjects definite numbers of workmen to definite functions.—C. 1.

PROPORTIONATE PRODUCE
With equal fertility and equally efficient exploitation of lands, mines and fisheries, the produce is proportionate to the size of the capital.—M.

Where equal capitals are employed the product is proportionate to the fertility. Hence, where capitals are equal victory goes to the proprietor of the more fertile soil.—M.

PROSTITUTION
Loudon declares the number of *prostitutes* in England to be between sixty and seventy thousand. The number of women of doubtful virtue is said to be equally large.—M.

The present family finds its complement in public prostitution. The bourgeois family will vanish as a matter of course when its complement vanishes, and both will vanish with the vanishing of capital.—C. M. *See* Family.

The factory workers in France call the prostitution of their wives and daughters the Xth working hour, which is literally correct. —M.

PROSTITUTION, ECONOMIC
Prostitution is only a specific expression of the general prostitution of the laborer, and since it is a relationship in which not the prostitute alone, but also the one who prostitutes, falls—and the latter's abomination is still greater—the capitalist, etc., also comes under this head.—M.

The abolition of the present system of production must bring with it the abolition of prostitution both public and private. —C. M.

PROTECTIVE TARIFF

This makes clear the great importance to industry of the elimination or reduction of customs duties on raw materials. The rational development of the protective tariff system made the utmost reduction of import duties on raw materials one of its cardinal principles. This, and the abolition of the duty on corn, was the main object of the English free traders, who were primarily concerned with having the duty on cotton lifted as well.—C. 3.

PROUDHON

Proudhon grappled recklessly with problems for the solution of which he lacked the most elementary knowledge. . . . That which he trumpets in your ears is his own glorification, wearisome nonsense and eternal rodomontade about his pretended "science." Add to this the awkward and disagreeable didactic pedantry, which serves for erudition.—P. P.

Proudhon's book reveals, if I may use the expression, a distinct muscular style. I believe this style to be its greatest value.—Ltr. to Schweitzer.

In a strictly scientific history of political economy Proudhon's book would hardly be worth mentioning, but sensational works of this sort play their role in the history of science just as much as in that of the novel.—Ltr. to Schweitzer.

The good side and the bad side, the advantage and the inconvenience, taken together, form for M. Proudhon the contradiction in each economic category.—P. P.

Instead of comprehending the economic categories as the theoretical expression of historic relations of production, corresponding to particular stages of development in the material production, Proudhon misunderstands them as pre-existing eternal ideas, arriving by this circuitous method again at the viewpoint of bourgeois economy.—Ltr. to Schweitzer.

PROVIDENCE

Providence, the providential end, that is the fine word with which we are presented today to explain the progress of history. In actual fact, this word explains nothing.—P. P.

PROVISIONS, PRICE OF
The prices of labor are much more constant than the prices of provisions.—M.

PSYCHOLOGY
A psychology for which this (industrial activity), the part of history most contemporary and accessible to sense, remains a closed book cannot become a genuine, comprehensive and real science.—M.

It will be seen how the history of industry and the established objective existence of industry are the open book of man's essential powers, the exposure to the senses of human psychology.—M.

PUBLIC WORKS
As in Egypt and India, inundations are used for fertilizing the soil of Mesopotamia, Persia, etc.; advantage is taken of a high level for feeding irrigative canals. This prime necessity of an economical and common use of water, which, in the Occident, drove private enterprise to voluntary association, as in Flanders and Italy, necessitated in the Orient, where civilization was too low and the territorial extent too vast to call into life voluntary association, the interference of the centralizing power of government. Hence an economical function developed upon all Asiatic governments, the function of providing *public works*.—D. T.

PUNISHMENT
Man begets his own production as the loss of his reality, as his punishment.—M.

PURCHASING POWER
The power of the capitalist is the purchasing power of his capital.—M.

Q

QUANTITY OF LABOR
The increase of the quantity of labor does not depend only on the number of workmen, but also on the length of the working day. The quantity of labor can therefore be increased without increasing the part of the capital that is converted into wages. —C. 4.

R

RADICALISM
To be radical is to grasp the root of the matter. But for man the root is man himself.—C. C.

RAILWAYS
The emergence of railways in the leading capitalist countries permitted these nations to enlarge their capitalistic superstructure out of proportion to the production at large.—Ltr. to Danielson.

The railways usually hastened immensely the development of foreign commerce.—Ltr. to Danielson.

Originally in the construction of modern railways it was the prevailing opinion, pursued by the most prominent practical engineers, that a railway would last a century and that the wear and tear of the rails was so imperceptible that it could be ignored for all financial and other practical purposes. But it was soon found that the life of a rail did not exceed an average of 20 years. —C. 2.

RATE AND MASS OF SURPLUS-VALUE
It is to be emphasized that with a capital of a given magnitude the rate of surplus-value may rise, while its mass is decreasing, and vice versa. The mass of surplus-value is equal to the rate multiplied by the number of laborers; however, the rate is never calculated on the total, but only on the variable capital, actually only for every working day. On the other hand, with a given

magnitude of capital-value, the rate of profit can neither rise nor fall without the mass of surplus-value also rising or falling.—C. 3.

RATE OF EXCHANGE

The rate of exchange is known to be the barometer for the international movement of money metals. If England has more payments to make to Germany than Germany to England, the price of marks, expressed in sterling, rises in London, and the price of sterling, expressed in marks, falls in Hamburg and Berlin. If this preponderance of England's payment obligations toward Germany is not balanced again, for instance, by a preponderance of purchases by Germany in England, the sterling price of bills of exchange in marks on Germany must rise to the point where it will pay to send metal (gold bullion) from England to Germany in payment of obligations, instead of sending bills of exchange. This is the typical course of events.—C. 3.

RATE OF PROFIT

The rate of profit is the motive power of capitalist production. Things are produced only so long as they can be produced with a profit. Hence the concern of the English economists over the decline of the rate of profit. The fact that the bare possibility of this happening should worry Ricardo, shows his profound understanding of the condition of capitalist production. It is that which is held against him, it is his unconcern about "human beings," and his having an eye solely for the development of the productive forces—it is precisely that which is the important thing about him.—C. 3.

Given the *rate of profit*, the absolute increase in the mass of capital depends on its existing magnitude. On the other hand, if its magnitude is given, the proportion of its growth, i.e., the rate of its increment, depends on the rate of profit.—C. 3.

RAW MATERIAL

The rate of profit depends partly on the good quality of the raw material. Good material produces less waste. Less raw materials are then needed to absorb the same quantity of labor. The laborer needs more time when using bad raw materials to process the same quantity.—C. 3.

If the subject of labor has, so to say, been filtered through previous labor, we call it raw material; such is ore already extracted and ready for washing. All raw material is the subject of labor, but not every subject of labor is raw material; it can only become so, after it has undergone some alteration by means of labor.—C. 1.

RAW PRODUCE
The greater demand for raw produce, and therefore the rise in value, may in part result from the increase of population and from the increase of their needs.—M.

In the manufacture of locomotives, every day the waste amounts to whole wagonloads of iron filings. These are collected and resold (or charged in account) to the same iron manufacturer who supplied the locomotive manufacturer with his principal *raw material*. The iron manufacturer again gives them solid form, adding new labor to them. However, in the form in which he sends them back to the locomotive manufacturer, these filings represent the part of the value of the product which replaces raw material. In this way not the same filings, but constantly a certain quantity of filings, move hither and thither between the two factories. This part forms in turn the raw material for each of the two branches of industry and, considered as value, only wanders from one shop to the other.—C. 4.

The *raw material* serves merely as an absorbent of a definite quantity of labor. By this absorption it is in fact changed into (a product).—C. 1.

REASON
Human reason, which is nothing less than pure, having only an incomplete view, meets at each step fresh problems to solve.—P. P.

If you base yourself on giving to Caesar the things which are Caesar's and to God the things which are God's, do not consider the mammon of gold alone but at least just as much free reason as the Caesar of this world.—L. A.

In capitalist society social reason always asserts itself only post festum.—C. 2.

REFLEXES
The religious world is but the reflex of the real world. . . . The juridical relation is but the reflex of the real economical relation.—C. 1.

REFORMERS
The piecemeal reformers either want to raise wages and in this way to improve the situation of the working class, or regard equality of wages (as Proudhon does) the goal of social revolution.—M.

REFUGEES
I have now criticized Gladstone, attracting some attention—just as I previously criticized Palmerston. The demagogic refugees here like to attack the Continental despots from a distant sanctuary.—Ltr. to Kugelmann.

REGRESSION
Man returns to live in a cave.—M.

RELATION, SOCIAL
There is a definite social relation between men, that assumes, in their eyes, the fantastic form of a relation between things. —C. 1.

Every one of your *relations to man* and to nature must be a specific expression, corresponding to the object of your will, of your real individual life.—M.

RELATIVE SURPLUS POPULATION
The relative surplus population exists in every possible form. Every laborer belongs to it during the time when he is only partially employed or wholly unemployed. Not taking into account the great periodically recurring forms that the changing phases of the industrial cycle impress on it, now an acute form during the crisis, then again a chronic form during dull times—it has always three forms, the floating, the latent, the stagnant. —C. 1.

RELATIVE SURPLUS-VALUE
The surplus-value arising from the curtailment of the necessary

labor-time, and from the corresponding alteration in the respective lengths of the two components of the work day, I call relative surplus-values.—C. 1.

RELIGION

Religion is the opiate of the people.—C. C.

In religion, man is governed by the products of his own brain.—C. 1.

Religion is the general theory of that world, its encyclopedic compendium, its logic is a popular form, its spiritualistic *point d'honneur*, its enthusiasm, its moral sanction, its solemn completion, its universal ground for consolation and justification.—C. C.

Religious distress is the expression of real distress and the protest against real distress. Religion is the sigh of the oppressed creature, the heart of a heartless world, just as it is the spirit of a spiritless situation.—C. C.

The basis of irreligious criticism is: Man makes religion, religion does not make man. In other words, religion is the self-consciousness and self-feeling of man who has either not yet found himself or has already lost himself again.—C. C.

Religion is only the illusory sun which revolves round man as long as he does not revolve round himself.—C. C.

In the religious world the productions of the human brain appear as independent beings endowed with life, and entering into relation both with one another and the human race.—C. 1.

In religion the spontaneous activity of the human imagination, of the human brain and the human heart operates independently of the individual—that is, operates on him as an alien, divine or diabolical activity.—M.

The state still can emancipate itself from religion if its overwhelming majority is religious. And the overwhelming majority does not cease being religious by being religious only in private. —J. Q.

If I know religion as alienated human self-consciousness, then what I know in it as religion is not my self-consciousness, but my alienated self-consciousness confirmed in it. I therefore know my own self, the self-consciousness that belongs to its very nature, confirmed not in religion but rather in annihilated and superseded religion.—M.

Man emancipates himself from religion politically by relegating it from public to private law.—J. Q.

RELIGION, ABOLITION OF
The abolition of religion as the illusory happiness of the people is required for their real happiness. The demand to give up the illusions about its condition is the demand to give up a condition which needs illusions. The criticism of religion is therefore in embryo the criticism of the vale of woe, the halo of which is religion.—C. C.

RELIGION, EMANCIPATION FROM
The division of man into Protestant and citizen, religious man and citizen is not a lie against citizenship or a way to circumvent political emancipation: it is political emancipation itself the political way of emancipation from religion.—J. Q.

RELIGION, HISTORY OF
Every history of religion that fails to take account of the material basis is uncritical.—C. 1.

RELIGION, PRIVILEGED
We have shown that political emancipation from religions permits religion to continue, though not privileged religion.—J. Q.

RELIGION AND PHILOSOPHY
Religion polemicizes not against a definite system of philosophy but against the philosophy generally of the definite systems. —L. A.

It seems that the wisdom of this world, philosophy, has more right to bother about the kingdom of this world than the wisdom of the other world, religion.—L. A.

If you make religion a theory of state right, then you make religion itself a kind of philosophy.—L. A.

If you presume to stand so high above religion as to have the right to separate the general spirit of religion from its positive definitions, what reproach have you to make to the philosophers if they want to make the separation complete, if they proclaim the universal spirit of religion?—L. A.

RELIGION IN AMERICA
The infinite splits of religion in the United States give it even the external appearance of a purely individual affair. It has been exiled from the sphere of the community as such and has been thrust among a crowd of private interests of which it is but one.—J. Q.

RELIGIOUS CONFLICT
The conflict in which man as a believer in a particular religion finds himself, with his own citizenship and with other members of the community, is reduced to the secular split between the political state and bourgeois society.—J. Q.

RELIGIOUS FREEDOM
Incompatibility between religion and human rights is so far removed from the concept of human rights that the right to be religious in a certain way, and the right to practice the worship of a given religion, are expressly enumerated among human rights. The privilege of belief is a universal human right.—J. Q.

RELIGIOUS SPIRIT
The religious spirit cannot become secularized for it is nothing but the non-secular form of the human spirit at a certain stage of its development. The religious spirit can realize itself only insofar as that stage of development of which it is the expression assumes a secular form. This is what happens in the democratic state.—J. Q.

RELIGIOUS WORLD
The religious world is but the reflex of the real world. . . . The religious reflex of the real world can only then finally vanish, when the practical relations of everyday life offer to man none

but perfectly intelligible and reasonable relations with regard to his fellow men and to nature.—C. 1.

RENT
Every new invention, every new application in manufacture of a little used raw material augments the rent of the land.—M.

The rent of land is established as a result of the struggle between tenant and landlord. We find that the hostile antagonism of interests, the struggle, the war is recognized throughout political economy as the basis of social organization.—M.

Wherever rent exists at all, differential rent appears at all times, and is governed by the same laws, as agricultural differential rent.—C. 3.

The more capital is invested in the land, and the higher the development of agriculture and civilization in general in a given country, the more rents rise per acre as well as in total amount, and the more immense becomes the tribute paid by society to the big landowners in the form of surplus-profits—so long as the various soils, once taken under cultivation, are all able to continue competing.—C. 3.

Rent results from the social relations in which exploitation is carried on. It cannot result from the nature, more or less fixed, more or less durable, of land. Rent proceeds from society and not from the soil.—P. P.

Rent is constituted by the equal price of the products of lands of unequal fertility in such wise that a hectoliter of wheat which has cost 10 francs is sold for 20 francs if the cost of production rises, for an inferior soil, to 20 francs.—P. P.

There is a direct constant rise in the rent of the land as a result of the course of industrial development; nevertheless, there must come a time when landed property, like every other kind of property, is bound to fall within the category of profitably self-reproducing capital—and this in fact results from the same industrial development.—M.

REPAIRMEN
There is a numerically unimportant class of persons, whose occupation it is to look after the whole of the machinery and repair it from time to time; such as engineers, mechanics, joiners, etc. This is a superior class of workmen, some of them scientifically educated, others brought up in the trade; it is distinct from the factory operative class, and merely aggregated to it.—C. 1.

REPRODUCTION
No society can go on producing, in other words, no society can reproduce, unless it constantly reconverts a part of its products into means of production, or elements of fresh products. —C. 1.

REPRODUCTION OF CAPITAL
The maintenance and reproduction of the working class is, and must ever be, a necessary condition to the reproduction of capital. But the capitalist may safely leave its fulfillment to the laborer's instincts of self-preservation and of propagation. All the capitalist cares for is to reduce the laborer's individual consumption as far as possible to what is strictly necessary.—C. 1.

REPULSION AND ATTRACTION OF CAPITAL
The splitting up of the total social capital into many individual capitals or the repulsion of its fractions one from another is counteracted by their attraction.—C. 1.

RESEARCH
Research must never appeal to the powers of comprehension of the masses, i.e., must never become popular and clear to itself. —L. A.

RESEARCH, SCIENTIFIC
Who should decide on the bounds of scientific research if not scientific research itself!—L. A.

RESISTANCE TO CAPITALIST DOMINATION
As the number of cooperating laborers increases, so too does their resistance to the domination of capital, and with it, the necessity for capital to overcome this resistance by counterpressure.—C. 1.

RESOLUTENESS, COMMUNIST
The communists are the most resolute section of the working class parties of every country, that section which pushes forward all others.—C. M.

RESPECTABILITY, CAPITALIST
Only as personified capital is the capitalist respectable.—C. 1.

RESTRICTION
All fetters and *restrictions* placed on manufacturers and foreign trade make manufactured commodities, etc., dearer.—C. 4.

RETAIL BUSINESS
Retail business deals with direct consumption.—C. 3.

RETRIBUTION
It is a rule of historical retribution that its instrument be forged not by the offended, but by the offender himself.—D. T.

REVIEWER
The uninformed reviewer tries to hide his complete ignorance and intellectual poverty by hurling the "utopian phrase" at the positive critic's head.—M.

REVOLT
Along with the constantly diminishing number of the magnates of capital, who usurp and monopolize all advantages of this process of transformation, grows the mass of misery, oppression, slavery, degradation, exploitation; but with this too grows the *revolt of the working class*, a class always increasing in numbers, and disciplined, united, organized by the very mechanism of the process of capitalist production itself.—C. 1.

REVOLUTION
Revolutionary upheavals periodically recur in history.—G. 1.

The already existing conditions of life of the various generations also decide whether the revolutionary upheavals that periodically recur in history are strong enough to overthrow the basis of all that is in existence; if these material elements of a complete overthrow, to wit, on one side the existing production forces and on the other the formation of a revolutionary mass which revolts not only against individual conditions of hitherto existing society but against the very "life-production" hitherto existing, the "whole of the activity" on which it is based—if these material elements are not to hand it is absolutely indifferent for practical development, as the history of communism proves, whether the *idea* of that revolution has already been formulated a hundred times.—G. I.

REVOLUTION, BOURGEOIS
The bourgeoisie cannot exist without constantly revolutionizing the instruments of production, and thereby the relations of production, and with them the whole relations of society. Conservation of the old modes of production in unaltered form was, on the contrary, the first condition of existence for earlier industrial classes. Constant revolutionizing of production, uninterrupted disturbance of all social conditions, everlasting uncertainty and agitation distinguish the bourgeois epoch from earlier ones. All fixed, fast-frozen relations, with their train of ancient and venerable prejudices and opinions, are swept away, all newly formed ones become antiquated before they can ossify. All that is solid melts into air, all that is holy is profaned, and man is at last compelled to face with sober senses his real conditions of life. —C. M.

REVOLUTION, COMMUNIST
The communist revolution is the most radical rupture with traditional property relations; no wonder that its development involves the most radical rupture with traditional ideas.—C. M.

REVOLUTION, COURSE OF
In the beginning, the (revolutionary) measures appear economically insufficient and untenable, but, in the course of the movement, they outstrip themselves.—C. M.

REVOLUTION, FUTURE
Doctrinaire and utopian predictions about the future revolution only divert us from the reality of the present class struggle. —Ltr. to Nieuwenhuis.

Eventually wages, which have already been reduced to a minimum, must be reduced yet further, to meet the new competition. This then necessarily leads to revolution.—M.

REVOLUTION, PROLETARIAN

The scientific observation of the disintegrating bourgeois society guarantees sufficiently the assumption that after the outbreak of the proletarian revolution the conditions for its next actions will be available.—Ltr. to Nieuwenhuis.

Bourgeois revolutions rush onward rapidly from success to success, their stage effects outbid one another, men and things seem to be set in flaming brilliants, ecstasy is the prevailing spirit; but they are short-lived, they reach their climax speedily, then society relapses into a long fit of nervous reaction before it learns how to appropriate the fruits of its period of feverish excitement. *Proletarian* revolutions, on the contrary, criticize themselves constantly; constantly interrupt themselves in their own course; come back to what seems to have been accomplished, in order to start over anew; scorn with cruel thoroughness the half measures, weaknesses and meannesses of their first attempts. —E. B.

REVOLUTION, SOCIAL

From forms of development of the productive forces the property relations turn into their fetters. Then begins an epoch of social revolution.—P. E.

REVOLUTIONARY CLASS

Of all the classes that stand face to face with the bourgeoisie today, the proletariat alone is a really revolutionary class.—C. M.

The revolutionary (proletarian) class holds the future in its hands.—C. M.

REVOLUTIONARY IDEAS

When people speak of ideas that revolutionize society, they do but express the fact, that within the old society the elements of a new one have been created, and that the dissolution of the old ideas keeps even pace with the dissolution of the old conditions of existence.—C. M.

REVOLUTIONARY MOVEMENT

That the entire revolutionary movement necessarily finds both its empirical and its theoretical basis in the movement of private property—in that of economy, to be precise—is easy to see. —M.

RICARDO

Ricardo, the creator of modern political economy in Great Britain, was convinced that political economy had nothing to do with questions of right (but of fact).—I. Q.

Ricardo's care for accumulation is even greater than his care for net profit, which he regards with fervent admiration as a means to accumulation. Hence too his contradictory admonitions and consoling remarks to the laborers. They are the people most interested in the accumulation of capital, because it is on this that the demand for them depends. If this demand rises, then the price of labor rises. They must therefore themselves desire the lowering of wages, so that the surplus taken from them, once more filtered through capital, is returned to them for new labor and their wages rise. This rise in wages however is bad, because it restricts accumulation. On the one hand they must not produce children. This brings a fall in the supply of labor, and so its price rises. But this rise diminishes the rate of accumulation, and so diminishes the demand for them and brings down the price of labor. Even quicker than the supply of them falls, capital falls along with it. If they produce children, then they increase their own supply and reduce the price of labor; thus the rate of profit rises, and with it the accumulation of capital. But the laboring population must rise in the same degree as the accumulation of capital; that is to say, the laboring population must be there exactly in the numbers that the capitalist needs—which it does anyway.—C. 4.

RICHES

A country is the richer the smaller its productive population is *relatively* to the total product; just as for the individual capitalist: the fewer laborers he needs to produce the same surplus, so much the better for him. The country is the richer the smaller the productive population in relation to the unproductive, the quantity of products remaining the same. For the relative smallness of the productive population would be only another way of expressing the relative degree of the productivity of labor.—C. 4.

ROBOT, THE WORKER AS
With the division of labor on one hand and the accumulation of capital on the other, the worker becomes ever more exclusively dependent on labor, and on a particular, very one-sided machine-like labor. He is thus depressed spiritually and physically to the condition of a machine and from being a man becomes an abstract activity and a stomach.—M.

ROMAN RELIGION
Epicurean, stoic or skeptic philosophy was the religion of the Romans of culture when Rome reached the zenith of its career. —L. A.

ROMANTICISM
Romanticism appears more and more as the "presupposition" of the critical criticism.—Ltr. to Engels.

RUINOUS COMPETITION
The bigger capitalist can even bear temporary losses until the smaller capitalist is ruined and he finds himself freed from this competition.—M.

RULE OF LANDED PROPERTY
The rule of landed property does not appear directly as the rule of mere capital. For those belonging to it, the estate is more like their fatherland. It is a constricted sort of nationality. —M.

RUSSIA
All strata of the Russian society are in a state of economic, moral and intellectual disintegration.—Ltr. to Sorge.

The movement is progressing in Russia faster than in all the rest of Europe.—Ltr. to Engels.

Russia will be so kind as to participate in the next revolution. —Ltr. to Engels.

RUSSIAN LANDOWNERS
As a result of the so-called emancipation of the peasants, the Russian landowners are now compelled to carry on agriculture with the help of wage-laborers instead of the forced labor of serfs.—C. 2.

S

SACRIFICE, PROLETARIAN
The raising of wages gives rise to overwork among the workers. The more they wish to earn, the more must they sacrifice their time and carry out slave-labor, in the service of avarice completely losing all their freedom, thereby they shorten their lives. This shortening of their life span is a favorable circumstance for the working class as a whole, for as a result of it an ever-fresh supply of labor becomes necessary. This class has always to sacrifice a part of itself in order not to be wholly destroyed.—M.

SATISFACTION, MODE OF
An object satisfies the wants directly as a means of subsistence, or indirectly as a means of production.—C. 1.

SAVING
Accumulate, accumulate! That is Moses and the prophets! "Industry furnishes the material which saving accumulates." Therefore, save, save, i.e., reconvert the greatest possible portion of surplus-value, or surplus-product into capital!—C. 1.

The less you eat, drink and read books, the less you think, love, theorize, sing, paint, fence, etc., the more you save—the greater becomes your treasure which neither moths nor dust will devour —your capital.—M.

SCARCITY
The greater the scarcity of the products offered relative to the demand, the dearer they are.—P. P.

SCIENCE
Modern industry makes science a productive force distinct from labor and presses it into the service of capital.—C. 1.

Contradictions in science are resolved by science itself.—J. Q.

Natural science will in time subsume under itself the science of man, just as the science of man will subsume under itself natural science; there will be *one* science.—M.

All science would be superfluous if the outward appearance and the essence of things directly coincided.—C. 3.

Like the increased exploitation of natural wealth by the mere increase in the tension of labor-power, *science* and technology give capital a power of expansion independent of the given magnitude of the capital actually functioning.—C. 1.

SCIENCE AND REVOLUTION
So long as they seek science and only make systems, so long as they are at the beginning of the struggle, they see in poverty only poverty, without seeing therein the revolutionary subversive side which will overturn the old society. From that moment science, produced by the historical movement and linking itself thereto in full knowledge of the facts of the case, has ceased to be doctrinaire and has become revolutionary.—P. P.

SCIENCE OF VALUE
This science consists exactly in elaborating the law of value. If one then wanted at the outset to "explain" all the phenomena which seem to contradict that law, one would have to offer a science before this science.—Ltr. to Kugelmann.

SCIENTIFIC
When I am active scientifically, etc.,—when I am engaged in activity which I can seldom perform in direct community with others—then I am social, because I am active as a man.—M.

SCIENTIFIC JOURNAL
It would be very pleasant if a truly scientific socialist journal were to be published. It would furnish us with a magazine for

criticism and counter-criticism in which theoretical issues could be discussed.—Ltr. to Engels.

SECULAR
In bourgeois society man is a secular being.—J. Q.

SECURITY
Security is the highest social concept of bourgeois society, the police concept that the entire society exists only to assure each of its members the preservation of his person, his rights and his property.—J. Q.

SEDUCTION, BOURGEOIS
Our bourgeois, not content with having the wives and daughters of their proletarians at their disposal, not to speak of common prostitutes, take the greatest pleasure in seducing each other's wives.—C. M.

SELF-ESTRANGEMENT
Every self-estrangement of man from himself and from nature appears in the relation in which he places himself and nature to men other than and different from himself. For this reason religious self-estrangement necessarily appears in the relationship of the layman to the priest, or again to a mediator, etc., since we are here dealing with the intellectual world. In the real practical world self-estrangement can only become manifest through the real practical relationship to other men. The medium through which estrangement takes place is itself practical.—M.

SELF-RESPECT
The feeling of regaining the ability to work does much for a man.—Ltr. to Engels.

SELLING
Sale is the practice of alienation. Just as a man, so long as he is engrossed in religion, can objectify his nature only by turning it into an alien and fantastic being, so, when he is dominated by egotistical needs, can he busy himself in production only by putting his products in the power of an alien being and bestowing upon him his own alien products the value of money.—J. Q.

SELLING AND BUYING
If selling and buying disappear, free selling and buying disappear also.—C. M.

SENSE PERCEPTION
Sense perception must be the basis of all science. Only when it proceeds from sense perception in the twofold form both of sensuous consciousness and of sensuous need—that is, only when science proceeds from nature—is it true science.—M.

SENSES
The forming of the five senses is a labor of the entire history of the world down to the present.—M.

Wherever the *sensuous affirmation* is the direct annulment of the object in its independent form (as in eating, drinking, working, etc.), this is the affirmation of the object.—M.

SENSUOUS WORLD
The more the worker by his labor appropriates the external world, sensuous nature, the more he deprives himself of means of life in the double respect: first, that the sensuous external world more and more ceases to be an object belonging to his labor—to be his labor's means of life; and secondly, that it more and more ceases to be means of life in the immediate sense, means for the physical subsistence of the worker.—M.

SEPARATION
Separation appears as the normal relation in this society. Where therefore it does not in fact apply, it is presumed and so far correctly; for in this society unity appears as accidental, separation as normal, and consequently separation is maintained as the relation even when one person unites separate functions.—C. 4.

SEPARATION OF CHURCH AND STATE
Was it not Christianity before anything else that separated church and state?—L. A.

SEPARATION OF LABORERS
The capitalist system presupposes the complete separation of the

laborers from all property in the means by which they can realize their labor. As soon as capitalist production is once on its own legs, it not only maintains this separation, but reproduces it on a continually extending scale.—C. 1.

SERVICES
Services may also be forced on me—the services of officials, etc. —C. 4.

SERVICES, ENJOYMENT OF
Certain services, or the use-values, resulting from certain forms of activity or labor are embodied in commodities; others on the contrary leave no tangible result existing apart from the persons themselves who perform them; in other words, their result is not a vendible commodity. For example, the service a singer renders to me satisfies my aesthetic need; but what I enjoy exists only in an activity inseparable from the singer himself, and as soon as his labor, the singing, is at an end, my enjoyment too is at an end. I enjoy the activity itself—its reverberation on my ear. —C. 4.

SEXUAL RELATIONS
The direct, natural, and necessary relation of person to person is the relation of man to woman. In this natural relationship of the sexes man's relation to nature is immediately his relation to man, just as his relation to man is immediately his relation to nature—his own natural function. In this relationship, therefore, is sensuously manifested, reducible to an observable fact, the extent to which the human essence has become nature to man, or to which nature has to him become the human essence of man.—M.

In the approach to woman as the spoil and handmaid of communal lust, is expressed the infinite degradation in which man exists for himself, for the secret of this approach has its unambiguous, decisive, plain and undisguised expression in the relation of man to woman and in the manner in which the direct and natural procreative relationship is conceived.—M.

Mill suggests public acclaim for those who prove themselves continent in their sexual relations.—M.

SHAKESPEARE
In *Timon of Athens*, Shakespeare excellently depicts the real nature of money.—M.

SHORTENING OF LABOR-TIME
The shortening of the working day is by no means what is aimed at, in capitalist production, when labor is economized by increasing its productiveness. It is only the shortening of the labor-time necessary for the production of a definite quantity of commodities that is aimed at.—C. 1.

SIGHT
The light from an object is perceived by us not as the subjective excitation of our optic nerve, but as the objective form of something outside the eye itself. But, in the act of seeing, there is at all events an actual passage of light from one thing to another, from the external object to the eye.—C.

SIMPLE REPRODUCTION
In the case of simple reproduction the surplus-value produced and realized annually, or periodically, if there are several turnovers during the year, is consumed individually, that is to say, unproductively, by its owner, the capitalist.—C. 2.

Apart from all accumulation, the mere continuity of the process of production, in other words, simple reproduction, sooner or later, and of necessity, converts every capital into accumulated capital, or capitalized surplus-value.—C. 1.

SKEPTICISM
The medical skepticism of the Parisian professors and students seems to be the order of the day.—Ltr. to Engels.

SLAVE CLASS
The worker gets the smallest and utterly indispensable part of the whole produce—as much, only, as is necessary for the propagation, not of humanity, but of the slave class of workers.—M.

SLAVE DEALER
The capitalist buys children and young persons under age. Pre-

viously, the workman sold his own labor power, which he disposed of nominally as a free agent. Now he sells wife and child. He has become a slave dealer.—C. 1.

SLAVE MARKET

The slave market maintains its supply of the commodity labor power by war, piracy, etc., and this rapine is not promoted by a process of circulation, but by the actual appropriation of the labor power of others by direct physical compulsion. Even in the United States, after the conversion of the buffer territory between the wage-labor states of the North and the slavery states of the South into a slave-breeding region for the South, where the slave thrown on the market thus became himself an element of the annual reproduction, this did not suffice for a long time, so that the African slave trade was continued as long as possible to satisfy the market.—C. 2.

SLAVERY

Slavery is an economic category as well as any other.—P. P.

Man has often made man himself, under the form of slaves, serve as the primitive material of money.—C. 1.

The purchase and sale of slaves is formally also a purchase and sale of commodities. But money cannot perform this function without the existence of slavery. If slavery exists, then money can be invested in the purchase of slaves. On the other hand, the mere possession of money cannot make slavery possible.—C. 2.

SLAVERY, BOURGEOIS

Direct slavery is the pivot of bourgeois industry as well as machinery, credit, etc. Without slavery you have no cotton, without cotton you cannot have modern industry. It is slavery which has given their value to the colonies, it is the colonies which have created the commerce in the world, it is the commerce of the world which is the essential condition of the great industry. Thus slavery is an economic category of the highest importance.
—P. P.

SLUMP

Whilst labor brings about the accumulation of capitals and with this the increasing prosperity of society, it renders the worker ever more dependent on the capitalist, leads him into competition of a new intensity, and drives him into the headlong rush of overproduction, with the subsequent corresponding slump.—M.

SMALL CAPITALIST
It is obvious that where industrial labor has reached a high level, and where therefore almost all manual labor has become factory-labor, the entire capital of a small capitalist does not suffice to provide him even with the necessary fixed capital.—M.

The small capitalist has the choice: (1) either to consume his capital, since he can no longer live on the interest—and thus cease to be a capitalist; or (2) to set up a business himself, sell his commodity cheaper, buy dearer than the wealthier capitalist, and pay increased wages—thus ruining himself, the market-price being already very low as a result of the intense competition presupposed.—M.

SMALL PROPERTY
While every social improvement benefits the big estate, it harms small property, because it increases its need for ready cash.—M.

SMITH, ADAM
Adam Smith, like all economists worth speaking of, takes over from the physiocrats the conception of the average wage, which he calls the natural price of wages.—C. 4.

Adam Smith discovered the division of labor.—P. P.

Engels was right to call Adam Smith the Luther of political economy.—M.

Adam Smith very acutely notes that the really great development of the productive power of labor starts only from the moment when it is transformed into wage-labor, and the conditions of labor confront it on the one hand as landed property and on the other as capital.—C. 4.

The capitalist, Adam Smith says, "could have no interest to employ the laborers, unless he expected from the sale of their work something more than what was sufficient to replace his stock to him."—C. 4.

Adam Smith's contradictions are of significance because they contain problems which it is true he does not solve, but which he reveals by contradicting himself. His correct insistence in this connection is best shown by the fact that his successors take opposing stands based on one aspect of his teaching or the other.—C. 4.

Adam's twistings and turnings, his contradictions and wanderings from the point, prove that, once he had made wages, profit and rent the constituent component parts of exchangeable value or of the total price of the market, he had got himself stuck in the mud and had to get stuck.—C. 4.

SOCIAL CONSCIOUSNESS
The social consciousness of past ages, despite all the multiplicity and variety it displays, moves within certain common forms, or general ideas, which cannot completely vanish except with the total disappearance of class antagonism.—C. M.

SOCIAL EVENTS
While every *social improvement* benefits the big estate, it harms small property.—M.

Man's reflections on the forms of *social life,* and consequently, also, his scientific analysis of those forms, take a course directly opposite to that of their actual historical development. He begins, post festum, with the results of the process of development ready to hand before him.—C. 1.

No *social order* ever perishes before all the productive forces for which there is room in it have developed; and new, higher relations of production never appear before the material conditions of their existence have matured in the womb of the old society.—P. E.

SOCIAL RANK
In the early epochs of history, we find almost everywhere a complicated arrangement of society into various orders, a mani-

fold graduation of social rank. In ancient Rome we have patricians, knights, plebeians, slaves; in the Middle Ages, feudal lords, vassals, guild-masters, journeymen, apprentices, serfs; in almost all of these classes, again, subordinate graduations.—C. M.

SOCIAL RELATIONS
In the social production of their life, men enter into definite relations that are indispensable and independent of their will.—P. E.

SOCIAL SCUM
The "dangerous class," the social scum, that passively rotting mass thrown off by the lowest layers of old society, may, here and there, be swept into the movement by a proletarian revolution; its conditions of life, however, prepare it far more for the part of a bribed tool of reactionary intrigue.—C. M.

SOCIALISM
A group of immature students and sophisticated doctors intend to instill a "higher ideal" objective to socialism, replacing its materialistic foundation by present-day mythology, especially by the goddesses of Justice, Freedom, Equality and Fraternity.—Ltr. to Sorge.

Socialism is man's positive self-consciousness, no longer mediated through the annulment of religion, just as real life is man's positive reality, no longer mediated through the annulment of private property, through communism.—M.

We have seen what significance, given socialism, the wealth of human needs has, and what significance, therefore, both a new mode of production and a new object of production have: a new manifestation of the forces of human nature and a new enrichment of human nature. Under private property their significance is reversed: every person speculates on creating a new need in another, so as to drive him to a fresh sacrifice, to place him in a new dependence and to seduce him into a new mode of gratification and therefore economic ruin.—M.

It will be seen how in place of the wealth and poverty of political economy come the rich human being and the rich human need. The rich human being is simultaneously the human being in need of a totality of human life-activities—the man in whom his own realization exists as an inner necessity, as need. Not only wealth, but likewise the poverty of man—given socialism—receives in equal measure a human and therefore social significance.—M.

SOCIALISM, BOURGEOIS

A part of the bourgeoisie is desirous of redressing social grievances, in order to secure the continued existence of bourgeois society. To this section belong economists, philanthropists, humanitarians, improvers of the condition of the working class, organizers of charity, members of societies for the prevention of cruelty to animals, temperance, fanatics, hole and corner reformers of every imaginable kind. This form of socialism has, moreover, been worked out into complete systems.—C. M.

The socialistic bourgeois want all the advantages of modern social conditions without the struggles and dangers necessarily resulting therefrom. They desire the existing state of society minus its revolutionary and disintegrating elements. They wish for a bourgeoisie without a proletariat.—C. M.

A more practical, but less systematic, form of bourgeois socialism sought to depreciate every revolutionary movement in the eyes of the working class, by showing that no mere political reform, but only a change in the material conditions of existence, in economic relations, could be of any advantage to them.—C. M.

In countries like France, where the peasants constitute far more than half of the population, it was natural that writers who sided with the proletariat against the bourgeoisie, should use, in their criticism of the bourgeois regime, the standard of the peasant and petty bourgeois, and from the standpoint of these intermediate classes should take up the cudgels for the working class. Thus arose the petty bourgeois socialism.—C. M.

SOCIALISM, CLERICAL

As the parson has ever gone hand in hand with the landlord, so has Clerical Socialism with Feudal Socialism.—C. M.

SOCIALISM, FEUDAL

Feudal socialism arose: half lamentation, half lampoon; half echo of the past, half menace of the future; at times, by its bitter, witty and incisive criticism, striking the bourgeoisie to the very heart's core, but always ludicrous in its effect, through total incapacity to comprehend the march of modern history.—C. M.

SOCIALISM, GERMAN
While this "true" (German) socialism thus served the government as a weapon for fighting the German bourgeoisie, it, at the same time, directly represented a reactionary interest, the interest of the German philistines.—C. M.

SOCIALISM, UTOPIAN
The utopian socialists reject all political, and especially all revolutionary, action; they wish to attain their ends by peaceful means, and endeavor, by small experiments, necessarily doomed to failure, and by the force of example, to pave the way for the new social Gospel.—C. M.

These proposals are of a purely utopian character. The significance of critical-utopian socialism and communism bears an inverse relation to historical development. In proportion as the modern class struggle develops and takes definite shape, this fantastic standing apart from the contest, these fantastic attacks on it lose all practical value and all theoretical justification. —C. M.

SOCIALIST GOVERNMENT
A socialist government can only gain power in a country when conditions are so that it can intimidate the bourgeoisie sufficiently.—Ltr. to Nieuwenhuis.

SOCIALIST MAN
Since for socialist man the entire so-called history of the world is nothing but the begetting of man through human labor, nothing but the coming-to-be of nature of man, he has the visible, irrefutable proof of his birth through himself, of his process of coming-to-be.—M.

SOCIALISTS
As the economists are the scientific representatives of the bourgeois class, so the socialists and communists are the theorists of the proletarian class.—P. P.

SOCIETY
If man is social by nature, he will develop his true nature only in society, and the power of his nature must be measured not by the power of separate individuals but by the power of society.—H. F.

Society itself—the fact that man lives in society and not as an independent, self-supporting individual—is the root of property, of the laws based on it and of the inevitable slavery.—C. 4.

The life-process of society, which is based on the process of material production, does not strip off its mystical veil until it is treated as production by freely associated men, and is consciously regulated by them in accordance with a settled plan. —C. 1.

SOCIETY, BOURGEOIS
Modern bourgeois society is divided into three great classes— capital, landed property, wage labor.—P. E.

SOCIETY, GROUNDWORK OF
A certain material groundwork of society or a set of conditions of existence are in their turn the spontaneous product of a long and painful process of development.—C. 1.

SOCIETY, HIGHER FORM OF
The capitalist creates those material conditions which alone can form the real basis of a higher form of society, a society in which the full and free development of every individual forms the ruling principle.—C. 1.

SOCRATES
Socrates may be called philosophy incarnate.—L. A.

SOIL
The soil (and this, economically speaking, includes water) in the virgin state in which it supplies man with necessaries or the means of subsistence ready to hand, exists independently of him, and is the universal subject of human labor.—C. 1.

SOIL, DETERIORATION OF
The greedy farmer snatches increased produce from the soil by robbing it of its fertility.—C. 1.

SOLDIER

Smith would say that the soldier's protective care is productive of defense, but not of the corn. If order was restored in the country, the ploughman would produce the corn just as before, without being compelled to produce the maintenance, and therefore the life, of the soldier into the bargain. The soldier belongs to the incidental expenses of production, in the same way as a large part of the unproductive laborers who produce nothing themselves, either spiritual or material, but who are useful and necessary only because of the faulty social relations—they owe their existence to social evils.—C. 4.

SOLVING AN EQUATION

An equation can only be solved when the elements to its solution are given.—Ltr. to Nieuwenhuis.

SOPHISTICATION

I am to blame for Proudhon's "sophistication," as the English denote the adulteration of commercial goods.—Ltr. to Schweitzer.

SOUTH AMERICANS

The brutal South Americans force their laborers to take the more substantial, rather than the less substantial, kind of food.—C. 1.

SPARTACUS

Spartacus appears as the most superb man in the whole history of antiquity.—Ltr. to Engels.

SPECIES, LIFE OF THE

The life of the species both in man and in animals, consists physically in the fact that man (like the animal) lives on inorganic nature; and the more universal man is compared with an animal, the more universal is the sphere of inorganic nature on which he lives.—M.

SPECULATION

At a certain high point the increasing concentration of capital in its turn causes a new fall in the rate of profit. The mass of small dispersed capitals is thereby driven along the adventurous road of speculation, credit frauds, stock swindles, and crises. —C. 3.

Speculation can withdraw masses of capital from one zone of business with extraordinary rapidity and throw them with equal rapidity into another. Yet with respect to each sphere of actual production—industry, agriculture, mining, etc.—the transfer of capital from one sphere to another offers considerable difficulties. —C. 3.

SPINNING MACHINE
A spinning machine has no use-value unless it is used for spinning, unless therefore it functions as a fixed component part of a productive capital. But a spinning machine is movable. It may be exported from the country in which it was produced and sold abroad directly or indirectly for raw materials, etc., or for champagne.—C. 2.

SPIRITUAL SUPERSTRUCTURE (UEBERBAU)
From the specific form of material production arises in the first place a specific (ideological super-) structure of society, in the second place a specific relation of men to nature. Their state and their spiritual outlook is determined by both. Therefore also the kind of their spiritual production.—C. 4.

SPONTANEOUS ACTIVITY
The worker's activity is not his spontaneous activity. It belongs to another; it is the loss of his self.—M.

Generatio aequivoca (spontaneous generation) is the only practical refutation of the theory of creation.—M.

STAGNANT SURPLUS POPULATION
The stagnant surplus population is characterized by maximum of working time, and minimum of wages.—C. 1.

STATE
Political economy in its classical period, like the bourgeoisie itself in its parvenu period, adopted a severely critical attitude to the machinery of the state, etc. At a later stage it realized and —as was shown too in practice—learnt from experience that the necessity for the inherited social combination of all these classes, which in part were totally unproductive, arose from its own organization.—C. 4.

The state is only justified insofar as it is a committee to administer the common interests of the productive bourgeoisie.—M.

In the *state*, where man counts merely as one of his kind, he is an imaginary link in an imagined chain of sovereignty, robbed of his individual life and endowed with an unreal generality.—J. Q.

STATE, BOURGEOIS
The perfect political state by its nature defines the life of man as of a particular kind, in opposition to his material life. In bourgeois society all the assumptions of this self-centered material life remain outside the sphere of the state.—J. Q.

STATE, CHRISTIAN
The so-called Christian state is a Christian denial of the state, not in any way the political fulfillment of Christianity. The state that continues to profess Christianity as a religion does not yet profess it in political form because it still behaves religiously toward religion. This means that it is not a genuine fulfillment of the human basis of religion, because it is still the product of unreality, of the imaginary shape of the human nucleus. The so-called Christian state is the imperfect state, and it treats Christianity as a supplementation and sanctification of its imperfection. It treats religion as a means to an end and becomes thereby hypocritical.—J. Q.

STATE, MODERN
Whereas the earlier teachers of state law construed the state out of ambition or sociability, or even reason, though not out of the reason of society but rather out of the reason of the individual, the more ideal and profound view of modern philosophy construes it out of the idea of the whole.—L. A.

STATE, RELIGIOUS
The truly religious state is the theocratic state.—L. A.

STATE AND RELIGION
Once the state includes several confessions with equal rights it cannot be a religious state without violating particular confessions; it cannot be a church which condemns adherents of another confession as heretics, which makes every piece of

bread dependent on faith, which makes dogma the link between separate individuals and existence as citizens of the state.—L. A.

The point here is not whether the state should be philosophized about, but whether it should be philosophized about well or badly, philosophically or unphilosophically, with prejudice or without, with consciousness or without, consistently or inconsistently, in a completely rational or half rational way. If you make religion a theory of state right, then you make religion itself a kind of philosophy.—L. A.

STATISTICS
Statistics is not able to make actual analyses of the rates of wages in different epochs and countries, until the conditions which shape the rate of profit are thoroughly understood. The rate of profit does not fall because labor becomes less productive, but because it becomes more productive. Both the rise in the rate of surplus-value and the fall in the rate of profit are but specific forms through which growing productivity of labor is expressed under capitalism.—C. 3.

STEAM
Steam and machinery revolutionized industrial production.—C. M.

STEEL RAILS
About 1867 began the introduction of *steel rails,* which cost about twice as much as iron rails but which last more than twice as long.—C. 2.

STIMULATION OF DEMAND
Under private property, every person speculates on creating a new need in another, so as to place him in a new dependence.—M.

STOCK EXCHANGE
Now you are a member of the stock exchange, and altogether respectable. My gratulations. I would like to hear you once howl among these wolves.—Ltr. to Engels.

STOCKS
Stock is called capital only when it yields to its owner a revenue or profit.—M.

STORAGE
The abidance of the commodity-capital as a commodity-supply in the market requires buildings, stores, storage places, warehouses, in other words, an expenditure of constant capital; furthermore the payment of labor power for placing the commodities in storage. Besides, commodities spoil and are exposed to the injurious influences of the elements.—C. 2.

STORCH
According to Storch, the physician produces health (but also illness), professors and writers produce enlightenment (but also obscurantism), poets, painters, etc., produce good taste (but also bad taste), moralists, etc., produce morals, preachers religion, the sovereigns labor security, and so on. It can just as well be said that illness produces physicians, stupidity produces professors and writers, lack of taste poets and painters, immorality moralists, superstition preachers and general insecurity produces the sovereign.—C. 4.

With *Storch* himself the theory of civilization does not get beyond trivial phrases, although some ingenious observations slip in here and there—for example, that the material division of labor is the precondition for the division of intellectual labor. How much it was inevitable that Storch could not get beyond trivial phrases, how little he had even formulated for himself the task, let alone its solution, is apparent.—C. 4.

STRATEGY
Concentration is the secret of strategy.—D. T.

STRIKES
Strikes have regularly given rise to invention and to the application of new machinery. Machines were, we might say, the arms which the capitalists used to defeat revolted labor.—P. P.

STRUGGLE, PROLETARIAN
The worker has to struggle not only for his physical means of subsistence: he has to struggle to get work, i.e., the possibility, the means, to perform his activity.—M.

SUBSISTENCE, MEANS OF
A quantum of the means of subsistence is absolutely requisite to keep the laborer in bare existence.—C. M.

For his maintenance the individual requires a given quantity of the means of subsistence. Therefore the labor-time requisite for the production of labor power reduces itself to that necessary for the production of those means of subsistence; in other words, the value of labor power is the value of the means of subsistence necessary for the maintenance of the laborer.—C. 1.

SUFFERING
Suffering, apprehended humanly, is an enjoyment of self in man.—M.

In general it has to be observed that in those cases where worker and capitalist equally suffer, the worker suffers in his very existence, the capitalist in the profit on his dead mammon.—M. You have been told that the sufferings of this life are not to be compared with the bliss of the future, that suffering in patience and the bliss of hope are cardinal virtues.—L. A.

SUN
The sun is the object of the plant—an indispensable object to it, confirming its life—just as the plant is an object of the sun, being an expression of the life-awakening power of the sun, of the sun's objective essential power.—M.

SUPERINTENDENCE
When comparing the mode of production of isolated peasants and artisans with production by slave labor the political economist counts this labor of superintendence among the *faux frais* of production. But, when considering the capitalist mode of production, he, on the contrary, treats the work of control made necessary by the cooperative character of the labor-process as identical with the different work of control necessitated by the capitalist character of that process.—C. 1.

The work of directing, *superintending*, and adjusting becomes one of the functions of capital, from the moment that the labor under the control of capital becomes cooperative.—C. 1.

SUPERIORITY, SOCIOLOGICAL
The landowner and the capitalist are everywhere superior to the worker and lay down the law to him.—M.

SUPERSEDING
A peculiar role is played by the act of superseding in which denial and preservation—denial and affirmation—are bound together.—M.

SUPERSTITION
It is not by atheism but by superstition and idolatry that man debases himself.—H. F.

SUPERSTRUCTURE, FINANCIAL
In the time of Louis XIV and Louis XV the financial, commercial, and industrial superstructure looked like a satire upon the miserable state of the agricultural production.—Ltr. to Danielson.

SUPERSTRUCTURE, LEGAL AND POLITICAL
The sum total of the social relations of the material production constitutes the economic (under-) structure (*Unterbau*) of society, the real foundation, on which rises a legal and political superstructure and to which correspond definite forms of social consciousness. The mode of production of material life conditions the social, political and intellectual life process in general. It is not the consciousness of men that determines their being, but, on the contrary, their social being that determines their consciousness. . . . With the change of the economic relations the entire immense superstructure (*Ueberbau*) is more or less rapidly transformed.—P. E.

SUPERVISION
The capitalist mode of production has been brought to a point where the work of supervision, entirely divorced from the ownership of capital, is always readily obtainable. It has, therefore, come to be useless for the capitalist to perform it himself.—C. 3.

Aristotle says that supremacy in the political and economic fields imposes the functions of government upon the ruling powers, and hence that they must, in the economic field, know the art of consuming labor power. And he adds that this supervisory work is not a matter of great moment and that for this reason the master leaves the "honor" of this drudgery to an overseer as soon as he can afford it.—C. 3.

SUPPLY AND DEMAND

In a final analysis, supply and demand bring together production and consumption, but production and consumption based upon individual exchanges.—P. P.

Supply and demand coincide when their mutual proportions are such that the mass of commodities of a definite line of production can be sold at their market-value, neither above nor below it. That is the first thing we hear.—C. 3.

The smaller the supply relatively to the demand, the higher the exchange-value or the price of the product rises.—P. P.

Supply and demand determine the market-price, and so does the market-price, and the market-value in the further analysis, determine supply and demand. This is obvious in the case of demand, since it moves in a direction opposite to prices, swelling when prices fall, and vice versa. But this is also true of supply. Because the prices of means of production incorporated in the offered commodities determine the demand for these means of production, and thus the supply of commodities whose supply embraces the demand for these means of production.—C. 3.

If supply and demand balance one another, they cease to explain anything, do not affect market-values, and therefore leave us so much more in the dark about the reasons why the market-value is expressed in just this sum of money and no other. It is evident that the real inner laws of capitalist production cannot be explained by the interaction of supply and demand, because these laws cannot be observed in their pure state, until supply and demand cease to act, i.e., are equated.—C. 3.

If the demand, and consequently the market-price, falls, capital may be withdrawn, thus causing supply to shrink. Conversely, if the demand increases, and consequently the market-price rises above the market-value, this may lead to too much capital flowing into this line of production and production may swell to such an extent that the market price will even fall below the market-value.—C. 3.

When political economy claims that demand and supply always balance each other, it immediately forgets that according to its own claim (theory of population) the supply of people always exceeds the demand, and that, therefore, in the essential result of the whole production process—the existence of man—the disparity between demand and supply gets its most striking expression.—M.

If demand and supply balance, the oscillation of prices ceases, all other conditions remaining the same. But then demand and supply also cease to explain anything.—C. 1.

It is the variations of demand and supply which fix for the producer the quantity in which it is necessary to produce a given product in order to get in exchange at least the cost of production.—P. P.

SUPPORT, BOURGEOIS
The bourgeoisie itself supplies the proletariat with its own elements of political and general education, in other words, it furnishes the proletariat with the weapons for fighting the bourgeoisie.—C. M.

SURPLUS LABOR
The productivity of capital consists in the first instance in the compulsion to perform *surplus-labor;* a compulsion which the capitalist mode of production shares with earlier modes of production, but which it exercises in a manner more favorable to production.—C. 4.

SURPLUS LABOR TIME
That part of the working day in which the workman's labor, being no longer necessary labor, creates no value for himself, but creates surplus value for the capitalist, I name surplus labor time, and to the labor expended during that time I give the name surplus labor.—C. 1.

SURPLUS-PRODUCE
The portion of the product that represents the surplus-value, we call "surplus-produce."—C. 1.

The action of labor power not only reproduces its own value, but produces value over and above it. This surplus value is the difference between the value of the product and the value of the elements consumed in the formation of that product, in other words, of the means of production and the labor power.—C. 1.

SURPLUS VALUE
The workman creates surplus value which, for the capitalist, has all the charms of a creation out of nothing. This portion of the working day, I name surplus labor-time, and to the labor expended during that time, I give the name of surplus-labor. —C. 1.

The creation of surplus value, and therefore the conversion of money into capital, can . . . be explained neither on the assumption that commodities are above their value, nor that they are bought below their value.—C. 1.

The aim of the capitalist is to produce not only value, but at the same time surplus value.—C. 1.

The value of a commodity is, in itself, of no interest to the capitalist. What alone interests him, is the *surplus value* that dwells in it, and is realizable by sale. Realization of the surplus value necessarily carries with it the refunding of the value that was advanced.—C. 1.

SUSTENANCE, HUMAN
Physically man lives on the products of nature, whether they appear in the form of food, heating, clothes, a dwelling, or whatever it may be. The universality of man is in practice manifested precisely in the universality which makes all nature his inorganic body—both inasmuch as nature is (1) his direct means of life, and (2) the material, the object, and the instrument of his life activity.—M.

SYNTHESIS
We have the thesis, the antithesis and the synthesis.—P. P.

T

TASKS
Mankind always sets itself only such tasks as it can solve; since, looking at the matter more closely, it will always be found that the task itself arises only when the material conditions for its solution already exist or are at least in the process of formation.—P. O.

TECHNOLOGY
Technology discloses man's mode of dealing with nature, the process of production by which he sustains his life, and thereby also lays bare the mode of formation of his social relations, and of the mental conceptions that flow from them.—C. 1.

THEOLOGIAN, CRITICAL
Even the critical theologian remains a theologian. Hence, either he had to start from certain presuppositions of philosophy accepted as authoritative; or if in the process of criticism and as a result of other people's discoveries doubts about these philosophical presuppositions have risen in him, he abandons them without vindication and in a cowardly fashion, abstracts from them showing his servile dependence on these presuppositions and his resentment at this dependence merely in a negative, unconscious and sophistical manner.—M.

Whenever discoveries (such as Feuerbach's) are made about the nature of his own philosophic presuppositions the critical theologian partly makes it appear as if he were the one who had accomplished this, producing that appearance by taking the results of these discoveries and, without being able to develop them, hurling them in the form of catch-phrases at writers still caught in the confines of philosophy; partly he even manages to acquire a sense of his own superiority to such discoveries by covertly asserting in a veiled, malicious and skeptical fashion elements of the Hegelian dialectic.—M.

To the theological critic is seems quite natural that everything has to be done by philosophy, so that he can chatter away about purity, resoluteness, and utterly critical criticism; and he fancies himself the true conqueror of philosophy.—M.

The critical theologian is either forever repeating assurances about the purity of his own criticism, or tries to make it seem as though all that was left for criticism to deal with now was some other immature form of criticism outside itself—say eighteenth-century criticism—and the backwardness of the masses, in order to divert the observer's attention as well as his own from the necessary task of settling accounts between criticism and its point of departure.—M.

THEOLOGY
Theology explains the origin of evil by the fall of man: that is, it assumes as a fact, in historical form, what has to be explained. —M.

The justice in history assigns to theology, ever philosophy's spot of infection, the role of portraying in itself the negative dissolution of philosophy—i.e., the process of its decay.—M.

THEOLOGY, PROTESTANT
There are conclusive proofs that the hatred of the Protestant theology for philosophers arises largely out of philosophy's tolerance toward the particular confession as such.—L. A.

THEORETIC NOTIONS
For the mass of human beings, i.e., for the proletariat, these theoretic notions do not exist and therefore do not need to be dissolved and if ever this mass has any such notions, e.g., religion, they have been dissolved long ago by circumstances.—G. I.

THEORY
Theory is fulfilled in a people only insofar as it is the fulfillment of the needs of that people.—C. C.

Theory is capable of gripping the masses as soon as it demonstrates *ad hominem*, and it demonstrates *ad hominem* as soon as it becomes radical.—C. C.

THINGHOOD
Because man equals self-consciousness, his alienated, objective essence, or thinghood, equals alienated self-consciousness, and thinghood is thus established through this alienation (thinghood being that which is an object for man and an object for him is really only that which is to him an essential object, therefore his objective essence).—M.

THINKING
Thinking and being are no doubt distinct, but at the same time they are in unity with each other.—M.

THOUGHT ENTITIES
The humanness of man's products appears in the form that they are products of abstract mind and as such phases of mind—thought entities.—M.

TIME
Time is everything, man is nothing; he is no more than the carcass of time.—P. P.

TIME-WAGES
The unit measure for time-wages, the price of the working hour, is the quotient of the value of a day's labor power, divided by the number of hours of the average working day.—C. 1.

TIMES, THE
The frantic roars of the "bloody old *Times*," as Cobbett used to call it—its playing the part of a furious character in one of Mozart's operas, who indulges in most melodius strains in the idea of first hanging his enemy, then roasting him, then quartering him, then spitting him, and then flaying him alive—its

tearing the passion of revenge to tatters and to rags—all this would appear but silly if under the pathos of tragedy there were not distinctly perceptible the tricks of comedy.—D. T.

TOIL, BURDEN OF
In proportion as the use of machinery and division of labor increases, in the same proportion the burden of toil also increases, whether by prolongation of the working hours, by increase of the work enacted in a given time, or by increased speed of the machinery, etc.—C. M.

TOOLS
The tool is not exterminated by the machine.—C. I.

The productiveness of labor depends not only on the proficiency of the workman, but on the perfection of his tools.—C. 1.

Tools of the same kind, such as knives, drills, gimlets, hammers, etc., may be employed in different processes; and the same tool may serve various purposes in a single process.—C. 1.

In handicrafts and manufacture, the workman makes use of a tool, in the factory tools make use of him.—C. 1.

TORTURE
With Hindus, whom their religion has made virtuosi in the art of self-torturing, the tortures of the sepoys inflicted on the enemies of their race and creed appear quite natural, and must appear still more so to the English, who, only some years since, still used to draw revenues from the Juggernaut festivals, protecting and assisting the bloody rites of a religion of cruelty. —D. T.

However infamous the conduct of the sepoys, it is only the reflex, in a concentrated form, of England's own conduct in India, not only during the epoch of the foundation of her Eastern Empire, but even during the last ten years of a long-settled rule. To characterize that rule, it suffices to say that torture formed an organic institution of its financial policy. There is something in human history like retribution; and it is a rule of historical retribution that its instrument be forged not by the offended, but by the offender himself.—D.T.

TOTAL PRODUCT
The total product of our community is a social product. One portion serves as fresh means of production and remains social. But another portion is consumed by the members as means of subsistence.—C. 1.

TOTALITY
Man, much as he may be a particular individual (and it is precisely his particularity which makes him an individual, and a real individual social being), is just as much the totality—the ideal totality—the subjective existence of thought and experienced society present for itself just as he exists also in the real world as the awareness and the real enjoyment of social existence, and as a totality of human life activity.—M.

TOWNS, DEVELOPMENT OF
The leaning of commerce toward the development of towns, and, on the other hand, the dependence of towns upon commerce, are natural. However, it depends on altogether different circumstances to what measure industrial development will go hand in hand with this development.—C. 3.

TRADE
Whatever is true of foreign trade, is also true of home trade.—C. 3.

TRADE UNIONS
Trade unions work well as centers of resistance against the encroachments of capital. They fail partially from an injudicious use of their power. They fail generally from limiting themselves to a guerrilla war against the effects of the existing system, instead of simultaneously trying to change it, instead of using their organized forces as a lever for the final emancipation of the working class, that is to say, the ultimate abolition of the wage system.—A.

The workers begin to form combinations (trade unions) against the bourgeoisie; they club together in order to keep up the rate of wages; they found permanent associations in order to make provision beforehand for occasional revolts.—C. M.

TRADING NATIONS
Trading nations, properly so called, existed in the ancient world only in its interstices.—C. 1.

TRADITION
The tradition of all past generations weighs like a nightmare upon the brain of the living.—E. B.

TRAFFIC FACILITIES
Particularly great traffic facilities and the resultant acceleration of the capital turnover (since it is conditional on the time of circulation) give rise to quicker concentration of both the centers of production and the markets.—C. 2.

TRAINING, INDUSTRIAL
In order to modify the human organism, so that it may acquire skill and handiness in a given branch of industry, and become labor power of a special kind, a special education or training is requisite.—C. 1.

TRANSFORMATION, ECONOMIC
The transformation of scattered private property, arising from individual labor, into capitalist private property is, naturally, a process, incomparably more protracted, violent, and difficult, than the transformation of capitalistic private property into socialized property. In the former case, we had the expropriation of the mass of the people by a few usurpers; in the latter, we have the expropriation of a few usurpers by the mass of the people.—C. 1.

TRANSFORMATION, IDEOLOGICAL
We cannot judge of a period of ideological transformation by its own consciousness; on the contrary, this consciousness must be explained rather from the contradictions of material life, from the existing conflict between the social productive forces and the relations of production.—P. E.

TRANSFORMATIONS, CAPITALIST
With the transformation of the slave into a free worker, the landlord himself is transformed into a captain of industry.—M.

TRANSITORY
Everything is transitory.—C. 3.

TRANSPORT
With the development of *transport facilities* not only is the

velocity of movement in space accelerated and thereby the geographic distance shortened in terms of time. Not only is there a development of the mass of communication facilities so that for instance many vessels sail simultaneously for the same port, or several trains travel simultaneously on different railways between the same two points, but freight vessels may clear on consecutive days of the same week from Liverpool for New York, or goods trains may start at different hours of the same day from Manchester to London.—C. 2.

TRANSPORT INDUSTRY

Quantities of products are not increased by transportation. Nor, with a few exceptions, is the possible alteration of their natural qualities brought about by transportation, an intentional useful effect; it is rather an unavoidable evil. But the use-value of things is materialized only in their consumption, and their consumption may necessitate a change of location of these things, hence may require an additional process of production, in the transport industry. The productive capital invested in this industry imparts value to the transported products.—C. 2.

What the transportation industry sells is change of location. The useful effect is inseparably connected with the process of transportation, i.e., the productive process of the transport industry. Men and goods travel together with the means of transportation, and this traveling, this locomotion, constitutes the process of production effected by these means.—C. 1.

TRINITY FORMULA

Capital—profit (profit of enterprise plus interest); land—ground-rent; labor—wages; this is the trinity formula which comprises all the secrets of the social production process. This trinity formula reduces itself more specifically to the following: Capital—interest, land—ground-rent, labor—wages, where profit, the specific characteristic form of surplus-value belonging to the capitalist mode of production, is fortunately eliminated.—C. 3.

TRUST

You can exchange trust only for trust.—M.

TRUTH

Is there not a universal human nature just as there is a universal nature of plants and heavenly bodies? Philosophy asks what is true, not what is acknowledged as such, what is true for *all* men, not what is true for individuals: philosophy's metaphysical truths do not know the boundaries of political geography: its political truths know too well where the "boundaries" begin to confuse the illusory horizon of a particular world and national outlooks with the true horizon of the human mind.—L. A.

TURKS
The courageous Turks have accelerated the revolutionary explosion by inflicting great damage to the name of the Russian dynasty as well as to the Russian army and Russian finances.—Ltr. to Sorge.

TURNCOAT, BOURGEOIS
In times when the class struggle nears the decisive hour, the process of dissolution going on within the ruling class, in fact, within the whole range of old society, assumes such a violent, glaring character, that a small section of the ruling class cuts itself adrift, and joins the revolutionary class.—C. M.

TURNOVER OF CAPITAL
The turnover of the fixed component part of capital, and therefore also the time of turnover necessary for it, comprises several turnovers of the circulating constituents of capital. In the time during which the fixed capital turns over once, the circulating capital turns over several times.—C. 2.

TWO CLASSES
The final consequence is the abolishment of the distinction between capitalist and landowner, so that there remain altogether only two classes of the population—the working class and the class of the capitalists. This huckstering with landed property, the transformation of landed property into a commodity, constitutes the final overthow of the old and the final consummation of the money aristocracy.—M.

U

UNDERSTRUCTURE *(UNTERBAU)*, MATERIAL
History does not end by dissolving itself in "self-consciousness" as "the spirit of the spirit," but there is present in it at every stage a material result, a sum of production forces.—G. I.

UNEMPLOYED
They stand at opposite poles—unemployed capital at one pole and unemployed worker population at the other.—C. 3.

Political economy does not recognize the unoccupied workers, the workman insofar as he happens to be outside this labor-relationship. The cheat-thief, swindler, beggar, and unemployed man; the starving, wretched and criminal workingman—these are figures who do not exist for political economy but only for other eyes, those of the doctor, the judge, the gravedigger and bumbailiff, etc.; such figures are specters outside the domain of political economy.—M.

UNEMPLOYMENT
The whole form of the movement of modern industry depends upon the constant transformation of a part of the laboring population into unemployed or half employed hands.—C. 1.

A glaring contradiction—there is a complaint of the want of hands, while at the same time many thousands are out of work, because the division of labor chains them to a particular branch of industry.—C. 1.

UNFITNESS, BOURGEOIS
The bourgeoisie is unfit any longer to be the ruling class in so-

ciety, and to impose its conditions of existence upon society as an overriding law. It is unfit to rule, because it is incompetent to assure an existence to its slave within his slavery, because it cannot help letting him sink into a state that it has to feed him, instead of being fed by him. Society can no longer live under this bourgeoisie, in other words, its existence is no longer compatible with society.—C. M.

UNHAPPINESS
Since a society is not happy of which the greater part suffers—yet even the wealthiest state of society leads to the suffering of the majority—and since the economic system (and in general a society based on private property) leads to this wealthiest condition, it follows that the goal of the economic system is the unhappiness of society.—M.

UNION OF WORKERS
Now and then the workers are victorious, but only for a time. The real fruits of their battles lie, not in the immediate result, but in the ever expanding union of the workers. This union is helped on by the improved means of communication that are created by modern industry, and that place the workers of different localities in contact with one another. It was just this contact that was needed to centralize the numerous local struggles, all of the same character, into one national struggle between classes.—C. M.

UNITED ACTION
United action, of the leading civilized countries at least, is one of the first conditions for the emancipation of the proletariat.—C. M.

UNITED STATES
The United States have now surpassed England in the rapidity of economic progress.—Ltr. to Danielson.

That the bourgeois society in the United States has not yet developed far enough to render the class struggle evident and understandable is most noticeably shown by C. H. Carey, the only American economist of repute.—Ltr. to Weydemeyer.

UNITED STATES AND RUSSIA
It is difficult to draw an analogy between the United States and

Russia. In the former the governmental expenses decrease daily and the public debt diminishes yearly; in the latter public bankruptcy seems to be inevitable. The former has liberated itself from pure paper money, while the latter has nothing better than paper money. The former again, shows an unprecedented industrial development, while the latter reverts itself to the time of Louis XIV and Louis XV.—Ltr. to Danielson.

UNITED STATES RAILWAYS
The railways of the United States were presented by the government not only with land necessary for their construction, but also with large stretches of property adjoining both sides of the tracks. The railways thus became great landowners, while the small immigrant farmers settled near them, so as to secure good transportation for their produce.—Ltr. to Danielson.

UNITY
The communist organization turns existing conditions into conditions of (centralized) unity.—G. I.

UNIVERSALITY OF MAN
The universality of man is in practice manifested precisely in the universality which makes all nature his inorganic body—both inasmuch as nature is (1) his direct means of life, and (2) the material, the object, and the instrument of his life activity.—M.

UNPAID LABOR
There is not one single atom of capitalist value that does not owe its existence to unpaid labor.—C. 1.

UNPRODUCTIVE LABOR
The largest part of society, that is to say the working class, must perform this kind of labor for itself; but it is only able to perform it when it has labored "productively." It can only cook meat for itself when it has produced a wage with which to pay for the meat; and it can only keep its furniture and dwellings clean, it can only polish its boots, when it has produced the value of furniture, house rent and boots. To this class of productive laborers itself, therefore, the labor which they perform for themselves appears as "unproductive labor." This unproductive labor never enables them to repeat the same unproductive labor a second time unless they have previously labored productively.—C. 4.

To the extent that capital conquers the whole of production, and therefore the home and petty form of industry—in short, industry intended for self-consumption, not producing commodities—disappears, it is clear that the *unproductive laborers*, those whose services are directly exchanged against revenue, will for the most part be performing only *personal* services, and only an inconsiderable part of them (like cooks, seamstresses, jobbing tailors and so on) will produce material use-values.—C. 4.

UNPRODUCTIVITY
How very unproductive, from the standpoint of capitalist production, the laborer is who indeed produces vendible commodities, but only to the amount equivalent to his own laborpower, and therefore produces no surplus-value for capital—can be seen from the passages in Ricardo saying that the very existence of such people is a nuisance. This is the theory and practice of capital.—C. 4.

Is it not a contradiction that the "violin maker, the organ builder, the music dealer, the mechanic, etc.," are productive, and the professions for which these labors are only "preparations" are unproductive?—C. 4.

UNSKILLED LABOR
A commodity may be the product of the most skilled labor, but its value, by equating it to the product of simple unskilled labor, represents a definite quality of the latter labor alone. The different proportions in which different sorts of labor are reduced to unskilled labor as their standard are established by a social process that goes on behind the backs of the producers, and, consequently, appear to be fixed by custom.—C. 1.

URBANIZATION, BOURGEOIS
The bourgeoisie has subjected the country to the rule of the towns. It has created enormous cities, has greatly increased the urban population as compared with the rural, and has thus rescued a considerable part of the population from the idiocy of rural life.—C. M.

USE
Use determines a thing's value.—M.

The use of products is determined by the social conditions in which the consumers are placed, and these conditions themselves rest on the antagonism of classes.—P. P.

USE-VALUE
Use-values become a reality only by use or consumption: they also constitute the substance of all wealth, whatever may be the social form of that wealth.—C. 1.

A commodity, such as iron, corn, or a diamond, is, so far as it is a material thing, a use-value, something useful. This property of a commodity is independent of the amount of labor required to appropriate its useful qualities.—C. 1.

USELESS POPULATION
Production of too many useful things produces too large a useless population.—M.

USURER
Hoarding necessarily appears along with money. But the professional hoarder does not become important until he is transformed into a usurer.—C. 3.

USURER'S CAPITAL
Interest-bearing capital, or, as we may call it in its antiquated form, usurer's capital, belongs together with its twin brother, merchant's capital, to the antediluvian forms of capital, which long precede the capitalist mode of production and are to be found in the most diverse economic formations of society.—C. 3.

USURY
Usury centralizes money wealth where the means of production are dispersed. It does not alter the mode of production, but attaches itself firmly to it like a parasite and makes it wretched. It sucks out its blood, enervates it and compels reproduction to proceed under ever more pitiable conditions. Hence the popular hatred against usurers, which was most pronounced in the ancient world where ownership of means of production by the producer himself was at the same time the basis for political status, the independence of the citizen.—C. 3.

UTILITY
Nothing can have value, without being an object of utility. If the

thing is useless, so is the labor contained in it; the labor does not count as labor, and therefore creates no value.—C. 1.

Value exists only in articles of *utility*, in objects: we leave out of consideration its purely symbolical representation by tokens. If therefore an article loses its utility, it also loses its value.—C. 1.

The utility of a thing makes it a use-value. But this utility is not a thing of air. Being limited by the physical properties of the commodity, it has no existence apart from that commodity.—C. 1.

The product offered is not utility in itself.—P. P.

UTOPIAN SOCIALISTS

Future history resolves itself, in their eyes, into the propaganda and the practical carrying out of their social plans.—C. M.

Such fantastic pictures of future society, painted at a time when the proletariat is still in a very undeveloped state, and has but a fantastic conception of its own position, correspond with the first instinctive yearnings of that class for a general reconstruction of society.—C. M.

V

VALUE
Value is the cornerstone of the economic edifice.—P. P.

The transformation of values into prices of production serves to obscure the basis for determining value itself.—C. 3.

VALUE OF LABOR
In the expression "value of labor," the idea of value is not only completely obliterated, but actually reversed. It is an expression as imaginary as the value of the earth. These imaginary expressions, arise, however, from the relations of production themselves. They are categories for the phenomenal forms of essential relations.—C. 1.

VARIABLE CAPITAL
That part of capital, represented by laborpower, does, in the process of production, undergo an alteration of value. It both reproduces the equivalent of its own value, and also produces an excess, a surplus-value, which may itself vary, may be more or less according to circumstances. This part of capital is continually being transformed from a constant into a variable magnitude. I therefore call it the variable part of capital or, shortly, variable capital.—C. 1.

VICE
The interest obtained from the vices of the ruined proletarians stands in inverse proportion to it. (Prostitution, drunkenness, the pawnbroker.)—M.

VILLAGE SYSTEM
Village communities were found to be, or to have been, the

primitive form of society everywhere from India to Ireland. The inner organization of this primitive communistic society was laid bare, in its typical form, by Morgan's crowning discovery of the true nature of the gens and its relation to the tribe. With the dissolution of these primeval communities society begins to be differentiated into separate and finally antagonistic classes.—C. M.

The so-called village system gave to each of the small Hindu unions their independent organization and distinct life.—D. T.

VULGAR ECONOMICS

Vulgar economy actually does no more than interpret, systematize and defend in doctrinaire fashion the conceptions of the agents of bourgeois production who are entrapped in bourgeois production relations. It should not astonish us, then, that vulgar economy feels particularly at home in the estranged outward appearances of economic relations in which these prima facie absurd and perfect contradictions appear and that these relations seem the more self-evident the more their internal relations are concealed from it, although they are understandable to the popular mind. But all science would be superfluous if the outward appearance and the essence of things directly coincided.—C. 3.

The vulgar economist does practically no more than translate the singular concepts of the capitalists, who are in the thrall of competition, into a seemingly more theoretical and generalized language, and attempt to substantiate the justice of those conceptions.—C. 3.

W

WAGE FLUCTUATION
The growing competition among the bourgeoisie, and the resulting commercial crisis, make the wages of the workers ever more fluctuating.—C. M.

WAGE-LABOR
The condition of capital is wage-labor. Wage-labor rests exclusively on competition between the laborers.—C. M.

The average price of wage-labor is the minimum wage, i.e., that quantum of the means of subsistence which is absolutely requisite to keep the laborer in bare existence as a laborer. What, therefore, the wage-laborer appropriates by means of his labor, merely suffices to prolong and reproduce a bare existence.—C. M.

WAGES
What are wages? They are the value of labor.—P. P.

Wages rise with the rising prices of the necessities of life. Wage advances are the consequence, not the cause, of advances in the prices of commodities.—C. 2.

According to the dogma of the economists, wages rise in consequence of accumulation of capital.—C. 1.

A forcing up of wages (disregarding all other difficulties, including the fact that it would only be by force, too, that the higher wages, being an anomaly, could be maintained) would therefore be nothing but better payment for the slave, and would not conquer either for the worker or for labor their human status and dignity.—M.

Taking them as a whole, the general movements of wages are exclusively regulated by the expansion and contraction of the industrial reserve army, and these again correspond to the periodic changes of the industrial cycle. They are, therefore, not determined by the variations of the absolute number of the working population, but by the varying proportions in which the working class is divided into active and reserve army, by the increase of diminution in the relative amount of the surplus population, by the extent to which it is now absorbed, now set free.—C. 1.

As the repulsiveness of the work increases, the wage decreases.—C. M.

Wages are determined through the antagonistic struggle between capitalist and worker. Victory goes necessarily to the capitalist. The capitalist can live longer without the worker than can the worker without the capitalist.—M.

An orchestra conductor need not own the instruments of his orchestra, nor is it within the scope of his duties as conductor to have anything to do with the "wages" of the other musicians.—C. 3.

WAGES, LAW OF

The higher wages stimulate the working population to more rapid multiplication, and this goes on until the labor market becomes too full, and therefore capital, relative to the supply of labor, becomes insufficient. Wages fall, and now we have the reverse of the medal. The working population is little by little decimated as the result of the fall in wages, so that capital is again in excess relative to them, or, as others explain it, falling wages and the corresponding increase in the exploitation of the laborer again accelerate accumulation, whilst, at the same time, the lower wages hold the increase of the working class in check. Then comes again the time when the supply of labor is less than the demand, wages rise, and so on. A beautiful mode of motion this developed capitalist production! Before, in consequence of the rise of wages, any positive increase of the population really fit for work could occur, the time would have been passed again and again, during which the industrial campaign must have been carried through, the battle fought and won.—C. 1.

WAITING
Everything comes to those who wait.—C. 2.

WANTS
In place of old wants, satisfied by the productions of the native country, we find new wants, requiring for their satisfaction the products of distant lands and climes.—C. M.

Natural wants themselves change continually. What variety there is, for instance, in the objects which serve as the staple food among different peoples!—P. P.

WAR
The war is recognized throughout political economy as the basis of political organization.—M.

About eighteen months ago, at Canton, the British government propounded the novel doctrine in the law of nations that a state may commit hostilities on a large scale against a province of another state, without either declaring war or establishing a state of war against that other state.—D. T.

WASTE
Waste is one of the circumstances that makes production by slave labor such a costly process.—C. 1.

What is wasted represents labor superfluously expended.—C. 1.

WASTE PRODUCTS
Rising prices of raw materials naturally stimulate the utilization of waste products.—C. 3.

Waste products—as for example cotton waste and so on—are fed to the fields as fertilizer or become raw material for other branches of industry, as for example linen rags (in the production) of paper. In such cases, part of an industry's constant capital may be directly exchanged for the constant capital of another industry. For example, cotton for cotton waste used as fertilizer.—C. 4.

The most striking example of utilizing waste is furnished by the chemical industry. It utilizes not only its own waste, for which it finds new uses, but also that of many other industries. For instance, it converts the formerly almost useless gas-tar into aniline dyes, alizarin, and, more recently, even into drugs.—C. 3.

WATER WHEEL
A water wheel is necessary to exploit the force of water, and a steam engine to exploit the elasticity of steam.—C. 1.

WEALTH
Taking two countries with equal populations and an equal development of the productive powers of labor, it would always be true to say that the wealth of the two countries must be measured according to the proportion of productive and of unproductive laborers. For that means only that in the country which has a relatively greater amount of productive laborers, a relatively greater amount of the annual revenue is reproductively consumed, and consequently a greater mass of values is produced annually.—C. 4.

Not too much wealth is produced. But at times too much wealth is produced in its capitalistic, self-contradictory forms.—C. 2.

The enjoyment of *wealth* seems to emerging capitalist society a superfluous luxury.—C. 4.

Since the production of surplus-value is the chief end and aim of capitalist production, it is clear that the greatness of a man's or a nation's wealth should be measured, not by the absolute quantity produced, but by the relative magnitude of the surplus-produce.—C. 1.

The wealth of those societies in which the capitalist mode of production prevails presents itself as "an immense accumulation of commodities."—C. 1.

There are nothing but general superficial analogies and relations between spiritual and material wealth.—C. 4.

WEALTH, CREATORS OF
The two primary creators of wealth are labor-power and the land.—C. 1.

WEALTH, GROWTH OF
When does a society find itself in a condition of advancing wealth? When the capitals and revenues of a country are growing.—M.

WEALTH, SOURCE OF
The original sources of all wealth are the soil and the laborer.—C. 1.

WEALTH OF SOCIETY
The wealth of a society is the result of the accumulation of much labor, capital being accumulated labor; the result, therefore, of the fact that his products are being taken in ever-increasing degree from the hands of the worker, that to an increasing extent his own labor confronts him as another's property and that the means of his existence and his activity are increasingly concentrated in the hands of the capitalist.—M.

The actual *wealth of society*, and the possibility of constantly expanding its reproduction process, do not depend upon the duration of surplus-labor, but upon its productivity and the more or less copious conditions of production under which it is performed.—C. 3.

WEAR AND TEAR
Wear and tear is first of all a result of use . . . Wear and tear is furthermore caused by the action of natural forces.—C. 2.

WHIM, CAPITALIST
The demand on which the life of the worker depends, depends on the whim of the rich and the capitalists.—M.

WINDMILL
The windmill gives you society with the feudal lord; the steam mill, society with the industrial capitalist.—P. P.

WIVES, BOURGEOIS
The bourgeois sees in his wife a mere instrument of production.—C. M.

WOMAN LABOR
The less the skill and exertion of strength implied in manual labor, in other words, the more modern industry becomes developed, the more is the labor of men superseded by that of women.—C. M.

WOMEN
Women, even when gifted with understanding, are curious creatures.—Ltr. to Engels.

WOMEN, COMMUNITY OF
You communists would introduce community of women, screams the whole bourgeoisie in chorus . . . Nothing is more ridiculous than the virtuous indignation of our bourgeois at the community of women which, they pretend, is to be openly and officially established by the communists. The communists have no need to introduce community of women; it has existed almost from time immemorial.—C. M.

It may be said that the idea of the community of women gives away the secret of the yet completely crude and thoughtless communism.—M.

WORK STOPPAGE
It has been objected that upon the abolition of private property all work will cease.—C. M.

WORKER AS CAPITAL
The worker has the misfortune to be a living capital, and therefore a capital with needs—one which loses its interest, and hence its livelihood, every moment it is not working. The value of the worker as capital rises according to demand and supply, and even physically his existence, his life, was and is looked upon as a supply of a commodity like any other. The worker produces capital, capital produces him—hence he produces himself, and man as worker, as a commodity, is the product of this entire cycle.—M.

WORKER AS COMMODITY
The demand for men necessarily governs the production of men, as of every other commodity. Should supply greatly exceed demand, a section of the workers sinks into beggary or starvation. The worker's existence is thus brought under the same condition as the existence of every other commodity. The worker has become a commodity, and it is a bit of luck for him if he can find a buyer.—M.

On the basis of political economy itself, in its own words, we have shown that the worker sinks to the level of a commodity and becomes indeed the most wretched of commodities; that the wretchedness of the worker is in inverse proportion to the power and magnitude of his production.—M.

WORKERS' ASSOCIATION

Our French members prove obviously to the French government the difference between a political secret society and a genuine workers' association. As soon as the government has arrested the members of the Paris, Lyons, Rouen, Marseilles, etc., committees, twice the number of committees announced themselves as their successors. They did it through provocative and brazen declarations in the newspapers (even disclosing their private addresses).—Ltr. to Engels.

WORKERS' COMBINATION

Combination among the capitalists is customary and effective; workers' combination is prohibited and painful in its consequences for them.—M.

The *workers' demonstrations* in London, which are marvelous in comparison with anything we have seen in England since 1849, are the work of the "International." Mr. Lucraft, for instance, the captain in Trafalgar Square, is one of our Council. This proves the difference between working behind the scenes by disappearing in public and the Democrats' way of making oneself important in public and doing nothing.—Ltr. to Engels.

The largest part of society is the *working class.*—C. 4.

WORKING CONDITIONS

Since the laborer passes the greater portion of his life in the process of production, the conditions of the production process are largely the conditions of his active living process, or his living conditions, and economy in these living conditions is a method of raising the rate of profit; just as we saw earlier that overwork, the transformation of the laborer into a work horse, is a means of increasing capital, or speeding up the production of surplus-value. Such economy extends to overcrowding close and unsanitary premises with laborers, or, as capitalists put it, to space saving; to crowding dangerous machinery into close quarters without using safety devices; to neglecting safety rules in production processes pernicious to health, or, as in mining, bound up with danger, etc. Not to mention the absence of all provisions to render the production process human, agreeable, or at least bearable. From the capitalist point of view this would be quite a useless and senseless waste.—C. 3.

WORKING DAY

The working day is . . . not a constant, but a variable quantity.—C. 1.

Hence it is that in the history of capitalist production the determination of what is a working day presents itself as the result of a struggle, a struggle between collective capital, i.e., the class of capitalists, and collective labor, i.e., the working class.—C. 1.

The sum of the necessary labor and the surplus-labor, i.e., of the periods of time during which the workman replaces the value of his labor power, and produces the surplus-value, this sum constitutes the actual time during which he works, i.e., the working day.—C. 1.

WORKSHOP

The knowledge, the judgment, and the will, which, though in ever so small a degree, are practiced by the independent peasant or handicraftsman, in the same way as the savage makes the whole art of war consist in the exercise of his personal cunning—these faculties are now required only for the workshop as a whole.—C. 1.

WORLD LITERATURE

National one-sidedness and narrow-mindedness become more and more impossible, and from the numerous national and local literatures there arises a world literature.—C. M.

WORLD MARKET

Modern industry has established the world market, for which the discovery of America paved the way. This market has given an immense development to commerce, to navigation, to communication by land.—C. M.

The specific aim of bourgeois society is the establishment of a *world market*, at least principally, and of a production founded on the world market.—Ltr. to Engels.

Developing the material forces of production and creating an appropriate *world market* is the historical task of the capitalist mode of production.—C. 3.

WORLD MONEY
National money discards its local character in the capacity of universal money; one national currency is expressed in another, and thus all of them are finally reduced to their content of gold or silver, while the latter, being the two commodities circulating as world money, are simultaneously reduced to their reciprocal value-ratio, which changes continually.—C. 3.

WRITER
A writer is a productive laborer not insofar as he produces ideas, but insofar as he enriches the publisher who publishes his works, or if he is a wage-laborer for a capitalist.—C. 4.

Y

YOUTHFUL LABORER
Capital wants larger numbers of youthful laborers, a smaller number of adults.—C. 1.

CARDINAL BERAN LIBRARY
ST. MARY'S SEMINARY

3 3747 00001 0501

Cardinal Beran Library
St. Mary's Seminary
9845 Memorial Drive
Houston, Texas 77024

WITHDRAWN

HX
39.5
.A38
1965

DATE DUE

8893

Marx, Karl
Karl Marx dictionary

HX
39.5
.A38
1965

Cardinal Beran Library
St. Mary's Seminary
9845 Memorial Drive
Houston, Texas 77024